...st be ...ded
...ow, or on the c... in th...
charged on overdue bo...
f...

Milner's young men

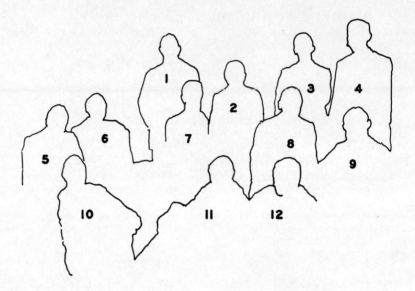

1. Hon. Robert H. Brand
2. Patrick Duncan
3. Herbert Baker (a close
   friend of many of the members of the kindergarten)
4. Lionel Hichens
5. Hon. Hugh Wyndham

6. Richard Feetham
7. Lionel Curtis
8. F. (Peter) Perry
9. Dougal O. Malcolm
10. John Dove
11. Philip Kerr
12. Geoffrey Robinson

Milner's young men: the "kindergarten" in Edwardian Imperial affairs / Walter Nimocks

HODDER AND STOUGHTON

To my wife, Susan Lee Nimocks

Preface

The failure of the Imperial Federation League in the early 1890's by no means ended enthusiasm for administrative reform within the British Empire. In fact, interest in reform, particularly reform meant to insure the continuation of the imperial connection in the face of growing Dominion nationalism, increased in proportion to the spread of the "new imperialism" of the Edwardian era. In the years before World War I new prophets stepped forward with schemes meant to prevent the disintegration of the Empire, and new groups appeared offering to educate the public on the perils which would result from a failure to take necessary action.

Among these groups was a coterie of young Oxford graduates called "Lord Milner's kindergarten." Drawn to South Africa during and after the Boer War to serve under Milner in the reconstruction of the two former Boer republics, they remained after the restoration of self-government in 1906 to work for Milner's goal of a united South Africa loyal to the British Empire. With the creation of the Union in 1909 the members of the group turned their attention to a much greater goal. Using methods perfected in the drive to unify South Africa and funds provided by friends of their patron Lord Milner, they organized a movement to achieve a similar sort of organic unity for the whole Empire. This movement—the round table movement—sought to establish an imperial government responsible to all the Dominions as well as to Great Britain, a government having control over matters of common interest to the otherwise independent member nations.

The early years of the round table movement were years of preparation: preparation of a specific proposal for imperial reform and of an organizational structure capable of mounting a great crusade for imperial unification. These preliminary activities came to a climax in the months just before the outbreak of World War I. Though the proposal for reform which had been drafted was acceptable to only a small portion of those associated with the movement, it was agreed within the kindergarten that the time had come to act. The kindergarten thus decided to delay no longer the instigation of a great campaign for closer union.

But the war made the implementation of this decision impossible. The public attention which might have been focused upon such a popular crusade was for the four years of the war directed towards a more immediate and crucial matter, and by war's end it was painfully clear to the kindergarten that the moment had passed. The impetus which the war and the peace conference gave to Dominion nationalism convinced most of the group that the sort of constitutional unity which they had envisioned in 1909 was impossible. Thus the goal which had been the *raison d'etre* of the kindergarten from its inception in South Africa was never achieved. Instead of organic unity came the Statute of Westminster and an increasingly tenuous Commonwealth association.

Despite the failure of their program to unify the Empire, members of the kindergarten continued throughout their lives the close bonds of their youth, those in England meeting frequently on social occasions and monthly as the editorial committee of the *Round Table,* the quarterly which they had created in 1910. As the years passed most of the group attained positions of prominence. Robert Brand (later Lord Brand) became a leading figure in London banking circles and a director of the *Times.* Richard Feetham climaxed a long legal career in South Africa with seven years on the bench of the supreme court of the Union. [Sir] Patrick Duncan also chose to remain in South Africa, where he spent a quarter of a century in the Union legislature and the last five years of his life as Governor-General. [Sir] Dougal O. Malcolm became president of the British South Africa Company, and Lionel Hichens guided the affairs of the great shipbuilding firm of Cammell Laird and Company. Lionel Curtis devoted his life to writing on imperial affairs and to the promotion of Atlantic unity and world peace. Geoffrey Dawson (earlier Robinson) was for a generation the editor of the *Times.* And Philip Kerr (Lord Lothian) served his country on a number of occasions, most prominently as ambassador to the United States in the crucial months of World War II when Britain faced Hitler singlehanded.

Though the kindergarten failed to achieve its original goal and *as a group* had little influence on Edwardian affairs, it was looked upon by some during World War I and the postwar years as a cabal of considerable power. The French politician Joseph Caillaux referred to it as a group of Oxford men, highly placed in British affairs, who met to conspire "the restoration of the tottering power of the caste to which they belong and the strengthening of the supremacy of Great Britain in the world."[1] Wilfrid Laurier is quoted as having said in 1917 that "Canada is now governed by a junta sitting in London, known as the 'Round Table,' with ramifications in Toronto, in Winnipeg, in Victoria, with Tories and Grits receiving their ideas from London and insidiously forcing them on their respective parties."[2] According to the *National Review*, the kindergarten, though it included "several men who mean well," was a "clique which encourages every centrifugal force in the British Empire."[3] To the editors of the *Morning Post* it was "a phalanx or palace-guard of idealists, who could be trusted by a sort of spiritual perversion to take a line injurious to British interests on every question."[4] Even Lloyd George was convinced of its influence: "It is a very powerful combination—in its own way perhaps the most powerful in the country. Each member of the Group brings to its deliberations certain definite and important qualities, and behind the scenes they have much power and influence."[5]

In light of such comments, one would assume that the students of Edwardian history had produced a considerable body of monographic literature on the subject. This, however, is not the case. Though an unpublished Ph.D. dissertation and three articles have appeared,[6] A. L. Burt's statement of more than a decade ago that

1. John Dove, "The Round Table: A Mystery Probed. Notes for a History of the Round Table," p. 2. An incomplete and unpublished typescript dated December 18, 1924, and in the possession of the *Round Table* editorial offices.
2. Richard Jebb, *Empire in Eclipse* (London, 1926), p. 8.
3. Quoted in Dove, "The Round Table: A Mystery Probed," p. 2.
4. April 10, 1923.
5. Quoted in *Lord Riddell's Intimate Diary of the Peace Conference and After, 1918–23* (New York, 1934), p. 329.
6. D. C. Ellinwood, Jr., "Lord Milner's 'Kindergarten,' the British Round Table Group, and the Movement for Imperial Reform, 1910–1918" (unpublished Ph.D. dissertation, Washington University, 1962); James Eayrs, "The Round Table Movement to Canada, 1909–1920," *Can. Hist. Rev.*, XXXVIII (March, 1957), 1–20; Carroll Quigley, "The Round Table Groups in Canada, 1908–38," *Can. Hist. Rev.*, XLIII (Sept., 1962), 204–24; Walter Nimocks, "Lord Milner's 'Kindergarten' and the Origins of the Round Table Movement," *South Atlantic Quarterly*, LXIII (Autumn, 1964), 507–20.

"the history of the Round Table movement has yet to be written"[7]
is largely true today. As A. M. Gollin wrote recently: ". . . this
curious band has yet to find its rhapsodist; but we may depend
upon it that he will put in an appearance in the fullness of time."[8]

The reader will have discerned by this point that my writing
style is somewhat less than rhapsodic. Even so, I have sought in
this book to describe and explain the most significant matters
relating to Milner's young men: why they came together and
stayed together, the part they played in bringing about South
African unification, their relationship with Milner and with other
Milnerite groups, the origins and goals of the round table movement, and the internal problems which contributed to the ultimate failure of that movement. In doing so I have acquired a debt
of gratitude to a number of people. I am particularly grateful to
those individuals and groups in Great Britain who made available to me the private papers upon which most of this study is
based: Mr. Dermot Morrah, the former editor of the *Round Table,* and the *Round Table* Editorial Committee for permission to
examine material in the files of the editorial offices; Professor Robinson of the Institute of Commonwealth Studies of the University
of London for access to the papers of Richard Jebb; Mr. C. T. Mc-
Innes, curator of historical records of the Scottish Records Office,
who made available to me selected letters from the papers of Lord
Lothian; the Warden and fellows of New College for access to the
Milner papers; Mr. Julian Amery for a copy of an important
letter from Curtis to his father Leo Amery; and most of all to Mrs.
Geoffrey Dawson, who was generous enough to collect the pre-
World War I papers of her late husband and turn them over to
me.

Many in England—members of the kindergarten and others
with special knowledge of the group—deserve my thanks for sharing with me their recollections. Among those who were most
helpful were—in addition to Mrs. Dawson and Mr. Morrah—Mr.
R. L. Richard, Mrs. Frederick Scott Oliver, Mrs. Lionel Hichens,

---

7. A. L. Burt, *The Evolution of the British Empire and Commonwealth from the
American Revolution* (Boston, 1956) , p. 925.
8. A. M. Gollin, *Proconsul in Politics: A Study of Lord Milner in Opposition and
in Power* (London, 1964) , p. 161.

Miss Jessica Westley, Sir Basil Blackwell, the late Sir Evelyn Wrench, and the late Lords Brand and Leconfield.

I am indebted to the *Round Table* Editorial Committee for permission to include the photograph of the kindergarten and to Sir Ivison Macadam for reading the typescript and suggesting improvements. I am grateful, also, to Mrs. Henry Parker, formerly on the staff of the *Round Table,* for her patience and many cups of coffee during the weeks in which I examined the records preserved at the *Round Table* editorial offices.

My thanks, too, to those scholars who have assisted me with advice and sometimes with research material. I would especially mention Professors Keith Sinclair of Auckland University; M. S. Donelly of the University of Manitoba; James Eayrs of the University of Toronto; L. M. Thompson of the University of California at Los Angeles; G. A. le Roux of the Republic of South Africa; DeWitt Ellinwood of the State University of New York at Albany; F. D. Schneider, Paul Hardacre, and H. L. Swint of Vanderbilt University; and Mary Ellen Miller and Carlton Jackson of Western Kentucky University.

To Western Kentucky University goes my thanks for money to cover the cost of typing the final draft.

Finally, I wish to express my gratitude to the Southern Fellowships Fund for the financial assistance which made it possible for me to conduct the research upon which this study is based.

Walter Nimocks

Centre College of Kentucky
August 10, 1967

Contents

Milner's young men

Chapter One. Alfred Milner

By the 1890's tensions which had been growing in South Africa between the British government and the two Boer republics, the Transvaal (since 1856 called the South African Republic) and the Orange Free State, had approached the flash point. When the explosion came in the last months of 1899, it attracted to South Africa many thousands of men from various parts of the British Empire and from all parts of the world. Along with the soldiers, speculators, and adventurers came servants of the Crown to assist in reconstruction once the fighting was ended. In this way the young men of Milner's "kindergarten" were brought into the center of imperial affairs and provided with a patron and leader and a cause which became the focus of their collective activity.

To understand the circumstances which drew them to South Africa, and to appreciate the effect of this experience upon their later activities, one should consider the reasons for the war between the Boer republics and the British government. Superficially, the conflict grew out of a disagreement about the political rights and economic treatment of foreigners, many of them British subjects, who had entered the Transvaal after 1886 to exploit the gold deposits on the Rand. These foreigners, called *Uitlanders* by the Boer population, claimed that their political rights were being denied. Though they constituted a sizable portion of the total Transvaal population and owned much of the taxable wealth of the country, they were prevented from influencing political affairs by a government which was obviously reluctant to grant them the right to vote. To President Paul Kruger, any other policy would have been fatal to the survival of Boer culture. The foreigners on the Rand would soon outnumber the *Afrikaners,* or white South Africans descended from early Dutch settlers. If franchised, the *Uitlanders* would thus achieve political control of a land which they had already come to dominate economically.

Political matters were not the only subject at issue. Economic disagreement arose over *Uitlander* complaints that the mining center at Johannesburg was forced to bear the tax burden for the whole country while at the same time its governmental needs were all but ignored by the government at Pretoria. The mining community further claimed that extortionate governmental officials and a state-controlled monopoly of mining supplies placed an unbearable burden on those who were bringing prosperity to a primitive land. To the Boers, however, it seemed only right that the rapacious, scheming strangers, who built cities where none were needed and broke the sod of the veld only to deface the land with mines, should bear the cost of government.

To many in Britain, such mistreatment of the *Uitlanders* was indefensible. Their welfare was supposedly protected by earlier agreements defining the relations between the Transvaal and Great Britain. The Pretoria Convention of 1881, by which the Gladstone government restored partial independence to the Transvaal after a brief period of British rule, imposed a number of limitations upon Boer sovereignty. Though it made no mention of circumstances under which foreigners might be naturalized, the agreement did state that self-government was "subject to the suzerainty of Her Majesty." A revision drawn up in London in 1884 did not repeat this earlier claim to "suzereignty," but the British government in following years chose to interpret the Convention in a way designed to justify a demand for more favorable treatment of the *Uitlanders*.

Although the issue of the political and economic rights of the British-oriented commercial element of the Transvaal population was an obvious source of irritation to both the British and the Boers, it was also a veil which hid the true dimensions of the conflict. In many ways the issue of the *Uitlanders* was a symbol of a deeper struggle which provides a more meaningful understanding of the causes of the Boer War. In its broadest context, the antagonism between the Boer republics and the British Empire arose from the effort made by each camp to extend its domination over all of Africa south of the Zambezi River. The Boer farmers of the Transvaal and the Orange Free State, though their attitudes were in many ways closer to the seventeenth than to the nineteenth century, were nevertheless infused with an aggressive, expansionist nationalism in perfect harmony with the fashion of their day. From pulpit, press, and lecture platform in the 1880's and '90's, they were assured of their superiority and stimulated by the shibboleth "Africa for the *Afrikaners*." In these same years many highly placed Englishmen came to harbor conflicting ambitions. Reflecting the new imperialism of the times, they were convinced of the British Empire's manifest destiny to civilize and control South Africa and determined that it would not be thwarted by a handful of narrow, unenlightened farmers. To both *Afrikaner* nationalists and British imperialists disagreement over the rights of an urban British minority in an *Afrikaner* state was only the most obvious sign of a deep-running struggle for control of South Africa.

The establishment of the Unionist government in June, 1895, brought to power in Great Britain men who were inclined to sympathize with those of their countrymen who held ambitious views concerning the role of the Empire in South Africa. Both the Prime Minister, Lord Salisbury, and his Colonial Secretary, Joseph Chamberlain, believed that the autonomy of the Boer states was an unnatural, and therefore temporary, condition. Both were convinced that the concessions to Boer independence which had been made at Pretoria in 1881 and London in 1884 were egregious mistakes. And both were frustrated by a situation which permitted the Boer republics to defy the British government time after time. This frustration and the growing realization by Chamberlain that the Transvaal government was increasing its economic, military, and diplomatic strength with dramatic speed perhaps account for the ease with which the new Colonial Secretary was drawn into an already half-born scheme to win by devious methods what could not be achieved by more forthright means.

Months before the formation of the Unionist government, *Uitlander* leaders in Johannesburg had gained the support of Cecil Rhodes, the Prime Minister of the Cape Colony, for a *coup d'état* designed to end forever the Boer domination of the Transvaal. According to the plan, a revolt of Johannesburg miners, financed by Rhodes and other Rand magnates, would signal the dispatch of a body of armed men waiting on the Bechuanaland frontier. Together the *Uitlanders* and the invaders would take control of the Rand and appeal to the British High Commissioner in Cape

Town for assistance in working out a settlement with the Pretoria government.

The details of the Jameson Raid, the efforts made to put it into effect, and its failure have been the subjects of intensive and extensive investigation.[1] This event played a significant part in precipitating war between Britain and the Boers by making maneuver and compromise by both governments more difficult. The complicity of the British High Commissioner, Sir Hercules Robinson, and the strong suspicion throughout the world that Chamberlain and perhaps the whole Salisbury government had some hand in the affair made the success of any future negotiations extremely doubtful.

In the Transvaal the tactical advantage presented by the failure of the Raid was used to the fullest. The old *voortrekker* Paul Kruger chose this moment to drop all pretense of forbearance and to adopt a policy of open defiance of British power. The importation of arms and ammunition, already at a level well above peacetime needs, was increased as the Transvaal government began to prepare for a war which many now regarded as inevitable. In adopting this new policy, Kruger's government was gratified to receive encouragement not only from Germany but also from *Afrikaners* in both the Orange Free State and the two British colonies. Many in Natal and the Cape Colony found the attraction of Boer nationalism to be stronger than ties of loyalty to the British Crown.

In London, too, the Raid caused a redefinition of policy. At the Colonial Office a feeling developed that the Raid had brought affairs in South Africa to a crossroads. From that point the future could take one of two directions. According to a Colonial Office memorandum, ". . . if South Africa remains as now a congeries of separate States, partly British Colonies and partly Republics, it will inevitably amalgamate itself into a [Boer-dominated] United States of South Africa." However, "if we can succeed in uniting all South Africa into a Confederacy on the model of the Dominion of Canada and under the British Flag, the probability is that that

1. See Melvin G. Holli, "Joseph Chamberlain and the Jameson Raid: A Bibliographical Survey," *Journal of British Studies*, III, No. 2 (May, 1964).

confederacy will not become a United States of South Africa."[2]

Obviously, powerful figures in the Colonial Office were convinced by "Jameson's criminal blunder"[3] that the British government could no longer pursue a course based on the hope that the enfranchisement of the *Uitlanders* would eventually place control of the Transvaal in friendly hands. This "natural process" of domination through immigration seemed unlikely even before the Raid; afterwards it was out of the question. But to substitute for the old passive policy one which entailed direct intervention by the imperial government was to accept a risk which might threaten the welfare of Great Britain and the Empire. Clearly, a more active policy would involve the possibility, if not the probability, of war in South Africa. The Colonial Office, though reluctant to precipitate a war, saw no alternative but to accept the risk. The Prime Minister, on the other hand, could not look with such equanimity upon a policy which, if implemented, might produce such serious consequences. Salisbury, who was also Foreign Secretary until 1900, understood clearly the extent to which the emergence of new powers in Europe and America had diminished Britain's pre-eminence in world affairs. Although he agreed with Chamberlain that South Africa was at a crossroads and that only a threat of force could preserve British interests there, he recognized that the matter could not be settled in a vacuum. South Africa was not the only area in which British interests were being threatened, and precipitate action there might open up far greater difficulties in other parts of the world.

The Colonial Office, therefore, had no choice but to act with moderation and wait for conditions to change. During the period of waiting, Chamberlain prepared for the moment when British power in South Africa might be asserted more effectively. An important step in this direction was to search for a replacement for Sir Hercules Robinson (by then Lord Rosmead), the High Commissioner in South Africa during the time of the Raid and the crucial months which followed. Rosmead, though old and in

2. Quoted in Ronald Robinson and John Gallagher, *Africa and the Victorians: the Climax of Imperialism in the Dark Continent* (New York, 1961), pp. 434–37.
3. *Ibid.*

poor health, had been involved in the plans of Rhodes, and his complicity, which considerably damaged the reputation of the British government, was even worse in Chamberlain's eyes because of the inept way in which Rosmead handled the negotiations in Pretoria immediately following the Raid. Chamberlain, with the concurrence of Salisbury, therefore began to cast about for a man with broad experience in colonial administration who could operate within a framework of policies established by the Colonial Office to restore British prestige and more effectively pursue British goals in South Africa. His attention quickly centered upon Sir Alfred Milner, the Chairman of the Board of Inland Revenue, whom he had first come to know in 1889, when the latter was in the Egyptian Finance Ministry. The favorable opinion thus formed was reinforced by Milner's splendid record in his later post.[4] When Chamberlain approached Salisbury in January, 1897, to ask his approval of Milner's appointment, he found that the Prime Minister had independently made the same choice.[5]

The announcement of Milner's appointment as Governor of the Cape Colony and High Commissioner for South Africa was released in February, 1897.[6] To the average Englishman Milner's name meant nothing, but among those who knew him and were aware of his ability the announcement was well received. The new High Commissioner had been born in Germany, the son of an English mother and a German-English father.[7] After an early education in Germany and London he entered Balliol College, at that time beginning its most outstanding era under Benjamin

4. Vladimir Halpérin, *Lord Milner and the Empire: The Evolution of British Imperialism* (London, 1952), pp. 88–89.
5. W. L. and J. E. Courtney, *Pillars of Empire: Studies and Impressions* (London, 1918), p. 149.
6. Halpérin, *Lord Milner*, p. 89. The Governor of the Cape Colony also served as High Commissioner for South Africa. As such he was charged with representing the British government "subject to instructions through a Secretary of State" in matters relating to British interests in all of South Africa. Cecil Headlam, ed., *The Milner Papers: South Africa* (London, 1931–33), I, 36. [Hereinafter cited as Headlam.]
7. There is no official biography of Milner. At his death he left instructions that none should be written. However, the Headlam edition of his papers dealing with South Africa contains a short biographical essay. Four biographical studies of Milner have recently appeared: Halpérin, cited above; Sir John Evelyn Wrench, *Alfred Lord Milner: The Man of No Illusions 1854–1925* (London, 1958); Edward Crankshaw, *The Forsaken Idea: A Study of Viscount Milner* (London, 1952); A. M. Gollin, *Proconsul in Politics: A Study of Lord Milner in Opposition and in Power* (London, 1964).

Jowett. At Balliol young Milner, an undergraduate between the years 1872 and 1876, developed personal ties which in some ways served as a substitute for a family throughout his life. A bachelor until four years before his death, he always looked upon Oxford as his home, and reserved a special affection for Oxonians young and old. He remained particularly close to his Balliol contemporaries, many of whom, like himself were stirred by Jowett to devote their lives to public service. Among them were the future Prime Minister, Herbert Asquith, the sociologist and economist Arnold Toynbee, St. John Brodrick, who later held various portfolios in the Unionist government, and Charles Gore, who became an Anglican bishop and a leader of the Anglo-Catholic movement.[8]

At Balliol Milner's industry and ability brought recognition and the respect and personal attention of Dr. Jowett. Under Jowett's tutelage, Milner received a series of academic honors, including a prize-fellowship at New College. According to the regulations then in effect, the recipient of this fellowship was permitted to live anywhere, pursue any profession, and after the first several years bear only the lightest of responsibilities to the college. The fellow received a stipend from the college until such time as he chose to marry. Milner had no personal fortune upon which to rely while devoting his life to important but unremunerative work. In his early years he therefore found this income of £200 of great value in that it provided him with a degree of economic security which he had never before known.[9]

Milner's academic career ended with his decision to enter the profession of law. He returned to London, and in 1881 was called to the bar. His career as a barrister, however, was both brief and briefless. Later that same year he became a member of the staff of the *Pall Mall Gazette,* a Liberal evening paper of sober reputation and small circulation. In 1883 the editor John Morley left journalism for politics, and was succeeded by his former assistant William T. Stead, a journalistic innovator and enthusiastic imperialist. With Milner as his assistant, Stead turned the *Pall Mall*

8. Headlam, I, 7.
9. Headlam, I, 11. According to Mr. R. C. Richard, assistant librarian of New College, this stipend was later returned as a donation.

Gazette into a lively but controversial journal which constantly supported social reform and what Stead called "the *Pall Mall* doctrine of Imperialism."[10] Stead later said that during the three years of their editorial association, he and Milner "edited England" by introducing many of the techniques which had become common in American newspapers.[11] Though Milner and Stead later disagreed over the Boer War, their relationship in the years before Milner's appointment as High Commissioner remained close largely as a result of their joint efforts to promote imperial unity.

By 1884 other activities were placing such demands upon Milner's time that he found it increasingly difficult to participate in the management of the *Pall Mall Gazette*. Though he continued for several years to contribute occasional articles, his association with Stead's paper became tenuous. In 1884 Milner became private secretary to George J. Goschen, at that time a leading figure in the Liberal party. He retained this position during the breakup of the Liberal party in 1886 and Goschen's subsequent appointment as Chancellor of the Exchequer in Lord Salisbury's second ministry.[12] On the advice of his patron, Milner made the only political race of his career in 1885. He stood as Liberal party candidate for Harrow only to be defeated by a thousand votes.[13]

In November, 1889, Milner was offered a position in the Egyptian Ministry of Finance. This appointment, made upon the recommendation of Goschen, was a turning point in Milner's career. The three years which he spent in the service of the Egyptian government ended in 1892 with his return to Britain as the Chairman of the Board of Inland Revenue.[14] He came home a seasoned colonial official with a splendid record as an administrator and with an attitude towards the Empire which was in keeping with that of the leading Conservative and Liberal Unionist politicians. It was these qualities which prompted Salisbury and Chamberlain to pick Milner as Rosmead's successor at Cape Town.

10. Quoted in Joseph O. Baylen, "W. T. Stead and the Boer War: the Irony of Idealism," *Can. Hist. Rev.*, XL (Dec., 1959) , 309.
11. *Ibid.*
12. Milner's relationship with Goschen is described in detail in Wrench, *Alfred Lord Milner*, pp. 67–95.
13. *Ibid.*, pp. 15–16.
14. *Ibid.*, pp. 96–110.

In choosing Milner, Salisbury and Chamberlain selected an administrator rather than a politician. Political circles in London were filled with ambitious men whose careers would have been advanced by such an appointment. But instead of making a choice from that group the Prime Minister and the Colonial Secretary offered this important post to a forty-three year old bureaucrat with many political connections but no desire to use whatever reputation he might earn in South Africa as a steppingstone to important political positions in Great Britain. In fact, by the time of his appointment Milner had begun to despise the party system, which seemed to him to be responsible for much of the trouble then besetting Britain and the Empire. His experience as an administrator had convinced him that, the state of politics being what it was in Great Britain, more could be accomplished outside than inside the circles of elective public office.

> I see that a man can do any amount of good public work, and be of the greatest service, without joining in the fray—can, in fact, be of greater service because he keeps himself in the background. Of course I have not . . . great wealth, but I have an independent position, a great number of influential friends, and, I fancy, that sort of influence myself which disinterestedness always gives. . . . My interests do not run on the lines of Party. & if I can help, in however small a way, to carry out the objects I have at heart, I do not care two straws how the politicians are labelled who execute them.[15]

This desire to remain aloof from party politics is in remarkable contrast to Milner's earlier race for Parliament and his deep involvement in political activities while working for Goschen. A partial explanation can perhaps be found in his temperament and personality. Milner was endowed with those qualities essential to an administrator. He was precise in all matters and possessed a logical and lucid mind. He digested and retained reports and memoranda easily, and was able to see through a plethora of confusing details to the heart of an administrative problem. But,

15. Milner to (Sir) George Parkin, Dec. 15, 1893, Private Papers of Sir George Parkin, Public Archives of Canada, Ottawa. An extract from this letter is found in Wrench, *Alfred Lord Milner*, pp. 146–47. A similar statement of Milner's antipathy for existing political institutions is found in Milner to Parkin, June 30, 1896, Parkin Papers.

according to the son of one of his most loyal followers, "his genius was of the autocratic kind, and in his heart he never recognised with much good humour the right of opposition."[16] These characteristics, the qualities of "a natural dictator,"[17] prompted his detractors in later years to comment upon Milner's rigid Teutonic mind and personality which were assumed to be derived in some way from his ancestry and his early education in Germany.[18] Whatever their origin, these characteristics influenced Milner's attitude toward the government and its operation. He looked with distaste upon political opportunism and parliamentary inefficiency, which seemed so frequently to frustrate the best efforts "of men . . . *with no axes to grind,* but with social position, knowledge of the world and a disinterested concern for the public good. . . ."[19]

Perhaps even more important in shaping Milner's aversion to politics was a growing conviction that the political institutions of Great Britain were inadequate to provide for the needs of the Empire. He felt that political leaders in London, determined to maintain the prestige and power of office, were frequently willing to accede to the short-sighted demands of the electorate in ways which damaged the welfare of the Empire. With so much time spent in considering petty domestic issues, the great problems of the Empire were denied the statesmanlike attention which they deserved.[20]

This concern for the British Empire which dominated Milner's mature life had reached full intensity by the time of his appointment to South Africa. From this point in his career, all of Milner's thought and action was directed towards its preservation and support. The Empire, which he referred to a few years later as "an influence, without an equal, on the side of humanity, civilization,

16. Julian Amery, *The Life of Joseph Chamberlain* (London, 1951), IV, 100.
17. *Ibid.,* p. 43.
18. R. C. K. Ensor, *England 1870–1914* (Oxford, 1936), p. 217 n.; Janitor [J. G. Lockhart & Lady Craik], *The Feet of the Young Men: Some Candid Comments on the Rising Generation, with an Epilogue 1929* (2nd ed.; London, 1929), p. 174. Evidence of the currency of this explanation is found in L. M. Thompson, *The Unification of South Africa 1902–1910* (Oxford, 1960), p. 5.
19. Milner to Mrs. Montefiore, Aug. 22, 1900, Private Papers of Alfred Lord Milner, New College, Oxford.
20. Milner to Parkin, June 30, 1896, Parkin Papers.

and peace,"[21] had become important to him during his days at
Oxford. Shortly after World War I Milner wrote:

> As an under-graduate at Oxford, I was first stirred by a new vision
> of the future of the British Empire. In that vision it appeared no
> longer as a number of infant or dependent communities revolving
> around this ancient kingdom but as a world-encircling group of
> related nations, some of them destined in time even to outgrow
> the mother country, united on a basis of equality and partnership,
> and united at least mainly by moral and spiritual bonds.[22]

A generation later these sentiments were widespread among
politically concerned students at Oxford, but in Milner's day they
were not widely held. In fact, his interest in the welfare of the
Empire often tended to divide him from most of his Oxford
contemporaries. In debates in the famous Oxford Union and in
discussions held by various political clubs, young Milner's opposition to the prevailing indifference to imperial issues was undisguised.[23] This deep concern for the Empire at a time when his
fellow students viewed it with suspicion perhaps reflects the early
stirrings of intellectual interest in the Empire developing at that
time among scholars and particularly historians at Oxford. But no
clear picture of Milner's early imperial commitment is possible
without reference to George Parkin, a lifelong friend and contemporary at Oxford. Parkin played an important part in awakening
in Milner's mind "a new vision of the future of the British Empire." Indeed, Leo Amery later wrote that "Parkin was, I believe,
mainly instrumental in first interesting [Milner] in Empire
problems."[24]

Eight years Milner's senior, Parkin came to Oxford from Canada in 1873 as a non-Collegiate student on a year's leave of
absence from the Collegiate School at Fredericton, New Bruns-
wick, where he was headmaster.[25] Though he was at Oxford for
only six months, Parkin aroused in his new friend a concern for
the future of the Empire and a desire that the connection between

21. Lord Milner, *Speeches Delivered in Canada in the Autumn of 1908* (Toronto,
1909), p. 93.
22. Alfred Lord Milner, *The British Commonwealth* (London, 1919), p. 5.
23. Headlam, I, 35; Wrench, *Alfred Lord Milner*, pp. 45–46.
24. L. S. Amery, *The Empire in the New Era: Speeches Delivered during an
Empire Tour 1927–28, with a Foreword by Lord Balfour* (London, 1928), p. 240.
25. Sir John Willison, *Sir George Parkin: A Biography* (London, 1929), p. 27.

Great Britain and the self-governing colonies be maintained. Parkin's own attitudes served as evidence to Milner that intense colonial nationalism need not preclude a much broader loyalty to an imperial family of equal sister nations. The extent to which Milner's thinking was shaped by the young Canadian headmaster is reflected in a letter written a quarter of a century later, when Milner was on his way to South Africa to assume his duties as High Commissioner. "My life has been greatly influenced by your ideas," he wrote, "& in my new post I shall feel more than ever the need of your enthusiasm and broad hopeful view of the Imperial future."[26]

The friendship formed at Oxford was ended only by Parkin's death in 1922. In their mature years, work on behalf of imperial unity drew the two together in a series of projects whose goal was a more rationally constituted imperial structure. Both were involved in the Imperial Federation League, Milner more or less indirectly, but Parkin as a full-time agent of the organization. Shortly before Milner's Egyptian appointment, Parkin set out on a speaking tour of Australia and New Zealand on behalf of the League. Following the completion of the tour, he remained in England until 1893 as the chief speaker and propagandist for the movement.[27] In the spring of that year, when it was apparent that the League was dying, Milner was instrumental in finding funds which enabled Parkin to continue his work on behalf of imperial federation.[28] Though the money thus raised was insufficient to support Parkin for long,[29] the two friends were reunited in common effort by Parkin's appointment in 1902 as administrator of the newly created Rhodes Scholarship system. Milner, an original trustee of the Rhodes estate, and Parkin were for the next twenty years intimately associated in the establishment of this program to unite more closely the English-speaking people.

Milner's early enthusiasm for the affairs of Empire was also undoubtedly stimulated by his contact with William T. Stead in

26. Milner to Parkin, April 23, 1897, Parkin Papers.
27. Willison, *Sir George Parkin*, pp. 56–88.
28. Milner to Parkin, April 29, 1893, and "Memorandum of a Conversation between Mr. Brassey, Mr. Parkin & Mr. Milner," June 1, 1893, Parkin Papers; Willison, *Sir George Parkin*, pp. 88–89.
29. Willison, *Sir George Parkin*, p. 89.

the years when the two labored together on the *Pall Mall Gazette*. In fact, while "editing England" they worked out a definition of "Empire" which each found to be satisfactory. What Stead wrote of in 1906 as "a voluntary association of free states, united by . . . ties . . . of mutual liberty,"[30] Milner had earlier defined in similar though more rhetorical terms as

> a group of sister Nations spread throughout the world, united and not divided by the ocean, each independent in its own concerns, all indissolubly allied for a common purpose, all free and willing subjects of the most ancient and august Monarchy in the world. . . .[31]

It was during Milner's three years in Egypt, however, that there "developed in him the passion of his life."[32] Heretofore his knowledge of conditions within the Empire and his understanding of "imperial mission" were arrived at second-hand. In Egypt, then being transformed under the authority of Sir Evelyn Baring, Milner observed the civilizing effect of British efficiency and imperial order. To his patron and friend Goschen he wrote from Egypt that

> as England is doing some of her best work in the valley of the Nile, I am glad to be of the company. The more I see of it, the more proud and convinced I become of the great service which 'jingoism' has rendered to humanity in these regions, and I touch my hat with confirmed reverence to the Union Jack. May I live to see it at Kassala!! Or, at very least, at Khartum.[33]

Upon his return to England in 1892 Milner wrote of his experiences in a work entitled *England in Egypt*. Called by one of his biographers "an Englishman's manual on Egypt," this book went through thirteen editions during the following decades.[34] In it Milner explained the background of British entry into Egypt and the reforms which had been instituted under British tutelage. But equally important, he provided there what Leo Amery later called "his first essay in preaching the gospel of creative imperialism."[35]

30. William T. Stead, *The Best or Worst of Empire: Which?* (London, 1906) , p. xi. Quoted in Baylen, *Can. Hist. Rev.*, XL, 314.
31. From a speech made by Milner in Durban, Oct. 28, 1901, Headlam, II, 287.
32. Crankshaw, *Forsaken Idea*, p. 29.
33. Milner to Goschen, Nov. 2, 1890. Quoted in Wrench, *Alfred Lord Milner*, pp. 105–6.
34. Halpérin, *Lord Milner*, p. 54.
35. *Ibid.*, p. 10. Foreword by L. S. Amery.

Though Milner insisted in the preface that "my aim is not to influence, but to inform—not polemical but didactic," the work nevertheless provides a clear statement of his mature attitude towards the British Empire. In it he justified British domination of Egypt and its continuation until the Egyptians proved their capacity for self-government, evidence of which he did not expect for many decades.[36] In cogent terms Milner expressed his serene conviction that "in the art of governing, Englishmen have a particular gift which is very much to their advantage," an advantage clearly in evidence in Egypt:

> In the art of government, the Englishman seems to be as handy and adaptable as he is clumsy and angular in society. There are other nations with equal and perhaps greater gifts for the creation of an ideally perfect administration. But I doubt whether any nation could have made anything at all of a system so imperfect, so incongruous and so irritating as that which we found in Egypt, and which we have not been permitted radically to alter. The logical Frenchman would have been maddened by its absurdities. The authoritative temper of the German would have revolted at its restrictions. It needed that incarnation of compromise, the average Briton, to accept the system with all its faults and to set to work quietly in his sensible, plodding way to do the best he could under the circumstances.[37]

Thus the man chosen to represent the Crown in South Africa during one of the crucial moments in the history of the Empire had qualities essential to his task. By both education and experience Milner was prepared to act with decision if not with tact on behalf of British interests. But more important, he was equipped with a philosophy of Empire which made him uniquely qualified to serve as an imperial proconsul in South Africa during the years ahead.

36. Viscount Milner, *England in Egypt* (11th ed.; London, 1904) , pp. 354–58.
37. *Ibid.*, pp. 355–56.

Chapter Two. The Boer War and the first arrivals

Shortly after his South African appointment was made public, Milner informed Parkin of "what I really feel about this new venture." He confessed that "any elation I might otherwise have felt at being selected for so big a task is quite swallowed up in my solemn sense of the great national interests at stake in this matter." It was clear, Milner wrote, that

> S. Africa is just now the weakest link in the imperial chain, & I am conscious of the tremendous responsibility wh. rests upon the man, who is called upon to try & preserve it from snapping. . . . I wish sincerely that the Empire could be represented by a stronger man. That not being possible, I am at least glad to think that it could not have found a more single-minded one, or one whose heart is more wholly in the work. I don't the least mind either the personal strain or the discomfort of having to live for years with mostly incongenial people. I am quite willing to be "all things to all men," if by any means the great cause can be furthered. But without the help of a higher power I know well that I, or anybody, may be unable to pull things through.[1]

Milner's lack of confidence, understandable in light of the great problems which awaited him in South Africa, was perhaps made more acute by his awareness of his own limitations. Despite his outstanding qualifications for the tasks which confronted him, Milner carried with him to his new appointment an admitted handicap: he knew very little about South Africa. He had neither been there, nor been officially involved in South African matters. Shortly after his appointment he thus admitted to Lord Selborne, Under-secretary at the Colonial Office, that "I have no claims as yet to pose as an authority on these subjects. My views are simply those of the man in the street."[2]

During his first months in South Africa, therefore, Milner moved with circumspection. For almost a year after his arrival in early May, 1897, he spent much of his time learning Dutch,

1. Milner to Parkin, April 23, 1897, Parkin Papers.
2. Milner to Selborne, March 20, 1897, Milner Papers.

conferring with leaders of all political opinions, and visiting as
many parts of South Africa as possible. This period of cautious
adjustment, in keeping with Chamberlain's decision "to stand
upon our rights and wait events," came to an end in the early
months of 1898. By then Milner had surveyed the situation and
had formed conclusions—conclusions which never changed in the
crucial period that followed. To Selborne he wrote that "my
opinions have been somewhat modified by a year of S. Africa."
For during that time he had come to realize that

> two wholly antagonistic systems—a mediaeval race oligarchy, and
> a modern industrial state, recognizing no difference of status be-
> tween various white races—cannot permanently live side by side
> in what is after all *one country*. The race-oligarchy has got to go,
> and I see no signs of its removing itself.[3]

The implication was clear. Milner had concluded that relations
between the imperial government and the Boer republics had
reached an impasse which seemed impossible to resolve without
force. As he explained to Chamberlain, "there is no way out of the
political troubles of South Africa except reform in the Transvaal
or war. And at present the chances of reform in the Transvaal are
worse than ever."[4] Once convinced of the brutal logic of these
alternatives, Milner never wavered. Though constrained to negotiate by instructions from the Colonial Office, he did so with
little enthusiasm and less success. Even at the famous Bloemfontein meeting with President Kruger in late May, 1899, Milner
conducted himself in a perfunctory way, certain that his antago-
nist had no intention of yielding on essential points. As Milner
predicted—or because of his predictions—an absence of reform
was followed by war. Both British and Boers rejected terms demanded by the other, and fighting began on October 11, 1899.

The transition from a political and diplomatic struggle to a
military one altered Milner's place in the determination of South
African affairs. During the war his position became second to that
of the military commanders, for the conduct of military opera-
tions was not within the province of the High Commissioner.
Even so, as the representative of the Crown Milner was involved
throughout the war in matters which would affect the develop-

3. Milner to Selborne, May 9, 1898, *ibid.*
4. Milner to Chamberlain, Feb. 23, 1898, *ibid.*

ment of South Africa after the fighting had ended and the generals had gone. Milner looked upon the war as a beginning, not an end. His real work would be the creation of a South African nation uniting the hitherto fragmented regions into a loyal element of the British Empire. As early as November, 1899, during the darkest weeks of the war, Milner turned his attention to the future, and began to lay plans for the task ahead. In a letter to a South African associate dated November 28, 1899, he wrote with startling clarity of the reconstruction which should follow the victory of imperial forces. For its summary of the program attempted by Milner during his remaining years in South Africa the letter deserves extensive quotation.

> It seems ill-omened to talk of eventual settlement when things are in such an awful mess. . . . Still, it must have an end and that end must be our victory. So though it may be premature, it is still necessary to think what to do with it. One thing is quite evident. The *ultimate* end is a self-governing white Community, supported by *well-treated* and *justly governed* black labour from Cape Town to Zambezi. There must be one flag, the Union Jack, but under it equality of races and languages. Given *equality* all round, English must prevail, though I do not think, and do not wish, that Dutch should altogether die out. I think, though all South Africa should be *one Dominion* with a common government dealing with Customs, Railways and Defence, perhaps also with Native policy, a considerable amount of freedom should be left to the several States. But though this is the ultimate end, it would be madness to attempt it at once. There must be an interval, to allow the British population of the Transvaal to return and increase, and the mess to be cleared up, before we can apply the principle of self-government to the Transvaal. . . . How long the period of unrepresentative government may last, I cannot say. I, for one, would be for shortening it as much as possible, but not before a loyal majority is assured. As for the Boer himself, provided I am once sure of having broken his political predominance, I should be for leaving him the greatest amount of individual freedom. First beaten, then fairly treated, and not too much worried on his own "plaats" in his own conservative habits, I think he will be peaceful enough.[5]

This statement, strikingly similar to proposals expressed a few weeks later by both Salisbury and Chamberlain,[6] clearly defined

---

5. Milner to Sir Percy Fitzpatrick, Nov. 28, 1899, Headlam, II, 35–36.
6. *Ibid.*, pp. 39–41.

the ultimate goals sought by Milner throughout the remainder of his stay in South Africa and the importance which he from the first placed upon a substantial increase in British settlers once the war was over. In fact, he came to look upon a favorable population balance as a key to success of the whole reconstruction program. "I attach the greatest importance of all to the increase of the British population," he wrote in late 1900. "If, ten years hence, there are three men of British race to two of Dutch, the country will be safe and prosperous. If there are three of Dutch to two of British, we shall have perpetual difficulty."[7] Milner's attitude concerning the significance of postwar immigration stemmed from his realization that the period in which the former republics could be governed as crown colonies would be brief. He feared that pressures in Britain and South Africa would rapidly mount for a restoration of popular government. And all too quickly the imperial government would be forced to accede. Then, even a constitution providing safeguards for civil and political rights could not prevent a restoration of Boer power unless population changes during the period of Crown control had tipped the balance in favor of British sentiment.[8] It was essential, therefore, that British immigration not only take place but take place quickly. But the problem of recruiting settlers, important though it was, was only one of many to be solved once the fighting had ceased. The gold mining industry had to be restored, for upon it had come to depend the prosperity of all South Africa. Hundreds of thousands of prisoners of war, civilians in concentration camps, and native laborers would be waiting for re-establishment. Burned farms had to be rebuilt, railroads and communications restored. And all these tasks had to be done in a way which would contribute to Milner's "*ultimate* end" of a united "self-governing white Community, supported by *well-treated* and *justly governed* black labour from Cape Town to Zambezi."

Aware of the proportions of such a reconstruction program, Milner in May, 1900, explained to the Colonial Secretary the steps which "any wise administrator" should take in this regard. At the

7. Milner to Major Hanbury Williams, Dec. 27, 1900, Milner Papers.
8. Milner to Chamberlain, Dec. 26, 1902, Julian Amery, *The Life of Joseph Chamberlain*, IV, 325; Milner to Herbert Asquith, Sept. 13, 1901, Milner Papers.

first opportunity military rule should end and civilian government be restored, for, "with few exceptions," Milner wrote,
"wherever soldiers are now doing civilian work, things are going
badly. The muddling of various military commandants under
Martial Law in the [Cape] Colony causes endless and needless
trouble."[9] Crown colony governments in the Transvaal and the
Orange Free State under civilian administration could, following
the defeat of the Boers, operate more flexibly and efficiently than
under military rule. Milner felt that finding the administrative
personnel for such governments would offer few problems. A
handful of British officials sent into each of the former republics
could do the job adequately, for in the Free State governmental
needs were few, and in the Transvaal local residents loyal to the
Crown were available for all but the most important positions.
"In spite of all the lies about them," the leading *Uitlanders* were,
according to Milner, "the ablest and honestest men in South
Africa, and quite the same type as leading men of business in our
home centres of industry."[10]

In fact, however, when Milner began several months later to
recruit administrators and civil servants to staff the Crown governments in the occupied republics the results were not what he
had led Chamberlain to expect. Necessary personnel was in many
cases recruited from the British civil service and from among
recent graduates of British universities rather than locally.
Among those who thus were drawn to South Africa were the
young men who later came to be called "Lord Milner's
kindergarten."

Milner's supporters and apologists later went to great lengths to
justify this action. According to Leo Amery:

> He was anxious to avoid a cut and dried administrative system; he
> was determined to enlist the very best brains and the greatest
> possible energy and adaptability for the unique task before him;
> he could not hope in every case to secure ripe experience as well.[11]

Other admirers insisted that at the time Milner had no choice but
to search outside South Africa for many of his crown colony

9. Milner to Chamberlain, May 9, 1900, Milner Papers.
10. *Ibid.*
11. Leo Amery, *The Times History of the War in South Africa* (London, 1900),
VI, 147.

officials. They pointed out that even before the war the government of the Transvaal had found it necessary to hire Hollanders and Germans to fill many important governmental posts left vacant by a shortage of trained and available Boers.[12] The situation facing Milner during and after the war, they insisted, was even worse. The war caused the Hollanders and Germans to scatter, and in its wake the appeal of private employment was so great that men of ability in South Africa found it possible to make several times as much working for the mines or in private business as they could as Crown officials.[13]

If Milner had difficulty finding suitable administrative personnel, it was not for want of applicants. In fact, by late 1901 he was prompted to write of a "cloud of applications" which had by then reached a figure of "many thousands."[14] Undoubtedly, these applications, some of them supported by letters of recommendation from such highly placed imperial administrators as Curzon and Cromer,[15] became the basis for many appointments. But the young men who later composed the kindergarten were all chosen in ways which were both more haphazard and more personal. Oxford friendships, contacts within the Colonial Office, and personal association with Milner were in these cases determinants. For instance, the first of the kindergarten to arrive in South Africa as a Milner appointee was J. F. (Peter) Perry, recently graduated from New College and a Fellow of All Souls and for a number of years a junior official in the Colonial Office. When Milner's "Imperial Secretary," (Sir) George Fiddes, was appointed to act as a liaison between Milner and the military commander, Lord Roberts, a replacement was needed on Milner's personal staff. In arranging with Chamberlain for Fiddes's transfer, Milner pointed out that he would "of course . . . have to be replaced here—and replaced if possible, by a man from home conversant with South

12. Cecil Headlam in *Cambridge History of the British Empire*, VIII, 553; W. Basil Worsfold, *The Reconstruction of the New Colonies under Lord Milner* (London, 1913), II, 212.

13. Selborne to the Colonial Secretary, received Nov. 26, 1906, *Further Correspondence relating to Affairs in the Transvaal and Orange River Colony* (in Continuation of Cd. 3025 and Cd. 3028), London: His Majesty's Stationery Office; June, 1907, p. 15; Worsfold, *Reconstruction under Milner*, II, 214.

14. Milner to Major W. Evans-Gordon, M.P., Dec. 27, 1901, Milner Papers.

15. Curzon to Milner, Aug. 22, 1901, and Cromer to Milner, Sept. 20, 1901, *ibid.*

African affairs, such as Perry."[16] Milner's request for Perry was perhaps a tribute to the ease and efficiency with which that young man had discharged his duties at the Colonial Office, for until his arrival in Cape Town in late July Milner knew him only through official correspondence and the latter's reputation.[17] As Imperial Secretary to the High Commissioner Perry was charged specifically with the administrative supervision of the native reserves of Basutoland, Swaziland, and Bechuanaland and with liaison between the imperial government and Southern Rhodesia.[18]

Two months after his arrival in Cape Town Perry was joined by a young associate also destined to become a part of Milner's kindergarten. On October 2, 1900, Lionel Curtis landed in Cape Town with a letter of introduction from Lord Welby, Chairman of the London County Council, under whom he had served briefly after Oxford.[19] Curtis, like Perry a product of New College, had come to South Africa earlier in the same year as a bicycle messenger in a military unit called the City Imperial Volunteers, but after the death of his older brother at Ladysmith he returned home before his unit to set his brother's affairs in order.[20] "Having fixed up his affairs," Curtis later wrote, "I was dying to get back and wanted to serve under Milner—as we all did."[21] He thus returned to Cape Town just as his old comrades in the C. I. V. were embarking for their voyage home,[22] and a week later Perry wrote to his intimate friend Geoffrey Robinson that "we roped him in to help in the office. . . ."[23] Assigned to Milner's personal

16. Milner to Chamberlain, May 9, 1900, *ibid.*

17. Perry to Robinson, Aug. 1, 1900, Private Papers of Geoffrey Dawson. Geoffrey Robinson, a member of the kindergarten and lifelong participant in round table activities, changed his name to Dawson in 1917 upon inheriting from his mother's family the Dawson properties in Yorkshire. He is identified as Robinson throughout this work.

18. Undated memorandum written by Robinson at the time of Milner's retirement in 1905 and left for his friend and Lord Selborne's private secretary Dougal O. Malcolm. A copy is to be found in the Dawson Papers.

19. Lionel Curtis, *With Milner in South Africa* (Oxford, 1951), p. vii. This account of Curtis's recruitment varies with that found in Leo Amery's autobiography, in which he wrote that Curtis was appointed in 1901 upon his recommendation. The Rt. Hon. L. S. Amery, *My Political Life*, Vol. I: *England before the Storm, 1896–1914* (London, 1953), p. 151.

20. Curtis, *With Milner in South Africa,* pp. v–vii.

21. Curtis to J. W. Shepardson, Dec. 25, 1948, Library, Royal Institute of International Affairs, London.

22. Perry to Robinson, Oct. 10, 1900, Dawson Papers.

23. *Ibid.*

staff as one of a number of private secretaries, Curtis discovered that Perry was not the only member of Milner's official family whom he had previously known. According to Curtis's diary, a young man named Basil Williams who "had been at B. N. C. [Brasenose College] 1893–97" was at that time "in the same position as myself at Government House."[24] The future historian and longtime associate of the kindergarten group had like Curtis previously been to South Africa as a soldier and had returned to work for Milner. Thanks to Perry's friendship, the two new members of the staff were able to adjust with ease to the conditions of wartime Cape Town.[25]

But their stay in Cape Town was a short one. Late in 1900 Milner prepared to move his headquarters to the north. Though the Boer troops had not then been swept from the two republics, Milner was determined to establish himself in Johannesburg at the first opportunity so that he might better supervise the reconstruction program. He designated Curtis to visit the recently occupied mining center to find suitable administration buildings and adequate quarters for the High Commissioner. Curtis's diary in November, 1900, records his trip to Johannesburg, where he selected as Milner's headquarters the magnificent estate of the mining magnate and financier H. Eckstein.[26] Called "Sunnyside" by its owner, the house and its park were in a hilly area on the northern outskirts of the city, far removed from the mining and commercial centers, and providing an impressive view across the veld to the capital of Pretoria some thirty miles away.[27] From March, 1901, when the move finally took place, until the establishment of union nine years later, Sunnyside was both the administrative center of British government in South Africa and the residence of the High Commissioner. And around it lived the officials of the government in whatever quarters they could find. As the months passed the problem of housing became less pressing, but in the hectic time just following the move from Cape Town members of Milner's staff faced housing difficulties of the

24. Curtis, *With Milner in South Africa*, p. 116. Quoted from his diary, Oct. 6, 1900.

25. Curtis, *With Milner in South Africa*, pp. 121–22.

26. *Ibid.*, pp. 156–57.

27. Milner to Mrs. Montefiore, March 22, 1901, Headlam, II, 235.

sort one would expect in a recently occupied city. Quarters of any kind were scarce and prices exorbitant. Perry and Curtis considered themselves fortunate to find a small house about three miles from Sunnyside which cost them £20 a month rent and £8 monthly for "two black boys." "The normal rent is £50 a month," Perry wrote to his friend Robinson, "but the tenant, being a renegade, instructed his agent to let it for anything he could get to anyone who would take care of it, lest the military should commandeer it & pay nothing, besides destroying the furniture."[28]

Just as the movement of Milner's headquarters was in progress Patrick Duncan, another member of the future kindergarten, arrived in South Africa. A Balliol man like Milner, Duncan had upon completion of his education joined the staff of the Board of Inland Revenue in 1894. At Somerset House he served as Milner's private secretary, thereby gaining the respect and affection of his superior and establishing a friendship which changed his life.[29] When casting about for able men to aid in the reconstruction, Milner offered to his old private secretary the post of Treasurer of the colonial government to be established in the Transvaal. Arriving in Cape Town in the middle of March, 1901,[30] Duncan conferred with Milner briefly and was soon settled in Pretoria. Despite his more mature years (he was thirty-one years of age), Duncan quickly formed close ties with both Curtis and Perry. Within two months of Duncan's arrival Curtis recorded in his diary his admiration for the Transvaal Treasurer, remarking that "Duncan is one of the people I should have appointed had I been the government."[31] Similarly, Perry registered his approval of Duncan, "whom I find very estimable & white all over."[32]

With the nucleus of crown colony governments established in the Orange River Colony and the Transvaal, and with the movement of his own headquarters complete, Milner was by May, 1901, able to take home leave for the first time in more than two years. The strain of the war had had a debilitating effect upon the High Commissioner which was a source of concern to his staff.[33] The

28. Perry to Robinson, March 29, 1901, Dawson Papers.
29. "Patrick Duncan," Round Table, No. 132 (Sept., 1943), p. 303.
30. Perry to Robinson, March 6, 1901, Dawson Papers.
31. Curtis, With Milner in South Africa, p. 235.
32. Perry to Robinson, May 17, 1901, Dawson Papers.
33. Perry to Robinson, Nov. 28, 1900, ibid.

demands of the forthcoming reconstruction thus made recuperation at this time essential. Furthermore, Milner wanted to confer with Chamberlain concerning the details of the reconstruction program and to seek through personal persuasion the support of those leaders of the Liberal party not doctrinaire in their opposition to the Empire.[34] After seeing to the establishment of his administrative machinery in the north, Milner sailed from Cape Town on May 8. On reaching Madeira he learned of the greeting Chamberlain planned for him upon his arrival in England. To scotch rumors that Milner was being recalled to make room for a High Commissioner less hostile towards the Boers, Chamberlain decided to make his return to England a Roman triumph. As a symbol to the world of the determination of the Crown to support the Milnerian program, almost the whole cabinet turned out to greet Milner upon his arrival at Waterloo Station. And immediately he was driven to an audience with the King at which he was made a Privy Councillor and created "Baron Milner of St. James's and Cape Town."[35] Initial plans for a restful holiday gave way thereafter to a series of public dinners and formal ceremonies which left little time for the peace and relaxation which Milner's weakened constitution so badly needed.

In spite of these claims upon his time and energy in England, Milner made a special effort to recruit able and energetic young men to assist him upon his return to South Africa. While he was conferring with political leaders and attending innumerable public functions, a young official from the Colonial Office, Geoffrey Robinson, was day after day "occupied chiefly in getting together a list of South African candidates for Lord Milner—from people already in the Service."[36] Nor did Milner fail to consider young men who were known to him personally or who were brought to his attention by his close friends at home. Among these was Leopold S. Amery, a Balliol man and chief South African correspondent of *The Times* throughout the most active part of the war. At the time of Milner's brief visit to England in 1901 Amery was engaged in the production of the widely respected *The Times*

34. Leo Amery, *The Times History of the War in South Africa*, VI, 13.
35. Julian Amery, *Life of Chamberlain*, IV, 32–34.
36. Robinson's diary, Aug. 14, 1901, Dawson Papers.

History of the War in South Africa. This commitment to Printing House Square made it impossible for him to accept Milner's invitation to return with him as his personal secretary. "I was naturally no less eager to go," Amery recalled years later, "both for the prospect of the adventure itself and because of the great personal affection as well as admiration I had conceived for one who, unofficially or officially, was to be my spiritual chief for the rest of his days."[37]

According to Amery, it was he who found for Milner "an admirable substitute in John Buchan."[38] The future novelist and biographer recorded in his memoirs that this summons was totally unexpected, for he had no reason to think that the proconsul of South Africa had ever heard of him. "But the name [of Milner] had been long familiar to me, for at Oxford men spoke it reverentially."[39] Upon his arrival in South Africa in late 1901 Buchan immediately formed close friendships with other young Oxonians on Milner's staff,[40] which perhaps accounts for his frequent inclusion in lists of kindergarten members. In fact, Buchan remained in South Africa only two years, returning to London in 1903 to enter the legal profession.[41] Though not a member of that group of young political activists called Milner's kindergarten, Buchan (later Lord Tweedsmuir) maintained throughout his life the associations formed in South Africa and reflected in his many novels and in his public career a devotion to the Empire derived in large measure from Milner.

Among Milner's close friends and frequent companions during his visit to England was George Wyndham, from 1900 to 1905 the Chief Secretary for Ireland.[42] In response to his request Milner received Hugh Wyndham (later Lord Leconfield), a tubercular young cousin of his friend who was anxious to serve the Crown and at the same time escape the rigors of the English climate.[43]

37. Leo Amery, *My Political Life*, I, 150 f.
38. *Ibid.*
39. John Buchan (Lord Tweedsmuir), *Pilgrim's Way: An Essay in Recollection* (Cambridge, Mass., 1940), p. 94.
40. *Ibid.*, pp. 99 ff.
41. *Dictionary of National Biography*, 1931–1940, p. 111.
42. Milner's diary, June and July, 1901, Milner Papers.
43. Interview with Lord Leconfield, March 8, 1960; Milner's diary, June 22, 1901, Milner Papers.

Thus, "a charming New College man called Wyndham"[44] joined
Buchan as one of the new private secretaries on Milner's staff,
where he remained until 1905.

It is not surprising that Geoffrey Robinson, whom the Colonial
Office put at Milner's disposal during this visit, should some
months later accept an invitation from Milner to join his official
family. Had there been no other inducement, it would have been
difficult for him to assist Milner in the recruitment of staff personnel without wishing to number himself among those selected. In
fact, however, Robinson, an intimate friend of Peter Perry, had
for over a year longed to forsake his unimaginative work in
London to join his All Souls associate on Milner's staff. An almost
unbroken series of weekly letters from Perry during their separation suggests the fervor of Robinson's efforts. On several occasions
Perry lamented the absence of an opening in South Africa which
would provide "the sort of job you want," but promised to find a
place for his friend as soon as possible.[45] It appears, however, that
the diligence with which Robinson served the High Commissioner
during these brief weeks in England was decisive, for shortly
thereafter his opportunity came. According to Robinson's diary
on September 24, 1901: "Found a tel. to M. C. from Ld. M. asking
him to let me go out as Private Sec. for a year at £1,000. Talked to
Ommaney [Sir Montagu Frederick Ommaney, Permanent Under-secretary for the Colonies] when he came up at 1 & found him
inclined on the whole to recommend it."[46] Two days later he
recorded that Chamberlain had given his approval, and on October 26, 1901, he sailed from Southampton. By the middle of
November he was settled in Johannesburg and thereafter quickly
integrated into Milner's organization as the High Commissioner's
"Secretary for Municipal Affairs."[47]

Thus by the end of 1901 there had gathered under Milner's
authority the nucleus of the kindergarten. Perry, Curtis, Duncan,
Robinson and Wyndham were brought from England by Milner;

44. Curtis, *With Milner in South Africa*, p. 323. Quoted from his diary, Oct. 19,
1901.
45. Perry to Robinson, Sept. 12, 1900, Feb. 3, 1901, and Good Friday, 1901,
Dawson Papers.
46. Robinson's diary, Sept. 24, 1901, Dawson Papers.
47. *Ibid.*, Oct. and Nov., 1901.

they were, however, to remain long after their patron had retired and with the addition of later arrivals to search for ways to promote the Milnerian dream of a united South Africa within an Empire of autonomous nations. But this was in the future. The tasks immediately before them involved the reconstruction of the former Boer republics. The experience thus acquired was to serve them well in their later activities.

Chapter Three. Reconstruction and the kindergarten

From the first it was obvious to Milner that Johannesburg, the heart of the mining industry and South Africa's largest center of population, was crucial to his reconstruction program. "A great Johannesburg," he said in 1902, "great in intelligence, in cultivation, in public spirit—means a British Transvaal."[1] Thus as soon as the city was occupied by British forces Milner began extending his control over municipal affairs. To hasten the replacement of military authority, for which he had only contempt, Milner created a Commission for the Constitution of Johannesburg even before he transferred his headquarters from Cape Town. This Commission had authority to examine conditions of local government and make recommendations for their improvement. On March 20, 1901, he appointed Lionel Curtis secretary of that body. Young Curtis, full of enthusiasm but with little appropriate experience, left immediately for Johannesburg to take up his duties. Less than a month later he and the members of the Commission presented the High Commissioner with a report calling for the creation of an appointed town council composed of leading Johannesburgers and the appointment of a town clerk having broad powers to establish a progressive municipal government.[2] After approving the plan on April 13, 1901, Milner appointed Curtis temporary town clerk until a more experienced and mature replacement could be found. In succeeding months, however, Curtis proved his fitness for the job, and in response to a request made by the town council in July, 1901, Milner made him permanent town clerk effective January of the following year.[3]

The complexity of this work and Curtis's inexperience soon convinced both Curtis and Milner that assistance was needed. Basil Williams was appointed Curtis's assistant—a needed step but one which caused the town clerk some embarrassment. "Very

1. *Times,* Jan. 11, 1902.
2. Curtis, *With Milner in South Africa,* pp. 204 f.
3. *Ibid.,* pp. 214, 236, 338.

weird feeling," he recorded in his diary, "having an assistant much older and cleverer than yourself."[4] The newly arrived Geoffrey Robinson was chosen from the group of private secretaries of the High Commissioner to be specifically responsible for municipal affairs.[5] For the following year he worked closely with Curtis to provide better liaison between the municipal government and the High Commissioner's office. Curtis's admitted inability to handle financial matters and his wish to find a place for an old friend prompted him to request the services of Lionel Hichens as town treasurer.[6] Hichens, a New College friend and comrade-at-arms of Curtis, was at that time serving in the Egyptian Ministry of Finance. Upon receipt of Curtis's wire containing Milner's offer he immediately accepted, and shortly thereafter assumed the position which he held for almost two years.[7] An active and enthusiastic member of the kindergarten, Hichens remained in South Africa until 1907 and later participated in the creation of the round table movement.

The problems which confronted Curtis and his staff were formidable. Johannesburg was, in the words of one kindergarten member, "simply the veldt with the grass rubbed off by passing vehicles."[8] Like all boomtowns, it had been created by a transient population bent upon quick wealth and indifferent to the needs of a settled community. To make matters worse, the Boer government had before the war coldly ignored the problems of the Transvaal's only city. "At Johannesburg everything a town needs had to be created," wrote one of the kindergarten over twenty years later, "and there was little or nothing on which to build."

> In such a climate the want of a water-borne sewage system was a public danger. There was no up to date tram or lighting service, no abattoir. There was not even a passable system of public health notwithstanding the existence of a large native quarter, an Asiatic location, and a large poor Dutch slum. There had never been any attempt at town planning.[9]

4. *Ibid.,* pp. 334, 336. Quoted from his diary, Jan. 13, 1902.
5. *Ibid.,* p. 328.
6. *Ibid.,* pp. 329, 334.
7. Leo Amery, *The Times History of the War in South Africa,* VI, 148.
8. J. R. M. Butler, *Lord Lothian (Philip Kerr) 1882–1940* (London, 1960), p. 14. The quotation apparently comes from a letter written by Kerr to his family in 1905.
9. Dove, "The Round Table: A Mystery Probed," pp. 5–6.

Milner, whose enthusiasm for municipal reform had been evinced during his days with the *Pall Mall Gazette,* was determined that this deplorable situation should not continue. And in Curtis he had a dedicated agent. Both were aware that the time for action was short, for the inevitable return of local government would end the dictatorship of the Crown government. Curtis and his staff, with Milner's concurrence, were thus forced to move swiftly. Even before his permanent appointment as town clerk, Curtis had worked out a plan for Milner's consideration which he regarded as basic to the development of the city. It called for the extension of the city limits of Johannesburg to include the whole metropolitan area, a plan which, if adopted, would bring under one municipal government the central part of the city, the many suburbs which had sprung up around the mining center, and the mines themselves with their company-owned native labor compounds.[10] Milner, always the supporter of centralization and governmental efficiency, approved Curtis's proposal, for he saw in it the only device by which the Johannesburg area as a whole could be provided with modern efficient government and with the tax receipts sufficient to pay for such government. But in doing so he incurred the opposition of the powerful Chamber of Mines, whose members regarded the extension of government authority over their property with undisguised hostility. Curtis, the instigator of the plan and the official directly involved in its implementation, remained from that time somewhat suspect in the eyes of the mining fraternity and property owners of the Johannesburg area.[11]

Hardly had Curtis, with the aid of Robinson, Hichens, and Williams, begun to reform and modernize Johannesburg when the town clerk contracted dysentery which failed to respond to treatment. In late April, 1902, therefore—just weeks before the Treaty of Vereeniging ended the war—Curtis returned to England on sick leave.[12] He was instructed by Milner to work through the Colonial Office while in England to find another assistant, this time one with legal training who could advise the

10. This plan is described in detail and appended to Curtis, *With Milner in South Africa.*

11. Dove, "The Round Table: A Mystery Probed," p. 6.

12. Curtis, *With Milner in South Africa,* p. 342.

town council on questions of law. A report of this search and its results was sent to Robinson by an Oxford friend in the Colonial Office:

> I think we have arranged the deputy town clerk business satisfactorily. Curtis has seen all the best candidates, but his name hasn't been allowed to appear officially. I remember Feetham, the man they have spotted as being the best, at New Coll. He is a white man and I should think a very able one. It gave rise to great surprise to recollect when he failed to get his 'first.'[13]

Richard Feetham, an old friend of Curtis and Hichens and later one of the most active members of the kindergarten, arrived in Johannesburg in the middle of 1902. According to Curtis, Feetham began at once to demonstrate an aptitude for municipal administration which impressed not only his English associates but the Johannesburgers on the town council as well. Milner decided early the following year, therefore, to move Curtis to Pretoria as Assistant Colonial Secretary charged with reforming municipal government in all the cities and towns of the Transvaal, enabling the town council of Johannesburg to make Feetham its town clerk.[14] Feetham served in this capacity until Milner's retirement and the restoration of responsible government in the Transvaal in 1905, whereupon he returned to the bar, mixing an active political career in Johannesburg with the practice of law.

By the time of Feetham's appointment as town clerk in 1903, Basil Williams, Curtis's assistant, had left Johannesburg to establish a new education system in the Transvaal.[15] Shortly thereafter, Lionel Hichens moved from town treasurer of Johannesburg to Colonial Treasurer of the Transvaal, replacing Patrick Duncan upon the latter's appointment as Colonial Secretary.[16] These vacancies on the town clerk's staff led to a search for an assistant for Feetham. Upon the recommendation of Sir William Anson, Warden of All Souls and at that time Minister of Education, John Dove was selected. Educated at New College before being called

13. Dougal O. Malcolm to Robinson, May 17, 1902, Dawson Papers.
14. Curtis, *With Milner in South Africa*, p. 344.
15. "Basil Williams (1867–1950)," *Dictionary of National Biography*, 1941–1950, pp. 957–58.
16. Leo Amery, *The Times History of the War in South Africa*, VI, 148.

to the bar, Dove was a close friend of Curtis, Feetham, and Hichens. He brought to South Africa a weakened body which it was hoped would be made strong by the warm dry climate of Johannesburg. Overwork, however, nullified the good effect of a healthy climate, so that by the time of his return to England in late 1910 his health was precarious. Even so, Dove remained at the heart of all kindergarten activities in both South Africa and England from his arrival in Johannesburg until his death in 1934.[17]

Milner's efforts to establish in Johannesburg the form of enlightened municipal government characteristic of many English cities thus brought to South Africa Lionel Hichens, Richard Feetham, and John Dove, and gave to Lionel Curtis valuable experience in governmental affairs. For the rest of their lives they were proud to claim membership in that fraternity called Lord Milner's kindergarten. It should be noted, however, that these men were not properly speaking members of Milner's staff. Though they thought of themselves as Milner's young men, and though several of them later joined Milner's staff in various capacities, they were at this time employees of the city of Johannesburg. As such they were distinct from that group of young officials who, like Geoffrey Robinson, Peter Perry, and Patrick Duncan, worked directly under the High Commissioner.

Robinson, after serving for a year as liaison between the High Commissioner's office and the municipal governments, found himself thrust into a position of intimate association with Milner. In April, 1903, while Milner was in England on a brief visit, his private secretary, "Ozzy" Walrond, became ill and was replaced by Robinson.[18] As Milner's private secretary charged with directing the office staff and caring for the myriad details of office routine,[19] Robinson, during the two years which remained before Milner's retirement, came to know Milner far more intimately than the other young Englishmen on his staff. Indeed, it might be

17. "John Dove," *Round Table*, No. 95 (June, 1934), pp. 463–68; Robert Henry Brand, ed., *The Letters of John Dove* (London, 1938), p. v.
18. Curtis, *With Milner in South Africa*, p. 344; Milner to Lady Edward Cecil, April 24, 1903, Milner Papers.
19. A description of these tasks is found in a long undated memorandum left by Robinson to his successor Dougal Malcolm at the time of Milner's retirement in 1905. A copy is in the Dawson Papers.

said that Robinson was the only member of the kindergarten who could claim friendship with Milner during the South African years. Letters from Robinson preserved in the Milner papers indicate an ease and informality borne of friendship while those from the other kindergarten members suggest admiration and awesome respect. As Milner's retirement approached, the High Commissioner was able to find a position for his young friend as editor of a leading pro-British South African newspaper, the Johannesburg *Star*.

Patrick Duncan, in South Africa at Milner's request to serve as Colonial Treasurer of the Transvaal, was in late 1903 appointed Colonial Secretary and shortly thereafter made acting Lieutenant-Governor.[20] Throughout the last years of Milner's rule, therefore, Duncan served as chief administrative officer of the crown colony government of the Transvaal. As such, he was answerable only to Milner, the Governor of both the Transvaal and the Orange River Colony as well as the High Commissioner. According to Amery, on Duncan "fell all the most responsible work of the [Transvaal] administration from the peace down to the grant of self-government."[21]

Milner's so-called Imperial Secretary, J. F. Perry, was charged with handling matters relating to Milner's position as High Commissioner. He was thus concerned with affairs in the native areas directly under British authority, particularly problems arising from the postwar need for native labor in the Rand mines. Adequate labor for the mining industry was vital to Milner's reconstruction plan, for upon the rapid restoration of Rand prosperity depended the influx of British settlers which Milner considered essential to the creation of a British South Africa.[22] To Milner the logic of the matter was clear. Settlers from Great Britain and the self-governing colonies would come to South Africa in sufficient numbers only if prosperity were quickly restored. The economic realities of South Africa being what they were, a restoration of prosperity meant a speedy restoration of the mining industry. To use Milner's term, it was the "overspill" from a revived mining

20. "Patrick Duncan," *Round Table*, No. 132 (Sept., 1943), p. 303.
21. Leo Amery, *The Times History of the War in South Africa*, VI, 148.
22. Leo Amery, *My Political Life*, I, 174.

community which would provide the capital and generate the commercial activity necessary to restore economic health to a war-torn area.[23]

At war's end, however, Milner found the restoration of gold production hampered by a shortage of unskilled labor. The vast reserve of native labor upon which the mines depended was no longer available. In the months immediately following the war, the demand for workers to help rebuild what had been destroyed during the struggle cut into the normal labor supply. In Johannesburg the matter was made worse by efforts of the mine owners to reduce wages, a step which the recently created Witwatersrand Native Labour Association insisted was necessary to compensate mine owners for profits lost during the war.[24] Milner's whole reconstruction program was thus threatened by a shortage of natives willing to go down into the mines.

As Milner's Imperial Secretary, Perry became deeply involved in efforts to end this shortage by recruiting natives in sufficient numbers from Basutoland and Swaziland. When these sources proved inadequate, Milner in late 1901 sent him to negotiate with Portuguese authorities for permission to obtain labor in Mozambique. By early 1902 Milner's confidence in the young All Souls scholar was rewarded with an agreement allowing the Rand Native Labour Association to recruit labor there in unlimited numbers. In return for payment by the mines of thirteen shillings a head, the Portuguese promised to assist in the recruitment and to maintain the same tariff and rail rate from the port of Lourenço Marques that had existed before the war.[25]

The agreement with the Portuguese seemed to solve the labor problems of the Rand. "This means," wrote Curtis with enthusiasm, "restarting the whole mining industry."[26] Recruitment in Mozambique, however, proved to be inadequate. As the situation grew progressively worse, the mine owners demanded the importa-

23. Milner's opening address to the Intercolonial Council, March, 1904, Headlam, II, 491.
24. Worsfold, *The Reconstruction of the New Colonies under Lord Milner*, I, xi–xiv.
25. Curtis, *With Milner in South Africa*, p. 341; Leo Amery, *The Times History of the War in South Africa*, VI, 27, 105.
26. Curtis, *With Milner in South Africa*, p. 341. Quoted from his diary, Feb. 18, 1902.

tion of Asian laborers who could be used until the mines were again in full operation and an adequate supply of African labor was again available. Following the restoration of normal conditions on the Rand, they insisted, the Asians could be returned to their homes without adding further to the already troublesome racial composition of South Africa.[27]

Milner's support of the plan to import "coolies" was reflected in a letter from Robinson to his family in early 1903.

> I think there's very little doubt now that it will come to Chinamen in time. It would release an immense quantity of niggers for agriculture etc. which they much prefer, & I think it ought to be quite possible to keep the yellow men for unskilled labour pure & simple & to ship them home again when they have done it.[28]

Such a project involved political dangers. The Liberal opposition in Great Britain might, if so disposed, use it with great effect to discredit the Unionist government. Milner postponed final decision, therefore, until late 1903 when he was able to get to London to discuss the matter with the new Colonial Secretary, Alfred Lyttelton, and with Liberal Imperialists like Grey, Haldane, and Asquith.[29] His conversations having proved successful, Milner acted in late October to secure the needed labor. Perry, who had recently resigned from Milner's staff to become chairman of the Rand Native Labour Association, was ordered to London to assist in the working out of administrative details with the Colonial and Foreign Offices.[30] Milner himself sailed for South Africa a month later to get the necessary support from that quarter.[31] On February 10, 1904, the Transvaal Legislative Council, a body appointed by the Crown, passed an ordinance permitting the importation of Chinese labor.[32]

Immediately, popular disapproval was manifested in Great Britain among those who considered the plan immoral and in those parts of the Empire where concern for the "yellow peril"

27. F. Drummond Chaplin, "The Labour Question in the Transvaal," *National Review*, No. 275 (Jan., 1906), pp. 835–49; Worsfold, *Reconstruction . . . under Milner*, I, xi–xiv.
28. April 5, 1903, Dawson Papers.
29. Headlam, II, 477.
30. Robinson's diary, Oct. 30, 1903, Dawson Papers.
31. Milner's diary, Nov. 28, 1903, Milner Papers.
32. Wrench, *Alfred Lord Milner*, p. 250.

was traditional. Liberal party politicians, in need of a campaign issue with emotional appeal, soon began to refer to "Chinese slavery" practiced in South Africa by the Rand millionaires with the support of the Unionist government. Such hostility seemed not to surprise Milner; even so, he found it impossible to credit honorable intentions to those who protested.

> There is an immense amount of cant about the "moral" evils attending Chinese immigration. . . . It is the pro-Boers and Little Englanders who are really at the bottom of the whole business, though they are leading the bulk of their well-meaning ignorant countrymen by the nose. [And] to say that Chinese labour is *a substitution for white labour* is, quite simply, a lie. The exact opposite is the truth. Without a substratum of coloured people, white labour cannot exist here, and when the very rich mines are worked out the country will return to its primitive barrenness—and to the Boer. And that is the true inwardness of the whole business.[33]

The passage of the necessary legislation was only a first step to solving the labor problem. "Whether the Chinese will come is another question," wrote one of Robinson's friends at the beginning of 1904. "And much of course depends on Piet [Perry]."[34] As chairman of the Rand Native Labour Association, Perry was responsible for recruitment. After completing arrangements in London he went directly to the China coast to direct the project.[35] Milner soon learned that his former secretary was arousing antagonism among the "old China hands" in his haste to speed the laborers on their way. In a cable to the High Commissioner the Colonial Secretary, Alfred Lyttelton, remarked that "suspicions [are being] aroused by numerous current falsehoods & possibly by activity of Perry. . . ."[36] Perry, however, defended himself to his friends, insisting that his actions were above criticism. The main source of difficulty, he declared, was the Chinese laborers themselves, who believed rumors that they were being recruited to fight against the Boers. Adequate volunteers became available only

33. Milner to the Right Reverend A. Hamilton-Baynes, the Bishop of Natal, Milner Papers.
34. Dougal Malcolm to Robinson, Jan. 9, 1904, Dawson Papers.
35. Perry to Milner, April 26, 1904, Milner Papers.
36. Secretary of State, Colonial Office to His Excellency the High Commissioner, March 4, [1904] (copy), Dawson Papers.

after the early recruits were able to report that "to their astonishment they find that they are being paid what they were promised and that the whole thing is a square deal."[37] Further problems were created, Perry insisted, by W. Evans, the Superintendent of Foreign Labor of the Transvaal colonial government, who was constantly hovering about and interfering with those who were attempting to secure the needed labor. Charged with protecting the Chinese, Evans seemed to Perry to be undermining the recruitment program with his overanxiety for the welfare of the "coolies."[38]

Despite these difficulties the Chinese miners began arriving on the Rand in June, 1904. Their number mounted steadily, reaching a peak in January, 1907, when almost fifty-four thousand were employed.[39] Perry could thus feel that his efforts had been successful. Milner, too, could look upon the "coolie" venture as a success, for in spite of the political difficulties which resulted, the importation of Chinese labor provided the mines with a supply of unskilled workers essential to their recovery. With their help the output of the Rand mines rose from less than £13,000,000 in 1903 to more than £27,000,000 in 1907.[40] The prosperity of the mining industry, so essential to the fulfilment of Milner's dream of a united South Africa within the British Empire, was thus belatedly but finally restored.

But even Rand prosperity and the expected influx of British settlers were not thought by Milner to lead automatically to the creation of *"one Dominion* with a common government dealing with Customs, Railways and Defence, perhaps also with Native policy. . . ."[41] It was essential that steps be taken to create a community of interests among the colonies if the fragmented states of South Africa were ever to become unified. Thus, in the years following the war Milner sought at all times to promote joint action among the colonies, particularly in matters concerning police and transportation. In fact, the Letters Patent establish-

---

37. Malcolm to Robinson, Jan. 14, 1905, Dawson Papers.
38. Perry to Robinson, Oct. 7, 1904, Dawson Papers.
39. Leo Amery, *The Times History of the War in South Africa,* VI, 111–28.
40. Thompson, *The Unification of South Africa,* p. 14; Leo Amery, *The Times History of the War in South Africa,* VI, 127.
41. Milner to Sir Percy Fitzpatrick, Nov. 28, 1899, Milner Papers.

ing the Transvaal and Orange River Colony governments specifically vested the High Commissioner with control of the South
African Constabulary, a joint police force, and with the administration of the railroads in both former republics. Milner's hand
was further strengthened in this regard by the availability of
British government funds to finance relief and reconstruction.
Like the control of the police and railroads, the money, in the
form of grants and loans amounting to tens of millions of pounds
sterling, gave to Milner a potent device with which to win the
co-operation of the South Africans.

In an administrative and financial sense the police, railroads,
and funds provided by Great Britain were interrelated. Much of
the money was specifically provided for railroad improvement by
repairing existing lines, extending the system into areas previously not served, and buying the stock of the Netherlands Railway Company, which held franchises granted by the former Boer
governments. The resulting Central South African Railways, a
system owned jointly by the Transvaal and the Orange River
Colony, was expected to produce revenue sufficient to pay not only
the cost of retiring the loans but also the expenses of the South
African Constabulary.

To administer these joint enterprises the British government
created in May, 1903, an Intercolonial Council composed of both
official and non-official representatives appointed from the two
Boer colonies. Milner intended that this body should relieve him
of many administrative chores associated with the railroads and
the police. More importantly, however, he saw in it an instrument
to force upon colonial leaders an awareness of the extent to which
all areas of South Africa were related. As Leo Amery wrote,
Milner expected the Intercolonial Council "to open a wider political horizon, [and] to create a South African habit of mind, as
distinct from a colonial one. . . ."[42]

Though Milner was the president of the council, it was necessary that a secretary be found to devote his full time to the affairs
of the body and to other less important intercolonial agencies
which were then being formed. This position was offered to one of

42. Leo Amery, *The Times History of the War in South Africa*, VI, 8.

Perry's close friends, The Hon. Robert Brand. A product of New College and a fellow of All Souls, Brand (later Lord Brand) was invited to South Africa late in 1902 upon the suggestion of Perry to assist in the establishment of the council and to serve as its secretary. He remained in charge of that body until the creation of the Union government in 1909.[43] In this capacity Brand won the respect of both Milner and the Afrikaner leaders and the affection of the young men of the kindergarten, who quickly drew him into their group. At the time of his retirement in 1905 Milner commended Brand, remarking to his successor that he was "a fellow of real ability, who has this particular business at his finger's end. You can safely lean on him, for he has not only a great mastery of all the rather complicated details, but a good grasp of the general policy."[44] The accuracy of this description was made increasingly apparent in later years as Brand in an unofficial way became a central figure in the creation of the Union constitution and in the delicate negotiations leading to its adoption.

As secretary of the Intercolonial Council, Brand was charged with the over-all responsibility for the affairs of that body. But the complexity of these affairs made it essential that he have the support of able specialists. To handle financial matters Lionel Hichens was appointed treasurer of the Council, thus adding to his already heavy duties as Colonial Treasurer of the Transvaal. Hichens served in this dual capacity until the establishment of responsible government in the Transvaal in early 1907, after which he returned to England and ultimately to a successful career in business.[45] Sir P. Girouard, who during the war had ably directed all British controlled railroads, was named Commissioner of Railways. Under the supervisory control of the Intercolonial Council he was charged with the details of railroad reconstruction and operation. In 1904, however, the antagonisms of the postwar years and the hostility of the Afrikaner members of the council brought about Girouard's resignation. An acting commis-

43. Lord Brand to Miss Dowling, April 8, 1947, *Round Table* Papers (papers on file at the editorial offices of the *Round Table* in London). This long letter contains Brand's comments upon and additions to the previously cited typescript by Dove entitled "The Round Table: A Mystery Probed."
44. Milner to Selborne, April 14, 1905, Milner Papers.
45. "Lionel Hichens," *Round Table*, No. 121 (Dec., 1940), p. 8.

sioner was appointed, but in the following year the office was abolished and the administration of the system was made the direct responsibility of a Railway Committee of the Intercolonial Council.[46]

Brand, who was made secretary of this committee, soon found that the demands of railroad administration left little time for his broader duties as secretary of the Intercolonial Council. He therefore appealed to the High Commissioner for an assistant with whom to share the load. Upon his suggestion, Milner appointed Philip Kerr, a young acquaintance of Brand who had been at New College while Brand was at All Souls.[47] Kerr (later Lord Lothian) had arrived in South Africa only three months before to join the Pretoria staff of Sir Arthur Lawley (Lord Wenlock), the Lieutenant-Governor of the Transvaal. Lawley, an old friend of Kerr's father, Lord Ralph Kerr, had suggested the position with the comment that although it offered little challenge to a young man of ability, it might quickly lead to something more suitable. At the time of Kerr's appointment to Brand's staff in April, 1905, Lawley was therefore pleased to write to his old friend that "the opportunity which I hoped might arise of his dropping into a congenial billet where there will be free play for his talents has arisen."[48]

In his new position Kerr demonstrated a keen mind and a capacity for hard work which soon made him invaluable to Brand.[49] And with Brand and other members of the kindergarten in Johannesburg he found a life far more pleasant than that which he had experienced during the three months spent on Lawley's staff in Pretoria. In a letter to his family he expressed his satisfaction and described some of the day-to-day office routine with which he and Brand were concerned:

> I really like this job very much. It is far pleasanter than being Assistant Private Secretary to Sir Arthur. . . . Up to the present I have been mainly getting into my head the threads of the work, and I have by no means got to the end of that yet, but I see my

46. Leo Amery, *The Times History of the War in South Africa,* VI, 137.
47. [Lord Brand], "Philip Kerr. Some Personal Memories," *Round Table,* No. 199 (June, 1960), p. 235.
48. Quoted in Butler, *Lothian,* p. 13. Also in Lawley's party was his young daughter Cecilia, who later married Geoffrey Robinson (Dawson).
49. Brand to Miss Dowling, April 8, 1947, *Round Table* Papers.

way in the future to getting a good deal to do. Brand is very nice and we get on first rate. There are five clerks under us so you see there is a good deal in one way or another that passes through our hands. The main work really concerns the Railways as a Railway Committee meet every week or fortnight to deal with all the questions which arise about the working of the lines. Of this Brand is Secretary and I have to help him. The other subjects are the guaranteed loan of £35,000,000 to the Transvaal and the South African Constabulary and all the combined services for the two Colonies like Repatriation, Surveying, Land Settlement, etc. There will be an Inter-Colonial Council meeting at the end of May or the beginning of June. . . . It is like a small Parliament of 25 people. They decide policy and allocate funds and debate on different matters. The session lasts about a fortnight, and the proceedings are published in the South African Hansard. So you see there is lots of work and lots of interest before me.[50]

Kerr's claim to membership in the kindergarten is indisputable. It cannot be said to derive from close association with Lord Milner during his South African days, however, for Kerr had almost no contact with the patron of the kindergarten until South Africa had been unified and the young men had returned to England. By the time Kerr arrived in South Africa the High Commissioner's retirement was already planned, and a week after his transfer to Brand's staff in Johannesburg Milner sailed for home. It is rather upon Kerr's close friendship with other members of the group and his active participation in the movements for South African and later imperial unification that his membership in the kindergarten is based.

Much the same thing might be said for the member of the kindergarten who was the last to arrive in South Africa. Dougal O. Malcolm, a young official of the Colonial Office, arrived in South Africa as private secretary to Milner's successor, the Earl of Selborne, a matter of days after Milner's departure.[51] He thus cannot be called a member of the kindergarten in the narrowest sense. But like Kerr, he was made a part of the group by co-optation because of his Oxford associations (he was a graduate of New College and a fellow of All Souls), his close friendship with Perry and Robinson, which was strengthened by common experiences at

50. Quoted in Butler, *Lothian*, pp. 13–14.
51. Malcolm to Robinson, June 11, 1905, Dawson Papers.

the Colonial Office, and his intense efforts on behalf of South African unification.

Though he had not reached South Africa in time to have "the chance of serving him [Milner] on the spot,"[52] Malcolm nevertheless "had the luck to do a little work for him for a few weeks"[53] in London in 1903. During Milner's brief visit to England to seek support for the importation of Chinese onto the Rand, Malcolm served as his temporary private secretary. Like his close friend Robinson two years previous, Malcolm was released from his normal duties at the Colonial Office and placed at the disposal of the High Commissioner. And like Robinson, he was prompted by this association to apply for a permanent position on Milner's staff. Here the similarity ended, for Malcolm was unable to find a place for himself despite efforts made on his behalf by Perry and Robinson. Malcolm's weekly letters to "Robin" suggest that it was the Colonial Office rather than the High Commissioner that prevented him from joining his friends. Whenever he brought the subject to the attention of his superiors he was told that he "couldn't be spared." "Naturally I am very sick about it," he informed Robinson, "but I am not going about the world with a grievance. . . ."[54]

Malcolm's arrival in South Africa completed the kindergarten circle. Others joined the group from time to time in brief association, but it was only Brand, Curtis, Dove, Duncan, Feetham, Hichens, Kerr, Malcolm, Perry, Robinson, and Wyndham whose membership was recognized by all the others.[55] The moment of transition when Milner was replaced by Selborne is, therefore, an appropriate point at which to comment upon the personal relationships which bound the group together. During these early

52. Malcolm to Robinson, June 4, 1904, Dawson Papers.
53. Malcolm to Robinson, Jan. 9, 1904, Dawson Papers.
54. Malcolm to Robinson, n.d. [mid-Nov., 1904], Dawson Papers.
55. The origins of the nickname "kindergarten" are obscure. Basil Worsfold assigned responsibility to the Cape politician and bitter enemy of Milnerism, J. X. Merriman, who, in the Cape parliament in September, 1902, spoke of the High Commissioner's "setting up a sort of kindergarten of Balliol young men to govern the country" (Worsfold, *Reconstruction . . . under Milner*, II, 219). Curtis gave credit to Sir William Marriott, a brilliant but eccentric lawyer "who was busy making trouble for Milner in Johannesburg" (Curtis, *With Milner in South Africa*, p. 342). Lord Leconfield (Hugh Wyndham), however, thought it was first used by Milner in a fatherly sense and then pounced upon by his enemies (interview with Lord Leconfield, March 8, 1960).

years in South Africa there developed a camaraderie within the kindergarten which was an essential element in their later activities on behalf of South African and imperial unification. This group indentification can be partly explained as a natural result of years of intimate association in various administrative affairs. Under the circumstances it would have been surprising if the young men had not been drawn into close friendships, for the comradeship born of common effort was strengthened by a sharing of living quarters and social life. From the beginning these young Englishmen, most of whom were in Johannesburg, chose to pool their funds to establish bachelor quarters around the headquarters of the High Commissioner at Sunnyside. The little house shared by the first of the group to arrive in South Africa— Perry and Curtis—was only the first of a number of such establishments. It was, in fact, a brief arrangement, for within six months an increase in rent by the owner and the approaching marriage of Perry had caused the two to look for separate quarters.[56] In August, 1901, Perry's bride arrived, escorted on the trip from England by Lord Milner.[57] Following their marriage they lived near Milner's headquarters in a house large enough to afford temporary shelter for Curtis,[58] and for Robinson, who lived with them briefly after his arrival in Johannesburg in late 1901.[59] Robinson, however, soon found more suitable quarters in a cottage on the edge of town which he shared with Basil Blackwood, the son of the diplomat and onetime governor-general of Canada, Lord Dufferin.[60] Somewhat older than Robinson and the other young civil servants working for Milner, Blackwood was regarded with affection by the members of the kindergarten though he did not take part in their political activities.[61] This domestic arrangement ended in early 1903 when the house was "sold to a German Jew—with a name something like Goldenfinger—who wants to come in at once."[62] After moving around a bit, Robinson for a

56. Perry to Robinson, June 7 and 21, 1901, Dawson Papers.
57. Perry to Robinson, Aug. 19, 1901, Dawson Papers.
58. Curtis, *With Milner in South Africa*, pp. 320–21.
59. Robinson's diary, Nov. 22, 1901, Dawson Papers.
60. *Ibid.*, Nov. 20, 1901.
61. John Buchan (Lord Tweedsmuir), *Pilgrim's Way: An Essay in Recollection* (Cambridge, Mass., 1940), pp. 101–4.
62. Robinson to his father, April 5, 1903, Dawson Papers.

while occupied a cottage in Perry's garden. By the middle of 1906, however, he had found a house of his own where he remained until his departure from South Africa in 1910.[63]

Other members of the group found lodgings in a house near Sunnyside rented by Hugh Wyndham.[64] Though the names of its occupants varied as the composition of Milner's group of assistants changed, Wyndham's house served as residence for many of the kindergarten until after Milner's retirement, whereupon Wyndham left Johannesburg to take up farming near Standerton on the Vaal River.[65] By then plans had been made for the establishment of what came to be called "Moot House," a dwelling-place for several of the young men and the seat of all kindergarten activities from that time until the achievement of South African unification. Moot House was, strictly speaking, the home of Richard Feetham, who from the first thought of it as a place where he and his friends might hold moots reminiscent of those held by the freemen of Anglo-Saxon England. By the time of Milner's retirement Feetham had decided to leave the Johannesburg municipal government in the hands of his good friend and assistant, John Dove, and take up the practice of law in Johannesburg. He acquired a piece of land in the Parktown suburb not far from Sunnyside and in late 1905 commissioned the young architect Herbert Baker to build a house suited to the needs of Feetham and his friends.[66] Baker, a friend of many of the kindergarten, gained fame in later years for his restoration of the Bank of England building and his design of the secretariat and legislative buildings at Delhi. His earliest successes, however, were in South Africa. Under the patronage of first Rhodes and then Milner he designed many dwellings and public buildings in which he attempted to recapture the primitive dignity of early Cape architecture.[67] Upon its completion in July, 1906, Moot House became the abode of Feetham, Brand, Kerr, Dove, and George Craik. Craik, though not a member of the kindergarten, was a New College friend of many of the group who had come to South

63. Robinson to his father, Nov. 26, 1905, and to "Aunt Kitty," June 17, 1906.
64. Robinson's diary, Nov. 22, 1901, Dawson Papers.
65. Interview with Lord Leconfield, March 8, 1960.
66. John Evelyn Wrench, *Geoffrey Dawson and Our Times* (London, 1955), p. 53.
67. "Sir Herbert Baker," *Dictionary of National Biography*, 1941–1950, p. 41.

Africa during the war in the same unit with Curtis and Hichens.[68] From 1903 to 1909 he served as legal adviser to the Transvaal Chamber of Mines and sometimes as acting secretary of that body before returning to London to become chief constable of the Metropolitan Police.[69] For three years after its completion Moot House served not only as the residence of Feetham and his four friends, but also as a shelter for others—both kindergarten and visitors from Great Britain—who were temporarily in Johannesburg. As Feetham had hoped, his home became the center of kindergarten activities and a meeting place of those seeking to bring about South African unification.

The life which these young men created for themselves in Johannesburg was at first filled with official duties which left little time for leisure. Time available for recreation was usually spent in the company of other young civil servants, for theirs was "almost exclusively a male set"[70] isolated from the company of socially acceptable young women. Perry was in fact the only member of the kindergarten to marry before the group began to drift apart with the establishment of the Union constitution. His wife, who might have been expected to become a frequent hostess and adopted sister to her husband's friends, seems to have played no part in the activities of the group. Little is known of her except that she bore Perry several children before their separation in 1907.[71] Following her departure for England Perry appears to have lived at Moot House when he was not traveling about tending to the affairs of the Rand Native Labour Association.

In this bachelor existence, recreation tended towards vigorous outdoor activity of the sort popular in South Africa. Members of the group made hunting trips and long treks into the interior in which they often conducted official surveys as they fulfilled a desire for adventure. Not surprisingly, in a land of expert horsemen, many sought exercise in the saddle. Following the example set by the High Commissioner himself, the young men rode almost daily, and at least one of them—Robinson—developed a

68. Curtis, *With Milner in South Africa*, pp. 46–47.
69. Robinson's memorandum to Malcolm written at the time of Milner's retirement, Dawson Papers; "Sir George Lillie Craik, 2nd Bt.," *Who's Who*, 1928, p. 679.
70. Lady Gwendolen Cecil to Kerr's mother, quoted in Butler, *Lothian*, p. 16.
71. Interview with Lord Leconfield, March 8, 1960.

reputation as an excellent polo player. But it should be noted that their lives were not completely devoid of the less robust social pleasures. From the very beginning of the war South Africa attracted important visitors in great numbers. Protocol and expediency frequently caused the High Commissioner to take time from his official duties to play the host at lawn parties and dinners. On such occasions the members of his staff were often invited. In addition to these events at Sunnyside, the young men were made welcome in the homes of leading members of the pro-British business community in Johannesburg.[72]

The joint administrative efforts, the shared quarters, and the leisure spent together are perhaps sufficient to account for the spirit of comradeship which developed among Milner's assistants. But it was the lingering influence of Oxford that gave to the kindergarten its unique qualities and its durability. It must be remembered that all eleven members of the group had been educated at Oxford and all but two of them at New College, which had in their generation replaced Balliol as the most esteemed of the Oxford colleges. Proud of their association with New College, they tendered their friendship to each other and to the sons of other Oxford colleges without reservation. This camaraderie was manifested in South Africa in "Oxford dinners" held from time to time by the kindergarten and their colleagues.[73]

The sentimental ties resulting from common experiences at Oxford in general and New College in particular undoubtedly bound the young men into a fraternity of expatriates. But a further cohesive influence derived from Oxford must be considered. Four members of the kindergarten (Brand, Perry, Robinson, and Malcolm) were fellows of All Souls as well.[74] Among these, therefore, the ties which they shared in common with their associates were reinforced by membership in what must be one of the truly unique institutions of the academic world. All Souls College was—and remains—quite unlike any other college at Oxford or Cambridge. It is a fellowship of mature scholars with

72. See Leo Amery, *My Political Life*, I, throughout; Curtis, *With Milner in South Africa*, throughout; both the Milner and Dawson diaries for 1901–1905.
73. Robinson's diary, Feb. 14, 1905, and April 4, 1906, Dawson Papers.
74. The close associate of the kindergarten and charter member of the round table, Leo Amery was a fellow.

no undergraduates and with few responsibilities to educational activities of the university. Some of its number remain in the ancient quadrangle next to New College, where they devote their lives to the study of history, philosophy, classics, and the law; while others enter the professions and public life. Those who leave the college retain their fellowships until the seven-year term expires, after which they become *quondam* or sometime fellows without a voice in the business of the college but a part of the brotherhood for the rest of their lives.[75] Of the quondam fellows A. L. Rowse wrote: "There are a number of them abroad in the world and the University; but wherever they wander, they still belong to the company . . . [of fellows], and when they come home, they come home to All Souls."[76]

The more active quondams frequently returned to the college for a quiet weekend of good food and stimulating conversation. On special days in the college calendar—particularly All Souls' Day—festive homecoming celebrations drew to the house an impressive list of journalists, prelates, scholars, lawyers, businessmen, politicians, and civil servants. At these "gaudies" were demonstrated the two outstanding characteristics of the foundation: its preoccupation with public affairs and the lodge-hall sort of fraternalism which bound the fellows together. "Politics in the widest sense," according to A. L. Rowse, has always dominated smoking room conversations at All Souls.[77] Given the nature of its membership it is natural that both the resident fellows and the quondams should be interested in economic conditions and international and imperial affairs as well as the details of party politics. It would have been surprising if their conversations had not centered upon such topics. The younger fellows, who at these occasions mingled with the great and near great "on a happy footing of equality,"[78] undoubtedly absorbed some of this preoccupation with politics and the concern for the public welfare which it represented. "One thing dominated them all—the sense of

75. A useful brief essay on All Souls and an account of its peculiar characteristics is found in A. L. Rowse, *The English Past: Evocations of Persons and Places* (New York, 1952), pp. 1–14.

76. *Ibid.*, p. 10.

77. *Ibid.*

78. Leo Amery, *My Political Life,* I, 63.

public duty"; Rowse remarked, "there was nothing they would not do if they were convinced it was their duty. This was the air they breathed. . . ."[79]

The fraternal ritual and brotherly sentimentality which it creates are difficult to describe, for there is little information available on these matters. Factionalism is undoubtedly a part of All Souls life. It appears certain, however, that the fellows are bound by vows of "brotherly love and concord" which apply outside the college as well as within.[80] And like other such fraternal organizations, the order has its ceremonies which symbolize the ancient traditions of the group. Central to these is the mallard, a bird which by tradition played a part in locating the place upon which the college was built in the fifteenth century. In memory of this legendary event seventeenth-century fellows wrote a song which is sung at All Souls gaudies.[81] And once a century in solemn procession the fellows of the college led by the "Lord Mallard"—in 1901 Archbishop Lang—tour the college grounds and buildings in search of the "sacred bird." Robinson, who attended the centenary ceremony in January, 1901, described the scene to his mother:

> About 40 members of the College turned up for it & we duly kept the Feast of the Sacred Bird, carrying him in effigy round the College by night with torches in hand & chanting the song. It was an odd mixture of solemnity & jocosity. I believe the procession round the battlements looked & sounded very impressive from below, but you would have laughed to see grave professors & canons & arch-deacons & undersecretaries—to say nothing of H. M. Minister at Teheran—scrambling round the pinnacles. However, there were no casualties & we got to bed somewhere round 3.[82]

These two characteristics of the college—its preoccupation with public affairs and its fraternal unity—are partly responsible for the occasional charge that since the latter part of the nineteenth century All Souls has formed a conspiratorial group bent upon the achievement of unworthy goals. Some of the critics of the

79. Rowse, *Appeasement: A Study in Political Decline, 1933–1939* (New York, 1961), p. 2.
80. Rowse, *The English Past*, p. 11.
81. Quoted in *Anatomy of Oxford: An Anthology*, comp. C. Day Lewis and Charles Fenby (London, 1938), p. 303.
82. Robinson to his mother, Jan. 16, 1901, Dawson Papers.

college have suggested that it has become a mutual advancement society whose primary interest is the promotion of its younger members to positions of power and wealth.[83] Others have insisted that All Souls, while posing as an academic society, is actually a cabal of upper-class intriguers intent upon manipulating the affairs of the British nation and Empire.[84] Both these suggestions are found expressed with satirical wit in a privately published little essay by the *Times* leader-writer, Charles W. Brodribb.[85] After making much of the fact that mallards are birds with unusual qualities that instinctively flock together, he forgets his ornithological analogy to comment upon the influence exercised by the fellows of All Souls.

> It may be safely said that there is no set of men, bound together by similar ties, which exerts a comparable influence in the world where things have got to get done. Having representatives in all departments of the State, in every profession and in all branches of knowledge (except, possibly, the physical sciences), and being also as a body diligent travellers, familiar with all languages, constitutions and legal systems, at home equally in Europe, in the Dominions and in America, and being able from their own body to give themselves the necessary introductions to almost any potentate in the world, they have an extraordinarily rich and deep common fund of information and intelligence which they are always pooling at their dinners—and they make a point of dining together a great many times a year—and having at the same time a natural genius for management, . . . they have taken upon themselves no less a task than that of forming an unofficial committee for running, or helping to run, the destinies of the British Empire.[86]

Though these accusations are rarely made by those who know the college and its members, it cannot be denied that in recent generations All Souls fellows have, by occupying positions of power, influenced British affairs to a remarkable degree. Few, in fact, would quarrel with C. P. Snow's remark that "it is to some extent because of the existence of All Souls that Oxford, all through the nineteenth and twentieth centuries, has been more intimately

83. Leo Amery, *My Political Life*, I, 63.
84. Rowse, *Appeasement, passim.*
85. *Government by Mallardry: A Study in Political Ornithology* (London, 1932), 8 pp.
86. *Ibid.*

linked to English governing circles than has Cambridge, which is considerably bigger and more handsomely endowed."[87]

The effect of All Souls upon the kindergarten is difficult to gauge. It seems likely, however, that the sense of public duty and enthusiasm for governmental service which All Souls instilled into its members helped to determine the direction of the kindergarten. The fact that four members of the kindergarten were also fellows of All Souls certainly accounts in part for the close and durable fellowship of Milner's young men. Throughout their stay in South Africa Perry, Brand, Robinson, and Malcolm remained keenly interested in the affairs of the college and particularly the election of new fellows.[88] "I have severe accesses of nostalgia for the common room of All Souls from time to time," Perry wrote to Robinson while the latter was still at the Colonial Office.

> I trust to return to England before I cease to be a living member of that beneficent foundation. About this time tomorrow for instance it will be bitter to think you are gathering in hall, making salad, & flocking round the Warden as he stands with his back to the fireplace.[89]

In their exile they attempted to meet on appropriate days to celebrate the college gaudies with appropriate toasts and feasting.[90] Amery recorded his memories of one such conclave:

> Of many cheerful evenings [during a 1907 trip to South Africa] the most joyous I can recall is an All Souls' Gaudy, celebrated in Johannesburg *super flumina Babylonis*, by Robinson, Peter Perry, Brand, and myself, ending in a drive by a glorious full moon, Peter and myself standing on the seat of the Cape cart and chanting Homer.[91]

This warm affection for All Souls, so obvious during the years in South Africa, did not end with the return of the kindergarten to England after the establishment of the Union of South Africa. Though Perry seems to have drifted away from his connection with the college, Malcolm and Brand maintained their ties with

87. In a review of A. L. Rowse's *Appeasement: A Study in Political Decline, 1933–39* published in the *New York Times Book Review*, Dec. 24, 1961, p. 3.
88. This interest is illustrated in the letters from Perry and Malcolm to Robinson in the Dawson Papers, particularly those from Malcolm dated March 1, June 19, and Aug. 9, 1902, and from Perry on March 6 and May 31, 1901.
89. Perry to Robinson, May 30, 1901, Dawson Papers.
90. Robinson's diary, June 12 and Nov. 3, 1906, Dawson Papers.
91. Leo Amery, *My Political Life*, I, 321.

All Souls throughout the following half century. Robinson even became an official of the college for a brief period following World War I. Following a dispute with Lord Northcliffe, Robinson in 1919 resigned from the editorial chair of the *Times*. From then until his return to Printing House Square in 1922 he served as Estates Bursar, in charge of the financial affairs of the foundation.[92]

In these later years Milner's young men imbued All Souls with a concern for imperial matters which proved distasteful to those members of the fellowship who followed the Gladstonian tradition.[93] With the help of their good friend and fellow Milnerian Leo Amery, they were able in the years after their return from Africa to find fellowships for Lionel Curtis, T. E. Lawrence, and Reginald Coupland. With a membership such as this it is understandable that All Souls came to resemble, in Brodribb's words, "an unofficial committee for running . . . the destinies of the British Empire."

This intimacy within the kindergarten, which was in such large measure derived from the influences of Oxford in general and New College and All Souls in particular, had little historical importance during Milner's tenure as High Commissioner. The kindergarten in those years was simply a small circle of young civil servants bound together by similar backgrounds and common interests. As its members began to take an active part in the constitutional development of South Africa following Milner's departure, however, this intimacy became an important factor in determining the success (and sometimes the failure) of their enterprises.

92. Conversations with Mrs. Geoffrey Dawson, 1960.
93. Rowse, *Appeasement,* p. 5.

Chapter Four. Milner's retirement and the re-establishment of Boer authority

In April, 1905, Lord Milner's tenure as High Commissioner for South Africa and Governor-General of the Transvaal and the Orange River Colony came to an end. Physical and mental strain were partly responsible for his departure, for Milner's health, which was never robust, had suffered during his years in South Africa. With a long rest a restored Milner might have been able to remain at the center of South African affairs until reconstruction was complete and South Africa united under British authority. As in many similar cases, therefore, "reasons of health" cannot be accepted as full and sufficient cause for retirement. Of more importance were changing political conditions in Great Britain, which convinced both Milner and the Colonial Office that his retention would only render less likely the achievement of the goals for which he had been striving.

The future of the Unionist government in Great Britain in 1905 was dark. Mounting resentment over internal failures and the anti-Imperialist sentiment which had been growing since the Boer War seemed to presage a Liberal victory in the next general election. In such an event there would certainly be no place for Milner, for his name had come to symbolize to the readers of the Liberal press the untold crimes supposedly committed in South Africa by the Unionist government. Milner thought, therefore, that his replacement should be chosen well in advance of the election and that he should have a record on imperial issues and the Boer War which would cause as little offense as possible to the Little Englander faction of the Liberal party. In this way he hoped that a High Commissioner of Milnerian views might weather the impending change at Westminster.[1]

Once he became convinced of the need for his retirement, Milner missed no opportunity to bring the matter to the attention of Alfred Lyttelton, Chamberlain's successor at the Colonial Office. The selection of a man to replace Milner was a difficult

1. Milner to Lyttelton, Nov. 30, 1904, Milner Papers.

task, for few men possessed the conflicting qualifications which the job demanded. Finally, after weeks of indecision in London, Milner's patience came to an end. In January, 1905, he asked Lyttelton by cable if he might "begin quietly to make my preparation for leaving in the second or third week in March? Unless there is some grave reason to the contrary, I am most anxious not to defer my departure."[2]

It was thus with satisfaction that Milner learned late in February of the appointment of the Earl of Selborne, an exponent of vigorous imperialism who had served as Chamberlain's Undersecretary from 1895 to 1900 before becoming First Lord of the Admiralty.[3] "Lord M. quite overjoyed," Robinson wrote to his father. "He had long given up all hope of getting anyone so good."[4]

Milner's last weeks in South Africa were mostly spent in a tour by rail of the four colonies during which he was showered with honors and subjected to speeches of praise by both the British and the Boers. Though certainly a welcome change "after years of malice & abuse," Robinson reported that Milner was not deceived by the motives behind such friendly treatment by the Afrikaners. "H. E. says, to go away for good is the next most popular thing to dying."[5]

His labors finally at an end, Milner sailed up the east coast of Africa in early April accompanied by Robinson, who was on his way to England before returning to Johannesburg to assume his editorial duties with the *Star*. Though pleased by the prospect of extensive leisure and satisfied with the choice of his successor, Milner left South Africa with depressed spirits. His public remarks contained expressions of optimism for the future of South Africa and for the ultimate success of the reforms which he had instituted. His personal correspondence, however, reflected a fear that unforeseen difficulties during the years of reconstruction were combining with the imminent political changes in Great Britain to frustrate the achievement of his goal of a united and prosperous South Africa firmly tied to the British Empire.

2. Milner to Lyttelton, Jan. 17, 1905, *ibid.*
3. Balfour to Milner, Feb. 23, 1905, *ibid.*
4. Robinson to his father, March 5, 1905, **Dawson Papers.**
5. *Ibid.*

During the years since the war South Africa had not developed as Milner had planned. Though the mining industry had gradually recovered after the introduction of Chinese labor, the economy of the country as a whole had not prospered. A severe drought in 1903 and 1904 had caused an agricultural depression and discouraged immigration. As a result, the influx of British settlers upon which the political future of South Africa was thought to depend had not materialized. The racial and ethnic composition within South Africa was thus much the same as it had been before the war. The crucial element in Milner's plan for a self-governing South Africa loyal to the British Empire seemed now forever impossible.

Of course no serious problems would result so long as the authority of the Crown was maintained. But Milner had known from the first that the period of imperial dictatorship would be short. Pressure from within Great Britain and from other parts of the Empire would force the restoration of autonomy to the former republics. The Boers would then reassert their power in the Transvaal and the Orange River Colony, and the sacrifices of the past seven years would be made meaningless. By the time of Milner's retirement the likelihood of what he feared most—the early establishment of responsible government—was great. A Liberal party victory in the next election would almost certainly be followed by an end to crown-colony status in the former republics. The Liberal party was committed to this by both ideology and expediency. Leaders like Sir Henry Campbell-Bannerman valued the imperial connection no less than the Unionists, but unlike the Unionists, they believed that only liberty and responsible government could weld the disparate elements of the Empire into a noble commonwealth of free men. They had long insisted that Afrikaner hatred of the imperial connection had been brought about by decades of mistreatment at the hands of Conservative governments in Great Britain and could be erased only by the swift restoration of self-government.

This ideological commitment to responsible government was reinforced by the realization that ever since the 1890's South Africa had been an important issue with which to arouse the voters. Reference by Liberal spokesmen to farm-burning and concentration camps—and later to "Chinese slavery"—had brought about victory after victory in the by-elections of recent years. As the Unionist government grew weaker, the emotional appeal of the South African question took on greater importance to Liberal campaign leaders. Victory at the polls would thus almost certainly be followed swiftly by concessions to the Boers and others in South Africa who demanded the immediate granting of self-government in the Transvaal and the Orange River Colony.

The realization of this, it has been seen, was partly responsible for Milner's retirement and the appointment of Selborne. It also explains the creation of letters patent at the time of Milner's departure providing for the establishment in both former republics of a limited form of self-government. This Lyttelton Constitution, as it came to be called, provided for a Transvaal government whose executive power would be retained by Imperial officials. The legislature was to be partly nominated and partly elected, with the elected members to be chosen through an electoral arrangement which would make it possible in the future for an increased British population to achieve legislative power. Like the appointment of Selborne, the Lyttelton Constitution was an effort at compromise. Its creators hoped that limited concessions to Boer demands made by the Unionist government might preclude far greater changes later.

It was, however, a scheme in which Milner could place little confidence. By the time of his arrival in England in July after a holiday with friends on Lake Como, the Unionist government was clearly sinking. As its position grew weaker, the attacks of the Liberals, centering on conditions in South Africa, increased. Under the circumstances, the provisions of the Lyttelton Constitution were unlikely to satisfy the Liberal party once it had gained the power to make far more extensive concessions.

Milner, a central figure in the events leading to the Boer War, and the official in charge of the unpopular reconstruction program, returned home as this political struggle approached its climax. To Liberal campaigners his appearance was a godsend. Here was the very man responsible for the "Chinese slavery" which, they assured the voters, was filling the pockets of greedy Rand magnates and damaging the reputation of the British

Crown. As a result Milner became, according to one observer, "the most unpopular figure of the day."[6] Even after the resignation of Balfour and the subsequent victory of the Liberal party in the election of January, 1906, Milner continued to be the target of radicals. Though the new Under-secretary of State for the Colonies, Winston Churchill, passed off the charge of slavery as a "terminological inexactitude," the matter of alleged mistreatment of Chinese laborers remained a subject of interest among backbench extremists of the Liberal party. When it was learned in London that shortly before his retirement Milner had permitted the administration of light corporal punishment in the Chinese compounds, and that this had led to instances of undeniable brutality, an attempt was made to destroy him. Without the approval of the government, a Liberal back-bencher on March 21, 1906, proposed in the House of Commons censure upon Milner for having sanctioned "the flogging of Chinese labourers in breach of the law, in violation of treaty obligations, and without the knowledge or sanction of His Majesty's Secretary of State for the Colonies."[7] Representing the government, Churchill offered an amendment which removed the formal censure but retained the spirit of the original motion by expressing the "condemnation of [the House for] the flogging of Chinese coolies in breach of the law."[8]

The passage of this measure was considered by Milner's friends to be only slightly less damning than the original motion. The editor of Milner's South African papers well illustrates the deep anger of Milner's friends and supporters in a comment which he made years later: "The mean and pitiful exhibition of party spite registered in the resolution of the House of Commons disgraced its authors and the House, not Lord Milner."[9] Immediately following the attack Milner received indications of warm support from all parts of the Empire. The House of Lords voted its deep

6. Viscount Cecil of Chelwood, quoted from personal conversation, Halpérin, *Lord Milner*, p. 154.

7. Great Britain, 4 *Parliamentary Debates*, CLIV (1906), 463–64.

8. *Ibid.*, pp. 487–99. The matter of "Chinese slavery" and the censure of Milner have for the first time been examined adequately in Gollin's recent *Proconsul in Politics*.

9. Headlam, II, 560. Similar sentiments are expressed by Milner's young friend Leo Amery in *The Times History of the War in South Africa*, VI, 178–79.

appreciation of his service to the Crown, a great public dinner with Chamberlain presiding was held in his honor on May 24, and shortly thereafter he received a testimonial bearing nearly four hundred thousand signatures.[10] From among the thousands of letters which he received from his admirers, Milner preserved a number from the young men of the kindergarten. Typical of their reaction to "the attacks of your enemies and the patronage of Mr. Winston Churchill" were the remarks of Patrick Duncan:

> That debate made people [in South Africa] angrier than anything that has happened since I knew them. I was at Maritzburg at the Customs Conference and as each man stopped to read the telegrams posted in the hall one could see his face set as if he had received a personal affront.[11]

The affection and admiration of the members of the kindergarten for their patron was at this time being manifested in a tangible way. Shortly after his retirement Milner received a letter from Curtis, who, as spokesman for a number of "your old followers," asked that he sit for a portrait to be painted by Maxwell Balfour, a young artist known to several of the kindergarten. Though they realized that Milner was "peculiarly connected with Balliol," Curtis said that it was the wish of the donors, "a few New College men who have served under you in South Africa," that the finished portrait hang in the hall of their college.[12] Further correspondence indicates that work on the portrait did not go well. Milner proved to be difficult over the matter of sittings, and the artist was delayed by bad health, which led to his death shortly after the work was completed. The result was a portrait of little merit which was hung as planned, though it was received with embarrassment by the donors and with little enthusiasm by the dons of New College.[13]

The demonstrations of high regard from the kindergarten and other admirers could not assuage the feeling of bitter defeat which gripped Milner during the first years of retirement. Although he took his seat in the House of Lords, he appeared infrequently and

---

10. Leo Amery, *The Times History of the War in South Africa*, VI, 178–79.
11. Duncan to Milner, April 13, 1906, Milner Papers.
12. Curtis to Milner, July 31, 1905, Milner Papers.
13. Various letters concerning this portrait were many years later given to New College by Curtis.

spoke rarely. He assumed his position as one of the trustees of the Rhodes estate, having been appointed by Rhodes himself. But even here his performance was for some time perfunctory.

What little enthusiasm Milner possessed following his return from South Africa was directed towards his duties in the City. His financial resources had been all but exhausted in South Africa, and, unwilling to follow the questionable tradition of appealing to the government for a pension, Milner was forced to find some means of supporting himself. He accepted several directorships in banking and industrial firms in whose interest he applied the administrative skill and judgment which he had acquired in his years of government service. The most important of these was the Rio Tinto Mining Company, a firm with large copper interests in Spain which had over the years grown into an enterprise of international importance.

Attempts to persuade Milner to take an active part in public affairs during the first year of his retirement almost always met with failure. The wounds inflicted by partisan attack and the bitterness caused by what seemed to him to be needless failure in South Africa caused him to close his mind to appeals for action. Though he claimed that he was "certainly not the victim of any kind of personal disappointment," Milner nevertheless declared to Curtis that

> there is a sort of blight on men of both parties, & indeed on public life generally. We are flogging dead horses, mumbling the formulae of the past. I can see no realisation of the facts of the present: there are certainly no big ideas—indeed I don't see ideas of any kind—with regard to the future. Not among politicians I mean. There are occasional spasms of vitality in the press and outside, wh. the party organisations on both sides seek to suppress.[14]

As a consequence Milner bluntly refused to assume a position of leadership in the Unionist party and even as late as the winter of 1906–1907 declined to pick up the reins of leadership of the Imperial Preference movement from the faltering hands of Chamberlain.[15] An appeal for him to lead a "non-party" political move-

14. Milner to Curtis, Aug. 25, 1905 (copy), Milner Papers. (Gollin, who had access to the Curtis papers, quotes this letter from that source. *Proconsul in Politics,* p. 102.)
15. Leo Amery, *My Political Life,* I, 298–99.

ment aimed at reforming the constitution and revitalizing the Empire elicited a flat refusal: "My intention is to keep myself absolutely free from all political engagements. The question whether I shall ever re-enter public life in any shape or form, is a very open one."[16]

Even the swiftly changing political situation in South Africa which followed his departure could not rouse Milner from his mood of withdrawal and bitter detachment. In the months following his retirement conditions there changed in ways which justified his pessimism about the future of the area. The Lyttelton Constitution, created at the time of Milner's retirement but not published for some months after his departure, was never put into effect. Before the letters patent could be implemented the Unionist government fell. Campbell-Bannerman's Liberal government upon taking office immediately set about doing just what Milner feared most: that is, establishing responsible government in the two former republics. On February 8, 1906, the Lyttelton Constitution was revoked, and in December of that year letters patent were issued creating a new constitution for the Transvaal.[17] The new charter differed from the Lyttelton Constitution in two significant ways. It provided for the rapid and extensive reduction of Crown authority, and it altered franchise qualifications and the composition of constituencies in ways which would work to the advantage of the predominantly Afrikaner rural population. The effect of these two alterations was, in Milner's opinion, to end forever the possibility of the British element's ever gaining power through a shift in population. Once in power the Boers would make certain that they remained there. The Transvaal—and for that matter, all of South Africa—would retain the imperial connection for a while. But quickly British influence, cultural and economic as well as political, would begin to decline. Then at some future time, when it suited the purposes of the Boers, ties to the Empire would be severed, and the dream of a united self-governing South Africa within the British Empire would be forever shattered.

16. Milner to F. H. Congdon, n.d. [Oct., 1905], Milner Papers.
17. Thompson, *Unification of South Africa*, p. 26. A similar constitution for the Orange River Colony (restoring the old name Orange Free State) was issued in June, 1907. *Ibid.*, p. 29.

Even this development, which seemed to undermine Milner's whole reconstruction program, failed to force him to action. To a friend he wrote in bitter dejection:

> I have done nothing but . . . write letters, . . . and mutter curses, not loud but deep, at the appalling mess which those bunglers are making of South Africa. Where is it all going to end? Well. My conscience is clear, though I have a sore heart—in that respect, though not otherwise.[18]

In public, however, Milner limited his protest to a brief statement in the House of Lords,[19] a mild article published in the *National Review*,[20] and a few public speeches filled with generalities about the need for imperial unity.[21]

To his young disciples in South Africa Milner explained that it was more than just fatigue and disillusionment that prevented him from acting:

> I have kept comparatively quiet about S. A. though I am boiling inside, simply from policy. I never open my lips about it at all unless I am absolutely compelled. I have come to the conclusion that, having regard to the overwhelming,—though fortunately decreasing, force of rotten Radical opinion, any little good I can do by calling the attention of our own feeble forces to South Africa is far more outweighed by the impetus which my criticism gives to renewed vicious activity of the other side. A time will come, no doubt, for slaying the Philistines, but it is no use hitting them when you cannot slay them, or even hurt them seriously. It only wakes them up.[22]

Milner's reaction to recent political changes dismayed the members of the kindergarten. Still deeply involved in the reconstruction program established by Milner, they found that the constitutional changes emanating from London were having a direct and immediate effect upon their lives. Robinson perhaps mirrored the frustrations of the whole kindergarten when he wrote that

18. Milner to Miss Bertha Synge, Sept. 13, 1906. Quoted in Wrench, *Alfred Lord Milner*, p. 265.

19. Great Britain, 4 *Parliamentary Debates*, CLXII (1906), 646–58.

20. "Great Britain and South Africa," *National Review*, No. 278 (April, 1906), pp. 209–18.

21. Viscount Milner, *Imperial Unity: Two Speeches* (London: The National Review Office, 1907).

22. Milner to Robinson, Jan. 11, 1907, Dawson Papers.

it really is an *exasperating* place what with this poisonous Govt. at home & rotters out here—people who *won't* see or *don't want* to see or can't be bothered—it is sometimes almost maddening. Besides, it is a horrid strain to keep one's temper & not let private feelings make one unfair in the paper.[23]

The source of greatest strain and exasperation for the kindergarten came from the renewed political activities which followed the restoration of self-government to the Transvaal. During the years of Milner's control internal politics in the two former republics was non-existent. From the time of the Treaty of Vereeniging until the return of responsible government the affairs of the Transvaal and the Orange River Colony were administered by officials of the Crown with the advice of appointed Executive and Legislative Councils. In these years of dictatorship there were no elections and no political activities in the usual sense. By the time of Milner's retirement in April, 1905, however, political groups in the Transvaal had begun to emerge.[24] These groups, adhering closely to ethnic and linguistic divisions of the white population, quickly took on the characteristics of political parties. Thus when responsible government was restored there existed political machinery necessary to wage an election contest.

The Afrikaner party, called *Het Volk* (the People), symbolized the revived sense of self-confidence which developed among Boer leaders as the memories of defeat began to fade. The catalyst which solidified Boer sentiment was Milner's determination to import Chinese labor to work the mines. Afrikaner leaders, recalling that Indians brought into Natal as temporary workers had been permitted to remain, were vigorous in their protests. The result was a meeting in May, 1904, at which was formed a political action group to press Afrikaner views upon the British government. With former Boer general Louis Botha acting as chairman, the group not only condemned the use of Chinese labor, but also passed a series of resolutions criticizing other actions of Milner's government and demanding the restoration of responsible government at the first opportunity. A subsequent meeting in January,

23. Robinson to "Aunt Kitty," April 22, 1906, Dawson Papers.
24. These paragraphs dealing with the emergence of Boer political influence and the reaction of English-speaking South Africans are derived largely from Thompson, *Unification of South Africa*, pp. 21 ff.

1905, resulted in the creation of *Het Volk*, a permanent political party designed to serve the interest of Afrikaners of the Transvaal. Botha became chairman of the formal organization, assisted by a committee composed mainly of former Boer generals. Among them was Jan C. Smuts, a young Cambridge-educated lawyer who had been State Attorney of the Transvaal before becoming a commando leader in the last part of the war. In the following year a similar group was formed in the Orange River Colony. Called *Orangia Unie*, this counterpart to *Het Volk* was led by former Orange Free State officials Abraham Fischer, Christiaan R. de Wet, and J. B. M. Hertzog. These two parties, along with the old established *Afrikaner Bond* in the Cape Colony, became the agencies of Boer political activity throughout South Africa, there being an insufficient number of Afrikaners in Natal to form an effective party.

While the English-speaking white people of the sparsely populated Orange River Colony were united in their support of the Constitutional party, those in the Transvaal divided their loyalty. The Transvaal Responsible Government Association was formed shortly after the announcement of the Lyttelton Constitution mainly by English-speaking residents of Johannesburg who opposed the compromise nature of that settlement. Though not in sympathy with the ethnic orientation of *Het Volk*, the "Responsibles" were opposed to the extension of colonial status, and as the name implies, demanded early self-government.[25]

The other major English-speaking faction in the Transvaal, the Transvaal Progressive Association, strongly favored the retention of British authority and opposed responsible government in the immediate future. Organized and supported by the leading financiers and mining companies of Johannesburg, the Progressive group became the party of Milnerian opinion.[26]

At the time of Milner's retirement the leaders of the Progressive party could take heart in the fact that under the electoral provi-

25. By the time of the initial election under the 1906 Transvaal constitution, the name had been changed to the Transvaal National Association. *Ibid.*, p. 28.
26. A concise Milnerian interpretation of party policy and organization is found in "Political Parties in the Transvaal," *National Review*, No. 267 (May, 1905), pp. 461–88. This article, signed "Transvaaler," was written by Robinson just before Milner's retirement.

sions of the Lyttelton Constitution it might be possible for them to win control of the legislature. In conjunction with a still powerful colonial government of Crown officials they might then proceed to the fulfilment of the Chamberlain-Milner program. The accession to power of the Liberal party in Britain and the subsequent revocation of the Lyttelton Constitution, however, cast gloom in the Milnerian camp, and particularly within the kindergarten. Even before the announcement of the new Transvaal constitution in late 1906 it was clear that any new charter would contain concessions to the Afrikaner population insofar as franchise and constituency provisions were concerned. And with the British-oriented population of the Transvaal split between the Responsibles and the Progressives, a victory of those supporting a Milnerian settlement seemed highly unlikely.

Defeat for Milner's followers in the election set for February, 1907, became virtually assured when it was agreed that neither the Responsibles nor *Het Volk* would contest those seats in which the other held considerable strength. In the event of victory for the coalition it was understood that Sir Richard Solomon, leader of the Responsible Government Association, should become premier. A man of considerable ambition, Solomon had before the war achieved some political success in the Cape Colony. Upon moving to Johannesburg he identified himself with those who supported the policies of the reconstruction government. The political change which brought him to leadership in the camp of the Responsibles thus seemed apostasy to the Progressives. Solomon, "who owes all he is to Lord Milner," was, according to Robinson, nothing better than a "contemptible beast" for his failure to support his former friends.[27] The intensity of Robinson's antipathy was derived in part from Solomon's attempt to carry some of the kindergarten with him. Hichens and Duncan were apparently approached by Solomon with the argument that, given the political situation as it existed at that time, only the rapid establishment of a self-governing Transvaal led by a united white population could prevent a return to the Boer-British struggle of prewar days. Though there was "an organized puffing [by

27. Robinson to "Aunt Kitty," Jan. 27, 1907, Dawson Papers.

the Responsibles] of Duncan & Hichens at the expense of the other members of the Eng. Co.,"[28] which for a while threatened to destroy the unity of the kindergarten, the result was satisfactory to Milner. By September, 1906—fully five months before the initial Transvaal election—Robinson was able to report that the lost sheep had returned.[29]

With the loyalty of Hichens and Duncan thus assured, every effort was made by the kindergarten in the campaign preceding the election of February, 1907, to garner for the Progressive party the greatest number of votes possible. The chance of victory was remote, but a good showing for the Progressives might convince both the Afrikaners in the Transvaal and the Liberals in London of the wisdom of moderation. In this campaign the kindergarten was not without influence. Its members, most of them still at work in various agencies of government, filled positions of responsibility which gave them certain advantages during the election campaign. Duncan, Hichens, and Curtis were still officials of the Transvaal.[30] Brand and Kerr continued to direct the affairs of the Intercolonial Council. Malcolm was at the right hand of the High Commissioner as private secretary of Selborne. And John Dove, Feetham's successor as Johannesburg town clerk, still managed the municipal affairs of the Transvaal's only city. The four members of the kindergarten who had by this time resigned from government work were no less effective. Perry, closely associated with the Progressive leaders in the Chamber of Mines, and Feetham, now a practicing member of the Johannesburg bar, were generous with their time and influence in support of Progressive candidates.[31] Hugh Wyndham, who became a farmer on the Vaal River after Milner's retirement, was himself a Progressive candidate for the Standerton district.

But most important of all the kindergarten insofar as ability to influence the election was concerned was Geoffrey Robinson. His appointment as editor of the Johannesburg *Star* had been arranged by Milner during the last weeks of his tenure in South

28. Robinson to Milner, March 31, 1906, Milner Papers.
29. Robinson to his father, Sept. 15, 1906, Dawson Papers.
30. Curtis resigned in the midst of the campaign to devote his full time to the promotion of South African unification.
31. Robinson to Milner, Feb. 3, 1907, Milner Papers.

Africa. The owners—Lionel Phillips (a "Raider" and former president of the Chamber of Mines) and other mining company directors—[32]were, like Milner, anxious that Robinson's sound Milnerian views be fully utilized.[33] Upon taking charge in November, 1905, Robinson immediately began to devote the editorial columns of the *Star* to the propagation of the Progressive point of view. Shortly thereafter he wrote with satisfaction that the paper was doing well "& annoying a good many people who deserve to be annoyed. I wrote an article today . . . [critical of] some of the Responsible Govt. Gentlemen, wh. will certainly produce several typewritten sheets of abuse Monday morning."[34]

This local influence was extended to worldwide proportions in 1906 by Robinson's appointment as South African correspondent to the *Times*. His association with Printing House Square, which proved to be of such importance to both Robinson and to the whole school of Milnerian imperialists, was reported with delight to his family. "Nothing has really pleased me more for a long time—," he wrote, "not since All Souls I think which I shall always look upon as the greatest possible stroke of fortune."[35] With advice and inside information supplied by fellow members of the kindergarten Robinson was thus able to use his dual position as editor and correspondent to influence opinions on imperial matters throughout the world while at the same time promoting the interests of the Progressive party and its candidates.

According to Smut's biographer, Sir Keith Hancock, the Progressive party openly exhorted those of British background to remain loyal to the program of Milner by pandering to their fears of revived Boer power. "It was the Progressive Party," he wrote, "which whipped up jingoistic and 'racialist' emotions among the English-speaking community."[36] Undoubtedly this was true, but it might be more accurate to say that frequent appeals to "racialist" emotion were made by both sides in this initial election, and personal attack on the reputation and character of candidates was

32. Robinson to Milner, Aug. 15, 1907, *ibid.*
33. Milner to Lyttelton, April 2, 1905 (copy), *ibid.*
34. Robinson to "Aunt Kitty," Dec. 16, 1905, Dawson Papers.
35. *Ibid.*, May 24, 1906.
36. W. K. Hancock, *Smuts: The Sanguine Years 1870–1919* (Cambridge, 1962), p. 202.

frequent. Wyndham, in fact, found it necessary before the election to file suit for £10,000 damage against the *Volkstem,* a leading Afrikaner newspaper, for saying that he had "abused his position on . . . [Milner's] staff to get his farm."[37] In the closing days of the campaign Robinson remarked that "dead cats and Madeira eggs are at a premium, & any man who can (accurately) recall the 'awful past' of an opposition candidate is a hero."[38]

Despite their efforts, the Transvaal election of February 20, 1907, was a resounding defeat for the Progressive party and for the kindergarten. *Het Volk* won an absolute majority of five over all other parties in the Legislative Assembly. With the support of their allies the Responsibles, the Afrikaner leaders were able to control forty-three of the sixty-nine seats in the Assembly. Richard Solomon, however, was defeated by the well-known mine owner and Progressive leader, Sir Percy Fitzpatrick. The promised premiership thus slipped through Solomon's fingers as Lord Selborne turned to Louis Botha to form a government. In the cabinet chosen by Botha were four members of *Het Volk* and two Responsibles. Solomon was rewarded with the post of Agent-General of the Transvaal in London.[39]

Defeat, though it was expected, was nevertheless painful to the kindergarten, for it brought with it changes which directly affected the lives of Milner's young men. Those who before the election held positions in the crown colony government quickly resigned to make way for appointees of the new administration. For Patrick Duncan this meant a return to England, but only a temporary one. It had been Duncan's desire for some time to make his home in South Africa. Milner had learned almost a year before the Transvaal election that because "he had no private means, and did not think that a man should look forward to making his living out of politics," Duncan "meant to go to the bar and practice in Pretoria."[40] After turning the affairs of the Lieutenant-Governor's office over to his successor, "Sinister Smuts,"[41]

37. Robinson to Milner, Feb. 10, 1907, Milner Papers.
38. Robinson to "Aunt Kitty," Jan. 27, 1907, Dawson Papers.
39. Thompson, *Unification of South Africa,* p. 28.
40. Copy of an unsigned letter to Sir Julius Wernher, Bart., Feb. 19, 1906, Milner Papers.
41. Robinson to "Aunt Kitty," March 10, 1907, Dawson Papers.

and receiving the affectionate tribute of his associates at a "kinderfest" held in his honor,[42] he left for London on March 9, 1907.[43] The next day Robinson wrote that "they jeered at Lord Milner's young men & . . . Smuts turns out to be exactly Duncan's age."[44] Following his admission to the bar in 1908, Duncan returned to the Transvaal to practice and to play an active part in the political affairs of South Africa from then until his death in 1943.[45]

Hichens, for four years the Colonial Treasurer of the Transvaal, resigned immediately after the election and, like Duncan, returned to England.[46] During the following three years he was on two occasions drawn into temporary government service: in 1907–1908 as a member of the Royal Commission on Decentralization in India, and in 1909 as the chairman of a committee to visit South Africa to evaluate the public service of Southern Rhodesia. It was not until 1910 that Hichens became involved in the enterprise which occupied him until his death in 1940. In that year he became chairman of the old shipbuilding firm of Cammell Laird and Co.[47] The restoration of self-government in the Transvaal and the subsequent victory of the Boers thus removed Hichens from the list of kindergarten members still active in South African affairs. Even so, he maintained close contact with his former associates, and upon their return to England following the campaign for South African unification, he once again became a participant in their activities.

Curtis, though he had resigned from the colonial government before the Transvaal election, found that his influence in governmental affairs was not altogether ended. At the establishment of responsible government he was appointed to the Legislative Council, the upper house of the Transvaal legislature. According to the new constitution, the members of the lower house—the Legislative Assembly—were from the first to be chosen by popular vote. But the Council was for the first five years of its life to consist

42. Robinson's diary, March 4, 1907, *ibid.*
43. *Ibid.*, March 8, 1907.
44. Robinson to "Aunt Kitty," March 10, 1907, *ibid.*
45. "Sir Patrick Duncan (1870–1943)," *Dictionary of National Biography,* 1941–50, p. 223.
46. Robinson's diary, March 27, 1907, Dawson Papers.
47. "Lionel Hichens," *Round Table,* No. 121 (Dec., 1940) , pp. 8–9.

of five members appointed by the governor, with vacancies filled by the governor on the advice of his ministers.[48] By this device the crown colony government, though its life ended in early 1907, was able to extend its influence over the next five years. Appointed by Selborne to the Council with Curtis was the Johannesburg lawyer, Richard Feetham. From this position of relatively minor power, Curtis and Feetham were able to join the elected Progressive party representatives in the Assembly to form the "loyal opposition." In the upper house the two *kinder* kept alive the Milnerian point of view by constantly criticizing the behavior of the newly appointed and frequently inexperienced ministers. Both of them skilful speakers, Curtis and Feetham were on a number of occasions able to put to use the experience which they had gained in the Oxford Union. During the first session of the legislature Milner learned of "the handling that . . . [H. C. Hull, the new Colonial Treasurer] got from Curtis and Feetham in that much-abused Upper House."[49] "To the intense delight of everybody," wrote another friend,

> the kindergarten gave him an awful dressing, the severity of it consisting, I am delighted to say, in the restraint & dignity with which it was administered. Feetham and Curtis handled him with the very best of judgment and taste, and with an ability to debate that reduced Hull to the level of a donkey in the Derby.[50]

Like Duncan and Hichens, John Dove found it necessary to vacate his official post. His resignation as town clerk of Johannesburg, however, did not result in his departure from South Africa. Rather, he moved to Pretoria, where as chairman of the Transvaal Land Settlement Board he took charge of various schemes promoted by the Progressives and their friends in England to increase the flow of settlers into the rural areas of South Africa.[51]

Robert Brand and Philip Kerr, secretary and assistant secretary respectively of the Intercolonial Council, were able to retain their positions under the new regime. Unlike Duncan and Hichens, who were officials of the Transvaal, and Dove, an appointed agent

48. Thompson, *Unification of South Africa*, p. 26.
49. Robinson to Milner, March 24, 1907, Milner Papers.
50. Fitzpatrick to Milner, March 25, 1907, Milner Papers.
51. A review of these activities is contained in Dove to Milner, April 1, 1909, Milner Papers.

of the municipality of Johannesburg, Brand and Kerr were employees of the semi-autonomous agency created by Milner to draw
the colonies closer together. They were thus not subject to summary dismissal. Until the dissolution of the Intercolonial Council
in June, 1908, in fact, both remained active in the affairs of that
organization. Brand as secretary was occupied with the over-all
supervision of the railway system and the constabulary which it
supported, but particularly with the threat of a rate and tariff war
between the pastoral regions in the interior and the more commercial colonies on the coast. Kerr, on the other hand, spent much
of his time and energy as secretary of the Indigency Commission.
This body, appointed by the Transvaal government to examine
the causes, extent, and cure of poverty among the white population of the country, consisted of seven members, among them
Curtis and Feetham.[52]

The Transvaal election in February, 1907, was only the first of
a series of electoral reverses for Milner's friends. In November of
that year there was an even more complete—though not unexpected—Boer victory in the Orange Free State. In that election,
the first under the new constitution, candidates of *Orangia Unie*
gained thirty of the thirty-eight seats in the legislature. The resulting government was headed by Abraham Fischer, an Afrikaner
lawyer and official of the prewar Free State government. And
within three months the Cape Colony Progressive (Unionist)
government of the "raider" Dr. Jameson was replaced by one
which was as hostile to Milner and his policies as that of either
Botha or Fischer. The re-enfranchisement of those citizens of the
Cape accused of being rebels during the war enabled the newly
created and Boer-oriented South Africa party to win in the general election in February, 1908. Jameson's government, on which
first Milner and then Selborne had heavily depended, was replaced by one headed by J. X. Merriman, an Englishman by birth
but an implacable foe of Milner, his policies, and his friends.[53]

There thus took place in British South Africa an almost complete political reversal between early 1907 and early 1908. Only
Natal of the four colonies associated with the Crown was still in

52. Butler, *Lothian*, pp. 20–27.
53. Thompson, *Unification of South Africa*, p. 29.

the hands of men sympathetic with Milner's policies by the later date. Until March, 1905, Milner's policies had dominated South Africa, and one would not have been overly sanguine at that time to expect a fulfilment of his goal of a South Africa with a white population predominantly British and with firm attachments to the British Empire. But by early 1908 the conditions were reversed. The vanquished were again in authority, and the possibility of accomplishing Milner's goals seemed slight. Expressing the feeling of Milnerites throughout the world, Leo Amery wrote:

> . . . it almost looked as if the Boers had regained at the ballot-box all that they had lost on the field and conceded at Vereeniging. To many British South Africans it seemed as if the ground had given way under their feet, and as if all the cost and sacrifice of the war, all the thought and effort of the reconstruction had been thrown away utterly. Once more their own divisions and the recklessness of party politics in England had led to the repetition on a larger scale of the disastrous folly of the Majuba surrender. What hope was there that England's fortune should retrieve such folly once again?[54]

That this was Milner's own feeling is clear from a long letter which he wrote to Robinson in September, 1907.[55] In an analysis of conditions in South Africa which was meant for the eyes of "any . . . of your friends to whom you wish to show it," Milner expressed the feeling of defeat he had borne since his retirement.

> My view is that the policy to which we devoted years of labour . . . must be regarded as a thing of the past. I never had any doubt about it from the first moment that the election return of January 1906 began to come in, tho the disaster has been more rapid and more complete than I imagined. . . .
> When our feeble forces, opposed to the strong & united forces on the other side, were suddenly subjected to a deadly fire from behind, when the whole power & influence of the British Gov. were thrown into the scale against the solution of the S. A. question in a British sense, the thing became perfectly hopeless, & a total collapse of what you may call the Milner policy &.fabric was inevitable. . . .
> But while the great, final & hopeless fight was on, we did not say

54. Leo Amery, *The Times History of the War in South Africa*, VI, 196.
55. Milner to Robinson, Sept. 14, 1907, Dawson Papers. This letter is published in abridged form in Wrench, *Alfred Lord Milner*, pp. 268-69.

so, even to one another. But now that it is over, we can afford to take stock of the situation frankly.

The loss of the struggle, but more importantly the weakness and failure of the imperial government, should be understood to have had an important effect upon the position of the British element of the South African population. In Milner's opinion, it was clear

> that the S. African British are entirely relieved by what has happened from any obligations to the mother country—& can afford to think only of themselves. . . . They should devote themselves wholly to the problem of making life in South Africa, regarded as more or less a foreign country, bearable for self respecting British men & women, not disposed to part with their own national feelings and traditions. If they could only stick together, even a considerable minority of them, they would, I think, be in a first-class position to do this . . . & at the same time to be materially very happy and comfortable. . . .
>
> The British party, if it continues to exist, would necessarily be an opposition party. . . . But there is opposition & opposition. Opposition to the Boers because they are what they are, i.e. Boers & not British, is out of date. The fight is no longer for predominance. That is settled. The point is that, accepting Boer predominance, not as a desirable thing, but as a fact, a British party, . . . can do a lot, & an increasing lot as the old issues recede, to influence any Transvaal or South African gov't. . . . I am not suggesting for a submissive attitude towards the gov't. . . . But, if I am against a submissive attitude, I am also against beating the air, and flogging dead horses. A vigilant, alert critical opposition, denouncing every injustice, exposing every job, but . . . leaving the door open to bargains, . . . & always looking to the possibility of ultimately becoming master of the situation, . . .—that seems to me under the altered circumstances the only possible line. And, in an evil world, not a wholly useless or unamusing one.

To his young followers, therefore, Milner could only advise a realistic appraisal of the South African situation and a concern for their own careers. "Of course on this side we shall continue to denounce the S. A. policy of this gov't. But it is one thing to condemn that policy, . . . [and] quite another for you over there to *waste your strength* upon it. For [you] have better work to do in making the best of your own position under the altered circumstances."

Milner's pessimism concerning the future of South Africa had long been known to the members of the kindergarten. In both correspondence and conversation with his protégés during their visits to England Milner had ever since his retirement expressed his conviction that the struggle to create a united South Africa, independent in internal affairs but loyal to the Crown and the Empire, was a thing of the past. Yet by late 1907 the members of the kindergarten had come to accept a far more optimistic view of South African prospects. Their experience during the more than two years since Milner's departure had caused them to look upon developments from a point of view which was quite different from that of their mentor. By the time Robinson and the kindergarten received Milner's letter advising them to quit "flogging dead horses" and concentrate instead upon "making the best of your own position under the altered circumstances," they had, in fact, become deeply involved in a scheme which they hoped might even yet bring to fruition the Milnerian dream of a unified South Africa wholly committed to the preservation of the British Empire.

Chapter Five. The Selborne memorandum

To the kindergarten in South Africa the establishment of responsible government in the former republics and the resulting restoration of Boer political power did not necessarily signal the final collapse of British interests. Milner's dreams for South Africa might yet be achieved, they insisted, but by methods other than those instituted by Milner during the immediate postwar years. It was true that changing conditions since Milner's retirement had destroyed all likelihood of achieving British control by the gradual development of a British-oriented population through the economic "overspill" from the mines. Chances of succeeding here had indeed ended even before the Liberal victory of January, 1906. The depression throughout South Africa which began in 1903, and the consequent failure of large-scale immigration schemes, had made inoperative the overspill theory months before the fall of the Unionist government. But new tactics now existed, the young men came to believe in 1906, which, if effective, would in the end produce the same results.

These new tactics involved the immediate consolidation of the various areas of British South Africa into one nation. Although unification would at first place Boers in authority over all of South Africa, it would, they believed, ironically cause their eventual political decline.[1] No matter which group stepped into power, unification would create conditions of economic prosperity and political security which had been lacking ever since the war. With prosperity and security would come British immigrants in greater and greater numbers. Assuming a constitution containing equitable franchise and constituency provisions, the result, they insisted, would be an eventual transfer of political power from the

1. In referring to the consolidation of British South Africa it was traditional until shortly before the creation of the Union constitution to use the terms federation, union, closer union, and unification interchangeably. As the movement approached a climax, however, the question of whether the form of government should be federal or unitary became an important issue. To prevent confusion I will therefore follow the established practice among historians of using unification in a general way to mean some form of consolidation the exact nature of which was yet to be determined.

Boer population to the British. The future of South Africa as a part of the Empire would thus be made secure by a step which on the surface seemed to be an abandonment of Milnerian goals. The logic of the idea could be reduced to this: ". . . both races hope for prosperity, prosperity means expansion, expansion means immigration, [and] immigration means British!"[2]

In their insistence upon the need for immediate unification the kindergarten ran counter to opinions of both Boer and British leadership in South Africa. The eventual establishment of a unified South African government had been a foregone conclusion ever since the end of the war. This had been a basic part of imperial policy throughout the struggle. But neither Boer nor British leadership in the postwar years had found it to its advantage to urge its early fulfilment. Though the *Afrikaner Bond* had as early as 1902 declared its support of "a federal union . . . [under] the supreme authority of the British Crown,"[3] Boer leaders recognized the advantage to postponement.[4] Time was running in their favor and much might be gained by waiting. If unification came before the restoration of self-government in the two former republics and before the Boer acquisition of power in the Cape Colony it would be created on terms favorable to the British element of the population. In their opinion, therefore, there was every reason during the postwar years to discourage the translation of general pronouncements favoring unification into reality.

Most leaders of British opinion, for their part, tended to oppose early unification for other reasons. Like Milner, they felt that unification would be safe only after an influx of British settlers sufficient to overbalance the present numerical strength of the Afrikaners. They agreed with Milner that unification

> may take years; it may take far longer than is generally supposed. In any case, I am not sanguine enough to anticipate that it can

2. A remark attributed to Sir Percy Fitzpatrick in Thompson, *The Unification of South Africa 1902–1910*, pp. 176–77.

3. Quoted in Basil Williams, *The Selborne Memorandum: A Review of the Mutual Relations of the British South African Colonies in 1907* (Oxford, 1925), p. xiii.

4. The explanation throughout this chapter and the next of Afrikaner political attitudes and activities concerning unification is derived almost exclusively from Thompson's excellent study of the subject.

possibly come in my time, and indeed, when you consider all the difficulties which have to be got over, while there is no reason to despair of the ultimate attainment of that end, I think more harm than good is done by expecting to see it come sooner than it possibly can come. . . . I have learned to be very patient; and I don't expect to see the accomplishment of my hopes during my residence in South Africa, or perhaps during my lifetime.[5]

Just why the kindergarten came to favor immediate unification despite the negative attitude of both Afrikaner and British leaders is difficult to determine. It may be, as Lionel Curtis later claimed, that the idea resulted from a chance reading of a biography of Alexander Hamilton written by an Englishman named Frederick Scott Oliver. Because of his own enthusiastic support of imperial federation, Oliver devoted the greater part of his book to an account of Hamilton's efforts to win support for a United States constitution granting adequate powers to the central government.[6] From this essay on the virtues of centralized government by an author who was then unknown to the kindergarten Curtis claimed that he and his friends derived the idea of immediate unification as the answer to the needs of South Africa.[7] It is indeed possible that Oliver's book was the germ of the plan, for it was reviewed in London in May, 1906,[8] and the kindergarten decision to work for unification seems to have been made in "June or July 1906."[9] It would have been possible for a copy of the book to have fallen into the hands of one of the kindergarten and thus have the effect described by Curtis. A fragment of evidence to the contrary, however, is to be found in Robinson's diary. There it is recorded that Robinson, one of the most active and energetic members of the group, did not read the Hamilton biography until September—long after the kindergarten had begun its closer union activ-

5. Remarks to the Bloemfontein Town Council, Jan. 25, 1904, Headlam, II, 501–502.
6. Frederick Scott Oliver, *Alexander Hamilton: An Essay on American Union* (London, 1906). I have used the "New Edition" published in New York in 1921.
7. Interview with Mrs. Oliver, June 16, 1960. Mrs. Oliver's information came from a letter written to her by Curtis shortly after her husband's death in 1934. That letter was probably the source for a similar statement found in the introduction to Stephen Gwynn, ed., *The Anvil of War: Letters between F. S. Oliver and His Brother 1914–1918* (London, 1936), p. 16. Oliver's association with Milner and his influence upon the kindergarten are examined in Chapter VIII below.
8. *Times*, May 11, 1906.
9. Williams, *Selborne Memorandum*, p. xvii.

ities.[10] Curtis's statement giving credit to Oliver was not made until after the latter's death. It thus may have been prompted by a wish to reward the memory of his late friend. But regardless of how the idea originated, it was agreed, according to Basil Williams, "that somebody ought to get busy preparing a memorandum stating clearly, by means of facts and statistics, the dangers of disunion in South Africa and indicating Union as the only remedy."[11]

This decision of the kindergarten was communicated to Milner in a long letter written by Curtis in August.[12] He explained that a kindergarten committee was preparing to draft a memorandum on government in South Africa. The proposed memorandum was to contain an analysis of the existing relationship among the colonies, a plea for unification, and a draft constitution suggesting the specific form which such unification might take. Curtis, having been appointed by the committee to be the draftsman of the memorandum, would travel widely in South Africa gathering material for the study and examining conditions in various colonies. Reports on each stage of his work were to be submitted to the committee for criticism, and in this way a draft of the full memorandum would be compiled. After agreement had been achieved on the draft, Curtis intended to visit Canada, the United States, and Australia "to review the draft in the light of experience gained in those countries."[13] Upon his return to South Africa the revised draft, representing the findings and opinions of not only Curtis but the whole kindergarten committee, was to be given to Lord Selborne to be used in whatever ways seemed most appropriate.

Curtis's letter to Milner outlining the plans for what came to be called the Selborne Memorandum had a dual purpose. First, the members of the kindergarten wished to inform Milner of their plans and to win his approval. But of more importance, they

10. Robinson's diary, Sept. 10, 1906, Dawson Papers.
11. Williams, *Selborne Memorandum*, p. xvii.
12. This letter is unfortunately missing from the Milner Papers at New College. Even so, it is possible to reconstruct in detail its contents from two letters found in the Dawson Papers. These letters written by Milner to the kindergarten are a point-for-point reply to Curtis's initial letter. Milner to Robinson, Aug. 21 and Sept. 21, 1906, Dawson Papers.
13. *Ibid.*, Sept. 21, 1906. Quoted by Milner from Curtis's initial letter.

wanted his assistance. Curtis's letter was an appeal to Milner for aid in securing financial support for the project from the Rhodes Trust in whose affairs Milner as trustee was becoming increasingly active. The first goal was achieved with only moderate success, for Milner's initial response on August 21 was far from enthusiastic. Although he expressed his general approval of the proposed memorandum, Milner made clear to his young friends that in his opinion the plan for immediate unification could hardly retrieve the fortunes of the British in South Africa. Concerning the matter of money, however, Milner consented to present the proposal to his fellow trustees at their next meeting.[14]

In a long letter written to the young men late in September, Milner announced that the Rhodes Trust would give £1,000 to the committee to support the study for one year. If at the end of that time the project had not been completed, however, the trustees would entertain a request for more money. It was understood that the Rhodes Trust would in no way attempt to influence the findings to be presented in the memorandum. In return, the trustees stipulated the following terms:

1. Lionel Curtis was to be the "Organizing Secretary" of the project. As such he would be expected to resign his position with the Transvaal government to give full time to the preparation of the memorandum.

2. They felt that Curtis could gain through reading sufficient understanding of the various forms of government which might serve as models for South Africa. His plan to visit Canada, the United States, and Australia was therefore unnecessary.

3. The work of the "Organizing Secretary" and the committee was to be closely supervised by Lord Selborne, who was to be kept informed of all steps taken.

4. The wisdom of passing the finished memorandum to Selborne for exploitation was questioned by the trustees. It was thought best to keep Selborne's part in its preparation secret, lest news of it, in Milner's words, "excite local prejudice against them [the kindergarten] on the score of 'dicta-

14. *Ibid.*, Aug. 21, 1906.

tion' [by the Crown]." It was agreed by the trustees, however, that a decision on this matter could be deferred until later.

5. The fact that the financial support for the project was coming from the Rhodes Trust was to be kept secret.[15]

With this act of assistance, Milner's participation in the creation of the Selborne Memorandum came to an end. During the preparation of the memorandum Milner was neither consulted nor even kept informed of the progress of the work. His diary and correspondence in that period contain no references, direct or indirect, to the kindergarten project, nor is there any indication in other sources that Milner was concerned with this study. It was not until after the Selborne Memorandum had been completed by Curtis and the committee, accepted by Selborne, and dispatched to the colonial governments concerned that Milner learned of its completion and of the recommendations which it contained. Only then did he learn from Robinson that "a complete memorandum on the present relations between the S. African states has been prepared by Curtis & hacked about by all of us & sent home [to the Colonial Office] & to the South African govts. by Lord S."[16]

Even before learning of the final decision of the Rhodes Trust, however, Curtis and his friends began to organize their activities. During the middle of 1906—as the Transvaal and the Orange River Colony moved closer to self-government—the young men were busy planning a project which, they believed, would turn this self-government to the advantage of the imperial connection. Throughout the month of August there were frequent meetings—often informal luncheons and dinners attended by a few, but sometimes "great confabulations"—at which all available members of the kindergarten gathered to discuss the memorandum.[17] By the first of September plans had apparently progressed far enough for the group to present its scheme to the High Commissioner. Selborne, though privy to the intentions of the group from the first, had reserved his approval and support until preliminary plans were arranged. His active support was gained at a crucial conference in his office on the first of September. Accord-

15. *Ibid.*, Sept. 21, 1906.
16. Robinson to Milner, Jan. 20, 1907, Milner Papers.
17. Robinson's diary, Aug., 1906, Dawson Papers.

ing to Robinson's diary, he and Feetham went to Sunnyside at 2:15 that day "for the first meeting of the deadly secret *Ctee* with Ld. S."[18] Others attending were Duncan, Hichens, Curtis, and Sir Cecil Rodwell.[19] The formal committee meeting was followed by dinner, after which those present "sat up till all hours talking."[20]

Selborne was apparently pleased with the plans of the young men, for at this meeting his support of their project changed from tentative to wholehearted. The love of Empire and the desire to be of public service which prompted the kindergarten were certainly derived for the most part from Milner. But it is equally certain that "it was to Lord Selborne that they owed assistance and encouragement" in their activities on behalf of South African unification.[21] Selborne's enthusiastic support, which contrasted so completely with Milner's tepid attitude, was prompted by the experience which he had gained since his arrival in South Africa. The problems which he had faced as High Commissioner were in many ways different from those that had plagued his predecessor. Like the kindergarten, he came to believe that under the circumstances early unification would serve the interests of the British Empire. The following year he explained this conviction in a letter to Duncan:

> Those who urge delay about Federation on the ground of the present political preponderance of the Dutch are most shortsighted. While the general instability of South Africa continues, all real prosperity will be impossible and all expansion, and the Dutch will continue to preponderate ad eternam . . . : there can be no expansion without stability; and there can be no stability without Federation. Q. E. D.[22]

Once committed to unification and to the memorandum designed to precipitate that unification, Selborne never wavered. From September, 1906, until the national convention three years later he remained steadfast in his support of the closer union movement.

18. Robinson's diary, Sept. 1, 1906, Dawson Papers.
19. Rodwell was Perry's successor as Imperial Secretary to the High Commissioner and an active participant in the production of the memorandum.
20. Robinson's diary, Sept. 1, 1906, Dawson Papers.
21. Worsfold, *The Reconstruction of the New Colonies under Lord Milner*, II, 397.
22. Selborne to Duncan, Nov. 30, 1907, Duncan Papers. Quoted in Thompson, *Unification of South Africa*, p. 80.

With the High Commissioner's concurrence, the tempo of activity accelerated. Curtis, though still Assistant Colonial Secretary in charge of municipal affairs, spent much of September and October traveling throughout South Africa on behalf of the committee. As "Organizing Secretary" he visited all four colonies to gather information and to assess the attitudes of various elements of South African opinion.[23] By the latter part of October he had resigned his governmental appointment in compliance with the requirements of the Rhodes Trust and had retired to Moot House to compose a rough draft of the memorandum.[24]

As Curtis worked to gather material and block out the report, other members of "the Conspiracy," as Robinson called the committee,[25] were able to make a contribution. Though busy with their various occupational tasks during the day, they were frequently able to meet together in the evenings.[26] At these "moots" ideas were analyzed and discussed; and Curtis's tentative conclusions were subjected to the ruthless criticism of the committee. "There is great secrecy about the whole thing," wrote Kerr. "Everything is so mysterious that it is bound to leak out. Curtis is really writing a great despatch, which is subjected to the criticism of what is known as the Moot, which consists of Lord Milner's Kindergarten. . . ."[27] Several years later Curtis described with pride the thorough editorial methods of the kindergarten in a letter to Leo Amery: "I should be afraid to say how many times I rewrote the Selborne Memorandum. . . ." The resulting document, he said, is "just like a bill which has been redrafted from the beginning to end in the course of its passage through committee, and by which all the members are prepared to stand as a result."[28]

Late in October the first part of Curtis's rough draft was complete. Robinson's diary records that on October 28 he attended "a

23. Williams, *Selborne Memorandum,* p. xviii.

24. In his brief history of the Selborne Memorandum, Basil Williams ignores the part played by the Rhodes Trust, remarking simply that "Mr. Curtis thought it wiser to work at the Memorandum as a private individual, since he would thereby have more freedom for future action." *Ibid.,* p. xviii n.

25. Robinson's diary, Sept. 27, 1906, Dawson Papers.

26. *Ibid.,* Sept. and Oct., 1906.

27. Quoted without citation in Butler, *Lothian,* pp. 22 f.

28. Curtis to Amery, March 29, [1909], Amery Papers.

great moot of the Federation Committee—Duncan, Hichens, Feetham, Curtis, Brand, Kerr, & self—& went solidly through L. C.'s first [chapter of the] 'egg.' "[29] In succeeding weeks the committee met to consider additional portions of "L. C.'s gigantic egg,"[30] each of which was printed in proof form to facilitate criticism by the committee and by Lord Selborne.[31]

By mid-December of 1906 "the Federation plot," as Robinson described it,[32] entered its final editorial stages. As the hotly contested Transvaal election approached, the formal committee presided over by Lord Selborne met to make such changes as were needed to produce a report consonant with the views of the High Commissioner.[33] This turned out to be a difficult and nerve-fraying task which was not completed until the first week of January. There were two causes for this delay. The first was Selborne's determination to shorten the paper by improving the organization and by removing all contentious material. The latter task seemed particularly important to Selborne, who, perhaps more than the younger men on the committee, was aware that references which might offend either of the two dominant white groups could only postpone unification and thus undermine the purpose of the memorandum.[34] These excisions and editorial revisions forced through by the High Commissioner contributed greatly to its influence as well as to its readability. Selborne has in fact been credited with injecting into the memorandum a humanitarian idealism which was altogether missing in the draft submitted by Curtis and his friends.[35]

A second cause for delay stemmed from Selborne's insistence upon keeping the Colonial Office informed of all developments concerning the committee and the memorandum. This cautious regard for chain of command seemed to some of the members of the committee to threaten the whole scheme. In describing the

29. The use of the word "egg" to describe memoranda and reports edited by Curtis and created by the kindergarten seems to have originated with this first co-operative effort of the group.
30. Robinson to Richard Jebb, Nov. 4, 1906, Personal Papers of Richard Jebb, Institute of Commonwealth Studies, University of London.
31. Williams, *Selborne Memorandum*, p. xix.
32. Robinson to Jebb, Nov. 4, 1906, Jebb Papers.
33. Robinson's diary, Dec. 13 and 22, 1906, Dawson Papers.
34. Williams, *Selborne Memorandum*, p. xx.
35. Thompson, *Unification of South Africa*, p. 67 n.

development of the memorandum to Milner, Robinson mentioned that "it was the sending home & thereby the possible stoppage of publication which caused the friction—only temporary, I hope—between Lord S. on the one hand & Duncan, Hichens & Curtis on the other."[36]

The finished memorandum, entitled "A Review of the Present Mutual Relations of the British South African Colonies,"[37] contained an interesting array of historical and statistical information along with the often repeated conclusion of the authors that no part of South Africa could be self-governing in a real sense until unification was achieved. It began with a historical survey of the region's early European settlements, the growth of disharmony between the Afrikaner and British elements, and the consequent development of artificial political boundaries dividing into four states a region meant by nature to form one nation. The authors concluded from this recitation of the past that only unification could enable the people of South Africa to solve the many economic, social, and political problems that confronted them.

In subsequent portions of the work these problems were analyzed in detail in a way calculated to substantiate the authors' conclusion that only unification could save South Africa. The railway and customs problems received particular attention, for nowhere in South African life, so the authors implied, was the need for unified government more obvious. For over half a century an almost endless succession of quarrels and crises had divided the interior states from the colonies along the coast. The result had been to widen the breach between the Boer-dominated interior and the British-oriented Cape Colony and Natal. It has also served as a standing invitation to hostile European powers to promote their own interests by fishing in the troubled waters of South Africa. The present customs union and partial consolidation of the railway system were useful in keeping friction at a minimum. According to the authors, however, they were only temporary expedients which were destined to collapse when it suited the interest of any of the colonies.

36. Robinson to Milner, Jan. 20, 1907, Milner Papers.
37. In "Papers Relating to a Federation of the South African Colonies," Cd. 3564, July, 1907, *Sessional Papers, 1907,* LVII (*Accounts and Papers,* XI). The memorandum is also published verbatim in Williams, *Selborne Memorandum.*

The native and labor problems, because of their interrelationship, were treated together. Every effort was made to convince the reader that nothing short of unification could solve the labor problem of the Rand—a truly South African problem which was as important to the citizens of Cape Town and Durban as to those of Johannesburg. In the same way the authors insisted that the native problem, at present the responsibility of five separate native affairs departments governed by five different native policies, could be handled successfully only when unification was achieved.

Rhodesia and other regions to the north of the four colonies presented another important reason for early unification. According to the authors, the experience of Canada and the United States should convince even the most provincial South African that the rational settlement of that area demanded the united action of a united South Africa. The Chartered Company would someday find itself able no longer to carry the burden of administering Rhodesia. Then serious friction among the colonies—and between the colonies and nations outside the Empire—would develop unless concerted action was possible. That concerted action could be achieved only through unity.

The memorandum ended with an urgent appeal for immediate consideration of the question. Unification could not be pushed aside for consideration at some undetermined time in the future. Changes taking place in the Transvaal and the Orange River Colony made it essential that South Africans now face up to the need for unified government and act upon that need before the restoration of responsible government in the former republics caused a hardening of sentiments which would make unification forever impossible.

The question of how best to utilize the finished memorandum was one which required careful consideration. The Rhodes trustees in their agreement with the kindergarten had discouraged the original plan to give the document to Selborne for publication over his signature. They feared that it would antagonize South Africans, always touchy about Downing Street interference. Members of the committee saw the wisdom of this suggestion, for they too were aware of the tender feelings which could be damaged by the slightest hint of imperial coercion. This sensitivity was doubly

keen inasmuch as the Transvaal was at that time in the midst of
its first postwar election campaign. Even so, Selborne and the
kindergarten were determined to use the memorandum to best
effect. They remained convinced that nothing less than the name
of the High Commissioner could provide the weight necessary to
accomplish their goal. It was agreed, therefore, that a way must be
found by which these two conditions might be reconciled. Perhaps
it might be possible for Selborne to circulate the memorandum
without causing offense if it could be made to appear that the
study had been conducted at the request of one of the four colonial governments. To create this fiction, Curtis in November,
1906, put aside his work on the rough draft of the memorandum
to visit L. S. Jameson, who was still at that time the Prime
Minister of the Cape Colony. He explained the progress which
had been made on the memorandum and sought Jameson's aid in
promoting its effective circulation.[38] Jameson was immediately
willing to co-operate, and on November 28 publicly requested
that the High Commissioner review the current conditions in
South Africa and the feasibility of creating a unified South African state.[39] Upon receipt, Selborne sent copies of Jameson's request to the governments of the other states—including Southern
Rhodesia—asking for their comment. He received no opposition
from the other colonies. On January 7, 1907, therefore, Selborne
distributed to each of the colonial governments a copy of the
memorandum with an accompanying letter reviewing the ficti-
tious origins of the study contrived by Curtis and the committee
and assuring the colonial governments that the memorandum in
no way represented an attempt by the imperial government to
force unification upon the people of South Africa. "It is my dear-
est conviction," Selborne wrote,

> that no healthy movement towards federation can emanate from
> any authority other than the people of South Africa themselves;

38. Thompson, *Unification of South Africa,* p. 67. He cites a letter to himself from
Curtis dated Jan. 18, 1952.

39. In succeeding years the legend of the origins of the memorandum was
somewhat improved by the addition of a "biracial" touch. The *State,* a magazine
begun by the kindergarten to promote closer union, recorded in its first issue that
Jameson had been prompted to make his request by a series of articles in the
Afrikaner newspaper *Ons Land.* Written by the editor F. S. Malan, the articles urged
immediate unification upon South Africa. *State,* I, No. 1 (Jan., 1909), 19.

but, when I am called upon by those occupying the most representative and responsible positions in the country to furnish such
material as is in my possession, for the information of the people
of South Africa, it is clearly my duty to comply with the request.[40]

Selborne frankly admitted in the cover letter that he had not
drafted the memorandum, and he praised highly the unnamed
group which had accomplished that difficult task. He did, however, accept full responsibility for the report, which he had carefully edited and to which he fully subscribed.[41]

Less than two weeks after the circulation of the memorandum
to the colonial governments Selborne sent round an appendix
entitled "South African Railway Unification and its Effect on
Railway Rates."[42] Though he denied responsibility for the report,
he did commend it to the colonial governments as "a valuable
contribution to the study of the railway problem in South Africa
by a gentleman who has had opportunities of giving very special
attention to this subject."[43] That gentleman was Philip Kerr,
Brand's assistant on the Intercolonial Council. In late 1906 when
the creation of the Selborne Memorandum was in progress Kerr
had been at work on an article for the initial issue of a new South
African railroad magazine. As the article took shape it was decided that the information it contained and the conclusions which
Kerr derived from that information might lend added weight to
the larger work. Thus Kerr's draft was expanded, edited by
Brand, Hichens, and Duncan, and finally turned over to the High
Commissioner for use as he saw fit.[44] This paper, which, according
to Kerr "is designed to prove that we can't get sound railway
management in South Africa until they are unified,"[45] recommended the creation of a state-owned railway system managed by
an independent commission which in turn would receive its authority from a unified South African government. Though its
reception by the public was overshadowed by its being appended
to the more widely known Selborne Memorandum, Kerr's study
nevertheless filled a useful purpose. At the 1908 constitutional

40. Cd. 3564, p. 5.
41. *Ibid.*, p. 9.
42. *Ibid.*, pp. 64–108.
43. *Ibid.*, p. 63.
44. Butler, *Lothian*, p. 22.
45. From a letter from Kerr to his mother. Quoted without citation in *ibid.*, p. 23.

convention at which the details of South African unification were settled, Kerr's report was used in determining the railroad provisions for the Union Constitution.[46]

Getting the memorandum and the accompanying report by Kerr in the hands of colonial politicians was an important step in the plans of the committee. But it was necessary that the dispatch be made public if it was to fulfil its purpose of allowing South Africans "a timely opportunity of expressing a voice upon the desirability, and, if acknowledged, the best means, of bringing about a central national Government embracing all the Colonies and Protectorates under British South African administration."[47] The publication of the memorandum, like its earlier circulation to the colonial governments, was accomplished with the aid of a South African politician. Instead of Jameson, it was thought wise to enlist the services of an Afrikaner leader whose name would generate some enthusiasm for unification among the Boer population. The problem of course was in finding one who would associate himself publicly at this time with a movement for closer union. It will be remembered that the major Afrikaner political figures had shown no interest in early unification. They were, in fact, not likely to promote the idea so long as British-oriented governments were in command in the various colonies. When the memorandum was completed in January, 1906, the Transvaal was in the process of gaining self-government but the initial election was several months away, the Orange River Colony was still a crown colony, and Jameson had not yet been forced to resign from the premiership of the Cape Colony.

The desired co-operation was nevertheless secured from a young Afrikaner leader from Cape Town named Francis S. Malan. A growing power in the *Afrikaner Bond* and the editor of the influential newspaper *Ons Land,* Malan had earlier broken ranks by coming out in support of immediate unification. His newspaper had published the previous August and September a series of six articles in which he supported unification as the only solution to South Africa's many problems.[48] Encouraged by these

46. Thompson, *Unification of South Africa*, pp. 285 f.
47. Cd. 3564, pp. 4 f.
48. Thompson, *Unification of South Africa*, p. 70.

articles, Curtis persuaded Malan to make a speech favoring unification. The speech, like the earlier articles in *Ons Land,* was
republished by Robinson in the *Star* and made the text of numerous editorials supporting unification.[49] Naturally, therefore, Curtis thought of Malan when early the following year he and the
committee were searching for an Afrikaner political leader to aid
them in getting the memorandum into the hands of the public. A
copy of the memorandum was sent to Malan three days before he
was to meet with Curtis. Shortly before his death Curtis described
the resulting interview:

> I found Malan sitting on Rhodes's bench with the Selborne Mem-
> orandum in his hand. He said nothing for five minutes. When I
> could bear it no longer I said, "Well?" "Publish it," he said. That
> was all that passed, and I hastened back to Groot Schuur
> [Rhodes's home which had been made the residence of the pre-
> mier] and told Dr. Jim [Jameson] what Malan had said.[50]

The formalities which made publication possible took place in
July. At the session of the Cape parliament Malan called upon the
government to table whatever information it might have concerning the matter of unification.[51] A week later the memorandum
finally became available to the press and to the general public.
The previous day Robinson recorded in his diary that he "spent a
solid 5 hours in the evening digesting the Federal 'Egg' for publication" in both *The Times* and his own *Star.*[52]

Though it appears that almost all the newspapers in South
Africa responded favorably,[53] it is of course difficult to gauge the
general public reaction. However, in Robinson's opinion—which
in this case is somewhat suspect—the public was enthusiastic in its
approval. His report, printed in *The Times* on July 6, 1907, reads:

> Lord Selborne's memorandum is admitted throughout the country
> to be a State document of extreme importance. It has been de-
> scribed as the most notable pronouncement of the sort since Lord
> Durham's historical report on Canada, and as being conceived in a
> spirit of constructive statesmanship. While there is some diver-

49. Wrench, *Dawson,* p. 56.
50. Thompson, *Unification of South Africa,* p. 70. He cites a letter to himself from
Curtis, Jan. 18, 1952.
51. *Ibid.,* p. 75.
52. Robinson's diary, July 2, 1907, Dawson Papers.
53. *Times,* July 5, 1907.

gence of view regarding the expediency and practicability of federation in the immediate future and the means by which it is
attainable, there is a consensus of opinion that the memorandum
sheds a new light on the whole subject, arrays the essential facts
lucidly and temperately crystallizes ideas which hitherto have
often been vaguely and indefinitely expressed and gives a strong
stimulus to a wider and more careful consideration of South
African federation as an immediate practical policy instead of a
remote ideal. The trend of South African thought, Dutch as well
as British, seems to be in this direction.

This favorable reception of the memorandum was undoubtedly
a source of satisfaction to the young men of the kindergarten.
Even so, there was little time for self-congratulation, for even
before the completion of that project steps were under way to turn
the sympathy for unification resulting from the memorandum
into political action.

Chapter Six. The kindergarten and the draft constitution

Within the kindergarten it had been understood from the first that the memorandum created by Curtis and the committee was to be only a first step. It was assumed that the circulation of the memorandum would generate interest in unification and focus attention upon the key issues involved. But at this point matters could not be left to themselves. It was essential that the momentum created by the memorandum be harnessed in a way that would not only lead to unification but to unification of a sort which would serve the interests of British South Africans and the Empire. In practical terms this meant that the kindergarten must establish an organization to take advantage of this enthusiasm while it was strong and before it was captured by those unsympathetic with the Milnerian program.

In early January, 1907, Curtis explained this situation to fellow imperial enthusiast Richard Jebb, remarking that "a few of us from various parts of South Africa are meeting on the 21st to concert measures."[1] The meeting to which Curtis referred was a dinner given by [Sir] Abe Bailey, mining promoter, land owner, leader in Progressive circles, and along with the Rhodes Trust one of the two most generous financial supporters of kindergarten activities.[2] Though his money was essential to the group, Bailey was nevertheless a source of constant concern and frequent embarrassment to the kindergarten. His lack of polish, education, and sometimes discretion, often combined with his enormous energy for "good causes" to create problems for his young beneficiaries. At the time of Milner's retirement Robinson described Bailey to Malcolm, his successor as private secretary to the High Commissioner:

> *Abe Bailey* You probably know him already. He is a good chap, frightfully strenuous and keen about everything which he takes

1. Curtis to Jebb, Jan. 2, 1907, Jebb Papers.
2. Outlines of Bailey's career are found in the *Dictionary of National Biography*, 1931–40, pp. 27–29; *Times*, Aug. 12, 1940.

up, and *does* a thing while other people are talking about it. (The most notable recent instance of this is his taking up a bond for £34,000 one morning last February, in order to acquire control over the "Rand Daily Mail," which the Responsible Government people would have had in another hour.) He is also extremely rich, more in land than in gold mines, . . . but unpopular in Johannesburg, probably because his past was more than usually lurid and with a larger number of victims than the average. However, he is *all right now* and worth a dozen other men if *he's kept right*. But of all men in the world he requires constant patting on the back and assurances that the mantle of Rhodes has fallen straight on to his shoulders.[3]

Bailey's dinner, which occurred during the climax of the Transvaal election campaign, was ostensibly a social event to welcome to Johannesburg the delegates to an intercolonial conference on defense against native rebellions. In fact, however, Bailey and the kindergarten had in mind a meeting of men of all political factions to form a nationwide closer union organization under kindergarten leadership. Particular effort was made, therefore, to draw prominent Afrikaner leaders to the dinner, for it was realized that without them no political movement towards union could gain the universal support necessary for success. In a letter of invitation to Botha, Duncan freely admitted that the dinner had a political purpose. He explained that those attending would be asked "to consider whether a movement can be made at the present time in which men of all political parties can join to help forward the cause of union."[4] Curtis was more specific in a similar letter to Smuts. He first reviewed the reasons for the early creation of a unified South Africa and then sought Smuts's approval for the establishment of an intercolonial body advocating immediate closer union and representing the leading elements of every faction of the white population. The organization, which might be nominally headed by the chief justices of the four colonies, should have two related functions: the collection of statistical informa-

3. Robinson to Malcolm (copy), n.d. [*ca.* April, 1905], Dawson Papers. A similar comment is found in the memorandum from Milner to Selborne dated April 14, 1905, a copy of which is found in the Dawson Papers.

4. Duncan to Botha (copy), Jan. 8, 1907, Duncan Papers. Quoted in Thompson, *Unification of South Africa*, p. 69.

tion, and the presentation of that information to the public in a periodical dedicated to unification.[5]

This attempt at forming a popular multiparty organization under kindergarten direction failed, however, for the Boer leaders refused to play their assigned part. They were determined to unify South Africa once Afrikaner control had been achieved in the Orange River Colony and the Cape Colony as well as in the Transvaal. Even so, Smuts, Botha, and their friends made clear by their refusal to sit at Bailey's table that they were little inclined to become pawns in a kindergarten scheme to steal their own advantage. Bailey's dinner and the plans associated with it convinced Smuts that

> there are sinister influences at work—submarine operations which will have to be carefully watched. Bailey wants to run Federation as a sort of Barnum policy to advertise himself; some other highly placed persons want to achieve their ambitious hopes, and others no doubt have purely personal ends to serve.[6]

This Boer refusal to co-operate was a serious blow to the plans of the kindergarten. A popular movement for unification which lacked the support of Afrikaner leaders would be worse than none at all, for it would certainly cause closer union to become a party issue with "racial" overtones. The kindergarten was thus forced to admit at least temporary defeat and to reform its plans in the light of Boer intransigence. On the eve of the Bailey dinner several members of the group met at Bedford Farm, the country home of Sir George Farrar, a mine owner and Progressive party leader, to confer with political leaders from the British community. Besides Farrar and members of the kindergarten, the meeting was attended by C. P. Crewe, a Unionist (Progressive) party leader from the Cape Colony, and J. G. Maydon, a strong supporter of closer union from Natal.[7] In a letter written later that same evening Robinson described to Milner the change in plans, saying that now "the idea is to form a small private committee in

5. Curtis to Smuts, Jan. 7, 1907, Smuts Papers. Cited in Thompson, *Unification of South Africa*, p. 69.
6. Smuts to J. X. Merriman, Jan. 25, 1907, Merriman Papers. Quoted in Thompson, *Unification of South Africa*, p. 74.
7. Robinson to Milner, Jan. 20, 1907, Milner Papers.

each Colony to help Curtis in collecting materials & to postpone any public propaganda, the formation of a league etc. till he has done so."[8] A national organization of the sort which had been previously contemplated was thus to be eschewed for the time being. Only one of the dual functions described by Curtis in his letter to Smuts now seemed feasible. The propagandist part of the program must wait until Boer co-operation was obtainable. Even so, important things might be accomplished in the meantime by the accumulation of statistical material—material which could be made use of at the proper time and in the most effective way.

Bailey's dinner on January 21 was an anticlimax. Its original purpose had been undermined by the attitude of the Boers and the subsequent change in plans of the kindergarten. The dinner was not altogether valueless, however, for those present were persuaded to make "a largish subscription on the spot to cover preliminary expenses. . . ."[9] This money was supplemented with £1,000 from the Rhodes Trust—the same £1,000, in fact, which the previous year had been given to support the creation of the Selborne Memorandum. Money for the memorandum, however, had apparently been obtained locally—probably from Bailey. Robinson was thus able to report to Milner that the Rhodes Trust grant for that purpose "is banked in the joint names of Feetham & myself & still untouched."[10] It was the wish of the kindergarten, he said, that the trustees permit them to apply the money to the expenses of the new project. They wanted an understanding, however, that its source might be made public if the need ever arose, for according to Robinson, "Curtis is beginning to feel a little nervous about having any resources at his back which he is unable to disclose."[11] The Rhodes Trust complied with the wishes of the kindergarten,[12] the money thus acquired later being used to defray publication expenses for the unification movement.[13] It seems unlikely, however, that the contribution was ever disclosed. The published accounts of both the closer union movement and of the

8. *Ibid.*
9. Robinson to Milner, Feb. 3, 1907, Milner Papers.
10. Robinson to Milner, Jan. 20, 1907, Milner Papers.
11. *Ibid.*
12. Milner to Robinson, April 17, 1908, Dawson Papers.
13. Curtis to Milner, Oct. 31, 1908, Milner Papers.

Rhodes Trust—even those written years later—fail to mention any connection between the two.

With a new strategy for the achievement of their goal, and with the financial backing to support that strategy, the kindergarten in the early months of 1907 set about its work. Curtis explained how he and his associates interpreted that task in a letter written the following year to Richard Jebb:

> A year ago when we set out to do this work we pointed out to those who have helped us that while the new Governments were finding their feet and while all the Governments were thinking of the position to take up with regard to the question of union which the Selborne memorandum has propounded, there would be no one whose business it would be in the meantime to collect and digest the facts and figures which would be necessary before any new plan of Government could be formed. We therefore set ourselves to do this work. . . .[14]

The collection and digestion of facts and figures was, as Robinson pointed out to Milner, to be conducted by Curtis with the aid of "a small private committee in each colony."[15] There is, however, no evidence to indicate that such committees of carefully chosen assistants were ever established. Nor is there any information to explain the failure of this part of the revised program. There is reason to believe, however, that an attempt was made to form such committees from an organization—the Fortnightly Club—previously created by the kindergarten in October, 1906.

As the kindergarten began its work on what became the Selborne Memorandum in August and September, 1906, at frequent meetings at Moot House plans were made and aspects of the question of unification were discussed. From time to time men not associated with the kindergarten whose assistance and support were needed were brought as guests to these moots with the hope that they would be impressed by the serious determination of the group and won over by the logical clarity of its position. By early October the kindergarten committee realized that these moots might have a greater impact if a formal organization were created at whose meetings a greater number could be influenced. The

14. Curtis to Jebb, March 16, 1908, Jebb Papers.
15. Robinson to Milner, Jan. 20, 1907, Milner Papers.

creation of such an organization would of course in no way prevent the continued operation of the original committee as an "inner moot" completely independent of the larger and more loosely organized body. Thus the Fortnightly Club was formed. At its initial meeting at Moot House on October 4, 1906, Richard Feetham stated that "the raison d'etre of this embryo society . . . [is] the discussion of political questions," which in South African terms meant unification.[16] Though the organization seems to have played no great part in either the creation of the Selborne Memorandum or the spreading of the closer union gospel, it continued to meet regularly throughout the remainder of 1906.[17] On at least two occasions that year the club heard papers relating to unification read by members of the kindergarten, Feetham and Perry.[18] Perry's paper concerning the labor problem as it related to unified government is unavailable and very likely lost, but Feetham's essay entitled "Some Problems of South African Federation and Reasons for Facing Them" still exists. Read at the inaugural meeting of the club, it contains the first reasoned public expression in support of unification by a member of the kindergarten and probably summarizes the thinking of the group at that time.[19]

Though the details of the matter are obscured by an insufficiency of evidence, it appears that in April, 1907—just three months after Boer intransigence forced a revision of kindergarten plans—an effort was made by the kindergarten to reorganize the Fortnightly Club into a Transvaal committee to gather information on unification and to advise Curtis.[20] For six months thereafter the club met regularly to hear papers which more often than not were written by kindergarten members and their associates.[21] It is probable that these papers and the information which they contained were digested by Curtis and used in publications on the question of unification. To that degree then the Fortnightly Club

16. Richard Feetham, "Some Problems of South African Federation and Reasons for Facing Them," p. 1.
17. These meetings are mentioned in Robinson's diary, Dawson Papers.
18. Robinson's diary, Oct. 4 and Nov. 1, 1906, Dawson Papers.
19. A summary of this paper is found in Thompson, *Unification of South Africa*, p. 62.
20. Robinson's diary, April 23, 1907, Dawson Papers.
21. Robinson's diary contains references to papers by Curtis on "Subject Races of the Empire" (May 9), Robinson on "The Strike" (June 6), and George Craik, a close associate of the group, on universities (Jan. 23, 1908).

might have been the "small private committee" for the Transvaal. There is no reason to think, however, that similar groups were established in the other colonies as had been originally planned. Available evidence contains not the slightest hint of such groups in the Cape Colony, Natal, and the Orange Free State.

The failure of the plan to form committees to assist Curtis and the kindergarten did not preclude the fulfilment of the more important part of the January, 1907, program. During the next two years the young men, operating along patterns developed for the creation of the Selborne Memorandum, were successful in collecting and digesting an enormous amount of information. This information, if not the conclusions which inevitably accompanied it, was used with considerable effect to influence South Africans in general and the handful of men who framed the unification agreement in particular.

The material so collected was published in 1908 in two books. One of these, entitled *The Framework of Union: A Comparison of Some Union Constitutions*,[22] contained the constitutions of the United States, Canada, Germany, Switzerland, and Australia with an analysis of their similarities and differences. Though published anonymously, Curtis later announced that the work had been edited by B. K. Long,[23] an Oxford friend of many of the kindergarten "who came out to South Africa as a teacher, went to the Bar, [and] became a Member of Parliament" in the Cape Colony.[24] This work, which is essentially free from editorial bias, was meant only to provide those interested in the question of closer union with a convenient source of information about federal constitutions and how they compared with each other.

Of far greater significance in the unification movement was the second of the two works, a two-volume book by Curtis entitled *The Government of South Africa*.[25] The first volume contained an analysis of the history, economy, social and racial composition,

22. Printed in Cape Town by the *Cape Times*, Ltd.
23. [Lionel Curtis], *The Government of South Africa* (South Africa: Central News Agency, Ltd., 1908), I, xi.
24. Robinson to A. W. Jose, Sydney, N.S.W. (copy), n.d., Dawson Papers. Long took a hand in later kindergarten publications before returning to England to join the staff of the *Times*.
25. Published in 1908 by the Central News Agency. Though no author or editor is listed on the title page, Curtis's name is found at the end of the introduction.

and political situation in South Africa. The approach to the subject and the conclusions presented were understandably similar to those found in the Selborne Memorandum. All the notes, documents, and supporting evidence upon which the contents of the first volume were supposedly based were published separately in the second volume. Work on this study occupied much of Curtis's time and energy in 1907 and the first half of 1908. As was the case with the Selborne Memorandum almost two years previous, Curtis was assisted by an editorial committee of Milnerites. The most active seem to have been Duncan, Brand, Kerr,[26] and [Sir] William Marris, a young official of the Indian government who in 1906 was "borrowed from India to set the Civil Service in order."[27] This group, joined occasionally by Robinson and others, edited the rough draft material submitted by Curtis.[28] As portions were completed they were "issued by instalments in provisional form, so that any errors which the original draft contained might be detected and set right."[29] Shortly after the publication of the fifth and last instalment in September, 1908, the revised work was published in its final two-volume form.[30]

In the introduction Curtis made every effort to assure the reader that this study had been done by a group of disinterested but public-spirited citizens who were keenly concerned for the political future of South Africa.

> The authors do not propose in these pages to formulate a definite scheme of union, but rather to provide information which will enable the reader to discuss such schemes whenever advanced. . . . The object of the book is attained in so far as it provokes discussion.[31]

Despite this disclaimer, the first volume of *The Government of South Africa* was a long argument in support of closer union. In chapter after chapter Curtis described past events and present

26. Statement by Sir George Farrar quoted in Closer Union Societies, *Proceedings at the Annual Meeting of the Association of Closer Union Societies at Johannesburg March 3, 4, and 5th, 1909* (Johannesburg), p. 3.
27. Lionel Curtis, *A Letter to the People of India* (Bombay, Calcutta, and Madras, 1917), p. 3. For a summary of Marris's career see the *Dictionary of National Biography*, 1941–1950, pp. 575–76.
28. Robinson's diary, Feb. 29 and March 31, 1908, Dawson Papers.
29. Curtis, *Government of South Africa*, I, ix.
30. *Cape Times*, Sept. 26, 1908.
31. Curtis, *Government of South Africa*, I, viii.

conditions in South Africa in a way calculated to convince the reader that unification was the only road to salvation. Curtis's failure to restrict himself to the collection and digestion of facts as was agreed in January, 1907, illustrates the paradox of his personality. One might conclude that in this instance—as well as in all others for that matter—Curtis was a propagandist in spite of himself. Undoubtedly he thought of his work as being factual and unbiased. Probably he had no intention of promising objective research but delivering propaganda. Curtis, however, was incapable of being objective about a matter in which he was deeply involved. Thus *The Government of South Africa* was, like all Curtis's supposedly unbiased analytical studies, actually a political tract.

In this case, however, the inconsistency may not be altogether chargeable to Curtis's deficiencies. As will be seen, by the time Curtis and the committee reached the final stages in the production of *The Government of South Africa* events had begun to move at such a rapid rate that another change in the tactics of kindergarten was required. By early 1908 it seemed that the time had finally come to bring the movement out into the open with the formation of a popular organization utilizing all the devices which had been so much a part of public agitation in Great Britain ever since the Chartist era. Thus *The Government of South Africa,* claiming to be unbiased but actually quite tendentious, may be a child of that transition in tactics.

To understand this change in tactics and its probable effect upon *The Government of South Africa,* it should be noted that in this work the kindergarten for the first time addressed itself in a serious way to the matter of just what sort of constitutional system should be created in South Africa. From the time unification was first considered there existed the question of whether the proposed South African state should be federal or highly centralized in form. It was generally accepted that South Africa, like other advanced countries with vast areas and relatively low population density such as the United States, Australia, and Canada, would become federated. All observers of South African affairs conceded that traditional friction among the four colonies and the particularist sentiment among much of the white population made a unitary "national" form of government very unlikely.[32] As the kindergarten became active in the unification movement it was forced to accept the logic of this. Though unitary government, as F. S. Oliver taught in his biography of Hamilton, would undoubtedly provide a form of government vastly superior to that created by federation, the realities of South African life dictated the latter. In his paper read to the first meeting of the Fortnightly Club on October 4, 1906, Feetham touched upon this matter in a way which made clear that he saw federation as the most likely form which South African unification would take. He remarked rather cryptically, however, that "whether any combinations may be possible or desirable which would reduce the number of units to be federated is, of course, another question."[33] Shortly thereafter Kerr in a letter to his mother repeated the current opinion that "federation is what will ultimately come. It is really only a matter of time. . . . Unification [unitary government] is practically speaking impossible. You could not now destroy the inter-colonial boundaries if you tried."[34]

As Curtis and the committee began to work on what came to be called *The Government of South Africa* they could find no reason to think that unification would come in any form other than federation. In fact, the book of source material entitled *The Framework of Union* contained constitutions of only those countries with federal governments. And the first instalments of *The Government of South Africa* which appeared in the middle of 1908 reflected this assumption as well. Later portions of that work, however, indicate a complete reversal on this important point. In these instalments the authors urged not only unification, but unification of a highly centralized form. In justifying this remarkable inconsistency Curtis explained in the introduction that when the project was begun the authors had believed that only federation was possible. Therefore the more desirable alternative was not proposed. But as their work progressed they came to realize that the burdens of federation would create structural weaknesses which would in the end destroy closer union.

32. Thompson, *Unification of South Africa*, p. 101.
33. Feetham, "Some Problems of South African Federation and Reasons for Facing Them," p. 8.
34. Butler, *Lothian*, p. 23.

"They [the authors] have felt obliged, therefore, to state conclusions which have been, as it were, forced upon them in spite of preconceived ideas."[35]

Curtis's explanation of this matter is perhaps correct insofar as it goes. It does not tell the whole story, however, for there were practical political considerations which were probably more than anything else responsible in this changed opinion of the kindergarten concerning the best form of unification. Those political considerations were the same ones which help to account for the hortatory tone of *The Government of South Africa*. Rapidly changing events were producing altered attitudes towards unification which prompted the kindergarten to conclude in the midst of the research project that unitary government, which had heretofore seemed out of the question, was, after all, within the realm of possibility. By early 1908 members of the kindergarten learned that leading Afrikaners were no longer opposed to immediate unification, that they were in fact quite interested in it. By then the affairs of both the Orange Free State and the Cape Colony were, like those of the Transvaal, safely in the hands of the Boers. The *Orangia Unie* had gained control of the Free State in November, 1907, and two months later an election in the Cape Colony had brought victory to the South Africa party and an end to the ministry of Jameson. By early 1908, therefore, the conditions which Afrikaner leaders considered essential for unification had come to exist. Now that a united South Africa would be an Afrikaner-dominated state, and now that responsibility for framing the constitution would be securely in Boer hands, the Afrikaner leaders were willing—even eager—to see unification achieved.[36]

The form of unification which they favored was not federal but unitary. Like the kindergarten, they were aware that there were advantages to be derived from a highly centralized government, even one which controlled an enormous area of sparse population. Insofar as South Africa was concerned, these advantages were both political and economic. Economically, the country lacked both the resources and the reservoir of trained public servants to

35. Curtis, *Government of South Africa*, I, x.
36. Thompson, *Unification of South Africa*, pp. 70–75, 139–40.

support a federal system. The establishment of a federal government over the existing state governments would place an unbearable burden on the people of South Africa. Politically speaking, the
federal system involved additional disadvantages. By its very nature federal government was a compact, the terms of which were
specified in a constitution. When questions of interpretation
arose, recourse to a higher authority would inevitably result.
This, the Afrikaners feared, might mean appeals to the Privy
Council in London and unwanted imperial intervention. Unitary
government, therefore, had attractions not found in federalism.[37]

Boer willingness to support immediate unification was, as will
be seen, known to the kindergarten as early as March, 1908. The
first significant result of this change in attitude, however, did not
appear until early May. At an intercolonial conference meeting in
Pretoria on May 4 to iron out some pressing rail and customs
problems Merriman moved that the

> following *communiqué* be issued to the press at once: The dele-
> gates from the self-governing Colonies have adopted the principle
> of closer union and undertake to submit certain resolutions to
> their Parliaments in reference thereto. They also undertake to
> recommend to their Parliaments the appointment of delegates to a
> National Convention for the purpose of framing a draft Constitu-
> tion.[38]

This resolution, which ultimately led to a National Convention
in late 1908 and early 1909, had been planned in advance by
Merriman and his associates from the former republics. Since
Smuts and the kindergarten were by then co-operating on various
matters relating to unification, it seems likely that Curtis and his
friends knew in advance of Boer intentions. This assumption is
supported by statements made by Kerr and Robinson at the time
of the Pretoria meeting.[39] It appears, however, that the kindergarten was not at this time aware that Afrikaner leaders had, like the
Milnerites themselves, come to look upon unitary government as
the most desirable form of closer union. The kindergarten seems
not to have understood this fact until the following month when

37. *Ibid.*, pp. 102–5.
38. Quoted in *ibid.*, p. 92.
39. Robinson's diary, May 5 and 6, 1908; Kerr, apparently to his family, n.d.,
quoted in Butler, *Lothian*, p. 27.

Botha and Smuts on the floor of the Transvaal Parliament spoke in vigorous support of a highly centralized unitary government.[40] It was at this time that Curtis and his committee were in the process of issuing *The Government of South Africa* in instalments. Thus, bold advocacy of unitary government by Boer leaders, rather than an objective reappraisal of South African conditions, as Curtis claimed,[41] probably explains the change in approach discernible in the latter portions of that work.

The Government of South Africa was meant to shape the opinions of those in South Africa who directed the affairs of government and influenced the thinking of the general public. Even so, it was thought wise to cast the widest net by selling the book at the lowest possible price. The price was set at ten shillings, a figure which the prospective buyer was assured would "scarcely cover the cost of printing and binding."[42] Such poor business practices were made possible by the £1,000 from the Rhodes Trust. In a letter to Milner in which he described the progress of the closer union movement, Curtis remarked that

> it would have been a tremendous drag on us if we had to raise the whole of the money required for the printing of 'The Government of South Africa' as [sic] a time when we wanted to appeal for fighting funds for the movement as a whole.[43]

It might be noted here that in the preparation of this publication, as in the case of the earlier Selborne Memorandum, Milner had nothing to do with the actual composition of the work and the conclusions which it presented. Certainly his imperial philosophy and his goals for South Africa had been passed almost unchanged to the kindergarten and were thus reflected in the book, but Curtis's letter quoted above and Milner's diary for those months show clearly that Milner's only direct involvement in this project was in raising money. During the crucial period shortly before the book began to appear in instalments Milner was not even aware that the project was under way. Returning from an extended vacation in Egypt and the Sudan, he asked Robinson for

40. Thompson, *Unification of South Africa*, p. 144.
41. *Transvaal Legislative Council Debates*, June 30, 1908, col. 39.
42. From an advertisement for *The Government of South Africa* printed on the flyleaf of the earlier *The Framework of Union*.
43. Curtis to Milner, Oct. 31, 1908, Milner Papers.

news, remarking, "I have not heard whether the Federation Paper project has materialized, or been abandoned."[44]

Events in South Africa moved swiftly in 1908. Within a month after the publication of the two-volume study representatives of the colonial governments sat down to begin hammering out a constitution for a South African nation. Shortly thereafter Curtis reported with pardonable pride that "the book has done more to shape the ultimate results than we could ever have hoped."[45] It was of course a gross exaggeration for him to claim that "without it the convention would simply have had to adjourn for want of information."[46] Nevertheless, he was not far from the truth when he asserted that "our figures in the Govt of South Africa [sic] are being used as the basis of all the financial calculations of the convention."[47]

The exact way in which this information became important in determining the form of the Union constitution was quite different from what Curtis's correspondents might have assumed. It was not the publication of the completed study and the reading of it by important South Africans that gave it significance. Rather, it was the utilization in its raw form of the material from which the finished study was composed which gave it historic importance. And in this process of utilization J. C. Smuts played the vital part. It was through Smuts, the principal architect of the South African constitution, that the kindergarten was able to influence the final outcome of unification.

Smuts had never won the affection of the kindergarten. From the first they had correctly understood that he was not only an implacable foe of Milner's policies but also the most politically able and energetic of all the Transvaal Boers. In their correspondence the kindergarten sneeringly referred to Smuts as "slim Janny," a nickname which followed him throughout his life.[48] But

44. Milner to Robinson, April 17, 1908, Dawson Papers.
45. Curtis to Richard Jebb, Dec. 6, [1908], Jebb Papers.
46. Curtis to Jebb, Sept. 30, 1908, *ibid.*
47. Curtis to Milner, Oct. 31, 1908, Milner Papers.
48. According to one of Milner's correspondents, "a 'slim' man is what we should call a slippery customer, foxy, deceitful, who gets his enemies, opponents and friends to believe in him . . . even though he means to give them away when it suits his advantage." From a copy of a memorandum dated Oct., 1910, by F. Hatten, Milner Papers. For a more refined but no more expressive definition of "slimness," see Hancock, *Smuts*, p. 274.

after the Boer decision made in early 1908 to support immediate unification, the relationship began to change. The kindergarten and the Transvaal Boers—particularly Smuts—quickly thrust aside their previous bitterness as the two groups began to co-operate in the interest of closer union. Towards this end Curtis and his editorial committee made available to Smuts their statistical reports and conclusions which were later to become *The Government of South Africa*. In describing the research activities of his committee to Richard Jebb, Curtis commented that "now we find the Transvaal Government reaching out their hands for our results. We are helping them in every way and as our diagrams and tables are produced, copies of them are sent to Smuts."[49] In preparing various draft proposals to be presented to the National Convention Smuts often relied on the statistical material provided by the kindergarten, for as Curtis remarked, ". . . it has been the only carefully prepared thing in the field."[50]

Kindergarten influence on the South African constitution was not altogether derived from the cold facts and dubious conclusions that flowed from Curtis's pen. A significant part was played in these affairs by Robert Brand, who throughout 1908 and 1909 worked closely with Smuts both before and during the protracted National Convention. According to material uncovered by L. M. Thompson, these two, along with F. Lucas, a Johannesburg lawyer, labored in the last six weeks before the Convention began in October to fashion a draft constitution which became the starting point for the debates of the Convention. Furthermore, Brand, along with Patrick Duncan, helped in a vital though unofficial way in working out a compromise settlement during the course of the Convention.[51] There was thus a personal, as well as a "literary," path over which kindergarten ideas passed from the minds of Milner's young men to the constitution of the Union of South Africa.

This effect is perhaps most clearly discernible in the constitutional provisions regarding the method of defining the constituencies of the South African legislature. To the kindergarten this

49. Curtis to Jebb, March 16, 1908, Jebb Papers.
50. *Ibid.*, Dec. 6, [1908].
51. Thompson, *Unification of South Africa*, pp. 157 ff.

point was vital, for upon its determination rested the success or failure of their plan for the achievement of Milnerian goals despite the initial control of the united government by the Boers. Unless the seats in the legislature were based upon constituencies of equal voting strength, and unless there was specific provision for periodic redistribution of those seats, the influx of British settlers resulting from unification would be meaningless. Members of the kindergarten along with other leaders of the British community were thus determined that the constitution enable the expected flood of immigrants to have a cleansing effect at the ballot box. In Curtis's terms:

> Our task now is to . . . make it impossible for those in power in both countries [South Africa and Great Britain] to carry a gerrymandered scheme of union.[52]

It was Brand's conviction—and perhaps that of his kindergarten associates as well—that proportional representation could best accomplish this. Throughout 1908 he wrote and spoke on behalf of an electoral system which, he claimed, would result in "not only the softening of the sharp line between town and country, but also the mitigation of the asperity of racial [British vs. Boer] conflicts."[53] That his arguments had a telling effect upon Smuts is clear, for the draft constitution presented to the Convention by the Transvaal delegation contained provisions for proportional representation.[54] This was accepted by the Convention, only to be rejected later by colonial legislatures. Even so, the constitution as finally composed contained an electoral process which was generally acceptable to the leaders of the British community.[55]

The members of the kindergarten were thus justified in their feeling of pride over the part played by their research and personal influence in the deliberations of the National Convention. The creation of an acceptable constitution by the Convention,

52. Curtis to Jebb, March 16, 1908, Jebb Papers.
53. From a paper by Brand published in the *Cape Times*, Sept. 26, 1908. It appears to have been republished twice: in the *State* (Special Constitutional Number), Feb. 12, 1909, pp. 19–33, and, according to Thompson, in pamphlet form for distribution to the delegates at the National Convention (Thompson, *Unification of South Africa*, p. 134 n.).
54. The basic issue of the electoral system to be used in a unified South Africa is found discussed throughout Thompson's work. Smuts's proposals on this matter, and Brand's part in shaping those proposals, are dealt with on pp. 126–35.
55. *Ibid.*, pp. 372–74.

however, did not bring to an end the struggle for unification. Before the constitution could be submitted to the Crown for enactment into law it was necessary to get the approval of the colonial legislatures. And this in large part hinged upon the feelings of the white population in general. The reaction of white South Africans to the charter created by the Convention was thus the next crisis to be met. And it was to this matter that the kindergarten turned its energies in the last month of 1908.

Chapter Seven. The closer union movement and the *State*

Just days before the first session of the National Convention in October, 1908, Curtis in a letter to Richard Jebb reminisced about the rapidity with which changes had occurred since he and his associates started "on this wild campaign just two years and a month ago." At that time they had all conceded that the task would be both difficult and protracted. They were prepared for a painfully slow struggle against complacence and indifference from the general population and outright hostility from Boer political leaders. Yet the march of events had been amazingly swift—so swift, in fact, that the struggle appeared to be won almost before it was begun. The mass of white South Africans seemed to be not at all opposed to the idea of immediate unification, and the Boer leaders, once their control was assured in all the colonies but Natal, became as vocal as the kindergarten in its support. "I scarcely dreamed [at the beginning] that the movement could make so much progress in so little time. But the grass was very dry and the flames ran the moment the match was dropped into it."[1]

Because of the dryness of the grass, Curtis and his friends had for some time been aware that their role in bringing about unification was to be far different from that which they had originally supposed. South Africa was going to be unified, and quickly; no cabal of young manipulators was needed to achieve that end. They liked to think that the Selborne Memorandum was the spark that started the flame, but whether this was so or not, the fact remained that by 1908 the fire was briskly burning. Under the circumstances, the challenge confronting the kindergarten became far less heroic but no less important insofar as the future of British interests in South Africa was concerned. It was to insure that the specific provisions contained in the constitution for the united government would make possible the ultimate restoration of British control through immigration.

1. Curtis to Jebb, Sept. 30, 1908, Jebb Papers.

Efforts to accomplish this by influencing Smuts's draft constitution have been previously examined. But other steps, this time aimed at the general public, were attempted as well. For in the last analysis, it was the people of South Africa who would direct the thinking of the delegates, and accept or reject the product of their deliberations. It was, therefore, Kerr wrote,

> important that there should be no delay in getting the question thoroughly laid before the public and thoroughly explained. If it isn't there is a danger of the Federal constitution being engineered by the Dutch alone, without much, or indeed any, public discussion, in such a way as to leave the British or more advanced section of the population at a disadvantage, and so perpetuate the racial trouble.[2]

To lay the matter before the public the kindergarten decided that the time had come to create the popular movement first attempted at the time of the Bailey dinner but postponed because of Boer opposition. Central to this movement was the creation of a local organization in each population center. These groups, combined into some sort of area-wide league, would provide the kindergarten with a powerful instrument with which to influence the nature of the unified government. Associated with the league would be a periodical publication to disseminate propaganda to the general public and esoteric information to the various branches.

> Perhaps the measure of most importance in connection with the preaching of Federation is a propagandist paper, which can rally the Federalists round it, and explain constantly to the public what's what and who's who. The general principles of the question have already been explained in Lord Selborne's Federation Memorandum, but the facts and the details constantly change and require to be explained.[3]

The first local organization, formed in Cape Town in May, 1908, was followed within a month by the creation of a second group in Johannesburg. In succeeding months the movement spread so rapidly that by January, 1909, there were twenty closer union societies, as they came to be called, in the cities and towns

2. Apparently a letter from Kerr to his family, mid-Sept., 1907. Quoted in Butler, *Lothian*, p. 28.
3. *Ibid.*

scattered throughout the four colonies.[4] By March of that year the number had risen to more than sixty.[5] As the drive to unify South Africa neared its climax there was thus a group in almost every settlement with more than a handful of white citizens. And each of these groups contained a full array of local leaders, both British and Boer, whose opinions on unification might be expected to carry weight with the rest of the white population.

The growth of these groups was not a spontaneous process. Hard work and much organizational skill were required to bring together such diverse elements of opinion. And much of the credit should go to Curtis. Following the completion of *The Government of South Africa* he applied his time and energy to the formation of branch groups. The fervor with which he badgered essentially apolitical farmers and businessmen into participation in the closer union movement later became a subject of amusement. One who was himself an object of these tactics recalled on the public platform how "Mr. Curtis had almost made himself a public nuisance by his enthusiasm. (Laughter and applause.) He had dragged them from their homes at all hours of the day and night and they had meetings innumerable and resolutions by the dozen."[6]

These groups, from the time of their origin until the acceptance of the draft constitution by all the colonies in June, 1909, served to increase and direct local interest in unification. Methods for accomplishing this were much like those used by the earlier Fortnightly Club in that regular meetings were held at which papers on various aspects of the constitutional question were read and discussed. The effect of these meetings on public opinion was extended by prominent newspaper coverage and the frequent publication in pamphlet form of closer union lectures and papers.[7]

During the first several months of their development the closer union societies had no central organization. Contact was maintained only through the correspondence and visits of the peripa-

---

4. *State*, I (Jan., 1909), 19 ff.
5. Closer Union Societies, *Proceedings*, p. 12.
6. *Ibid.*, pp. 49–50.
7. "The Closer Union Societies and Their Work to Date," *State*, I (Jan., 1909), 104–12.

tetic Curtis. While the first session of the National Convention was meeting in Durban, however, representatives of eleven groups gathered there to form the Association of Closer Union Societies.[8] At this meeting, which was organized and promoted by Curtis,[9] the apparatus was created for the direction of the movement along the lines most congenial to the goals of the kindergarten. Curtis and W. H. Low of Cape Town were named Joint Honorary Secretaries, one responsible for the administration of the affairs of the Association in the north and the other in the south.[10] In keeping with the organization's purpose of generating local enthusiasm for closer union, an effort seems to have been made to create as many offices as there were provincial leaders of opinion. The list of delegates, vice chairmen, and members of various committees named by the convention is quite long. A glance at this list would in no way indicate the extent to which the kindergarten dominated the organization, however, for except for Duncan and Feetham no members of that group were named.

Before adjournment the delegates to the inaugural meeting of the Association of Closer Union Societies agreed that the Johannesburg society should produce a journal designed to create enthusiasm for unification and to serve as a house organ for the Association.[11] It will be recalled, however, that this decision had been made by the kindergarten long before the Association was formed and was announced in this manner only to make it appear that the Association was the creative force. Careful readers of *The Government of South Africa* could discern this from a remark made by Curtis in the introduction:

> Arrangements are on foot . . . to continue the supply of information initiated in these volumes in the form of a monthly magazine, which will serve to focus the work of the Closer Union societies, and will enable the statistical tables contained in the appendices to be brought up to date from time to time.[12]

The creation of a new magazine is an expensive matter. In this case, however, money seems to have presented no serious prob-

8. "The Closer Union Movement," *ibid.*, p. 24.
9. Closer Union Societies, *Proceedings*, p. 10.
10. *Ibid.*, p. iii.
11. "The Closer Union Movement," *State*, I (Jan., 1909) , 24.
12. Curtis, *Government of South Africa*, I, x.

lems, for Abe Bailey, whose generosity had been previously demonstrated, agreed to support the project. In Bailey's obituary
published in the *Round Table* in 1940 the anonymous writer—
apparently Curtis—described how this came about. Though
couched in the bland phrases favored by members of the kindergarten when describing the activities of their group, the account is
substantially accurate.

> In 1908, when the question of the union of the four separate
> governments in South Africa had not yet entered the field of
> practical politics, young men in various parts of South Africa were
> beginning to organise Closer Union Societies. Abe Bailey said to
> some of them: "I am a South African. I mean to be in on this
> movement. The time has come to realise the dreams of Cecil
> Rhodes. You young men are doing the writing, but you will want
> funds to run these Closer Union Societies. I can't write books,
> but I can write cheques. Go off, think it over, and tell me how
> I can help with money."
> Surprised and touched at this offer, the young men discussed
> at length what should be done about it. The intention had been
> that the Closer Union Societies should be self-supporting, and
> should be financed from the contributions of their members. But
> in those days there was no South African newspaper, nor even a
> magazine, which circulated through all the Colonies or indeed
> through more than one of them. The greatest need of the move-
> ment was some organ which people in all Colonies could read,
> and which would keep the South African, as opposed to the local
> and colonial, point of view before their minds. To create such a
> magazine, and on lines sufficiently attractive to command a wide
> circulation from the outset, was beyond the limited means of the
> Closer Union Societies. It was therefore agreed to suggest to Abe
> that he should guarantee the capital required for the purpose up
> to £3,000; but on one condition only, that a full public announce-
> ment of the fact should be made in advance. To this stipulation
> for publicity Abe was strongly opposed on the ground that he
> wanted to aid the movement entirely for its own sake, and not
> for the sake of "kudos" (a Greek word which had strangely found
> its way into current slang at that time). It was pointed out to him
> that everyone would see that a magazine of the type required
> could not hope to pay its way for some years. Everyone would see
> that the money required to finance it had been furnished by some-
> one, and great distrust would arise if the promoters were unable
> to say how the money to produce it was found. Abe, who had
> always an eye for realities, saw this point and agreed that a

magazine called *The State* should be founded, and that full publicity should be given in advance to the fact that he was providing the funds to finance it.[13]

To edit the magazine the kindergarten was able to secure the
full-time services of Philip Kerr, who was soon to be made jobless
by the dissolution of the Intercolonial Council. Though he had no
previous editorial experience, Kerr agreed to take charge with the
understanding that he would be initially assisted by Curtis and
would throughout have access to the counsel of the kindergarten.
After the breakup of the Intercolonial Council in June, 1908, and
a three-month visit with his family in England, Kerr set to work
on the *State*.[14] In September he and Curtis established an office in
Cape Town where they, with the occasional help of their friends,
struggled during the following few weeks to improvise a periodical with both popular appeal and political purpose. Kerr described to Brand the fever of activity which resulted:

> Curtis arrived on Wednesday and as you may imagine we have
> been in a whirl of brilliant ideas, altered plans and desperate
> anxiety to be at work. However things are shaping themselves
> gradually. I always seem to play the part of the drag on the
> coach. It is a thankless one, but I am fit for no other. One feels
> hopelessly useless and second rate, if one can only see difficulties
> and counsel delay and never suggest how the work may be hurried
> on or obstacles overcome. However that feeling is one of false
> pride, I think. My reason generally comforts me. There is so much
> push and drive in Curtis and the rest, that one need have no
> qualms about urging caution and delay, whenever one considers
> it a suitable course. There is no danger of opportunities being
> lost for the want of anybody to grasp them.[15]

Almost as soon as they got down to work the original plan for
"a weekly paper . . . on the line of the Outlook or Spectator"[16]

13. "Sir Abe Bailey," *Round Table*, No. 120 (Sept., 1940), pp. 743–44. Among
historians there is considerable disagreement concerning the actual amount of
Bailey's financial support. According to Worsfold, *Reconstruction of the New
Colonies under Lord Milner*, II, 415, Bailey gave £5,000 "to defray expenses of
publication" of the *State*. On the other hand, Thompson, in *Unification of South Africa*, speaks of "a donation of £6,000 by Abe Bailey" [p. 309], while Butler states that
Bailey agreed to support the venture only if the expenses exceeded revenues from
advertisements and "funds Curtis had raised in England" [*Lothian*, p. 31]. In none
of these works is a citation offered to substantiate the statement referred to.
14. Butler, *Lothian*, pp. 27–30.
15. Quoted in *ibid.*, pp. 30 f.
16. Kerr to his parents, May, 1907. Quoted in *ibid.*, p. 28.

was discarded as impractical. It was replaced with one for a monthly to be printed simultaneously in both Dutch and English. Thereafter, the days of Curtis and Kerr were filled with the countless activities necessary to create such a magazine. Translators had to be secured and a search for contributors instituted. Decisions concerning format were called for, and facilities for distribution throughout South Africa had to be found. And all within a few weeks, for early publication was essential if the magazine was to have the effect which its creators intended. Fortunately, Curtis and Kerr were able to lean on their kindergarten associates for advice on these matters. Throughout November and December there were frequent meetings at Bailey's Cape Town home at which those of the kindergarten who were in that city to attend the second session of the National Convention offered counsel on editorial problems.[17]

By the latter part of December these efforts began to bear fruit. The first number of the *State,* bearing expressions of good will from virtually all South African leaders both Boer and British, appeared a week before Christmas. In a statement of policy entitled "By Way of Introduction," the editor explained that " 'The State' is primarily the organ of the Closer Union Societies";[18] it would thus devote considerable attention and space to the news of the Association. Its secondary function, however, was to offer to the people of South Africa a forum upon which to debate the many questions associated with unification. And in doing this, the *State,* like the societies which it represented, would be open to all views, observing strict impartiality in questions of politics and "race."[19]

Succeeding issues of the *State* carried administrative news of the Association and of the formation of new societies. In addition there was in each number a long editorial column entitled "The Month" in which Kerr examined the events of the past month insofar as they influenced unification. The remaining pages were filled with a potpourri of material, some having relevance to the

17. Robinson's diary, Nov. 24 and 25, and Dec. 12, 1908; John Dove to his sister, Mrs. Pinching, Dec. 20, 1908 (quoted in Robert Henry Brand, ed., *The Letters of John Dove* [London, 1938], p. 21) .
18. *State,* I (Jan., 1909) , 1.
19. *Ibid.,* p. 3.

issue of closer union and some apparently included to give the magazine more general appeal. Several of the politically oriented articles were signed by members of the kindergarten, while the contents and style of a number of the unsigned pieces suggest a similar origin.[20] The material of general interest consisted of poetry, short stories, reminiscences, and essays on South African history. But even here political motives were not completely absent, for these items were carefully chosen to foster among South Africans a feeling of national unity and pride. "South African," not Afrikaner or British, architecture was praised. Examples from the past of harmonious relations between British and Boers were described. And the omnipresent native problem was presented in a way meant to convince the two European groups that only unity in spirit as well as in government could prevent eventual black domination. "In a word," wrote Basil Williams, the *State* was meant to help white "South Africans to think of South Africa as a whole and as a country of which to be proud."[21]

With the publication of the initial issue in December, 1908, Kerr and his friends could afford a moment of self-congratulation. So far the project seemed to have gone well—surprisingly well, in fact. In writing to Milner, Kerr remarked that

> there are doubtless many secret ambitions carried at heart, but it is something to find Botha, Smuts & Farrar, Abraham Fischer & Moor & Merriman [,] Malan & Jameson writing letters to a bilingual paper, edited by an Englishman, urging their own supporters to try it. So far as we can see at present we shall sell 1000 Dutch copies.[22]

The *State* had been in existence less than two months when the Cape Town session of the National Convention came to an end with the publication of a draft constitution to be submitted to the colonial legislatures for ratification. This charter, as has been noted, was generally acceptable to the kindergarten members and their political associates. Though less than the "one vote—one value" sought by the Milnerites, the electoral provisions contained in the draft constitution were adequate to their needs. In return

20. In the first four volumes there are articles signed by Brand, Duncan, Wyndham, and Perry, as well as Kerr.
21. *Selborne Memorandum*, p. xxiv.
22. Kerr to Milner, Dec. 22, 1908, Milner Papers.

for a clause making the state officially bilingual, Boer delegates
agreed to electoral districts of equal voting population with provisions for a variation of 15 per cent above or below that figure under
certain circumstances. A modified form of proportional representation would obtain, with a redistribution of seats taking place at
five-year intervals.[23] Under these circumstances the kindergarten
members and their friends were confident that in time the influx
of immigrants from Great Britain would enable British influence
to dominate. As a result, the report of the Convention was greeted
with almost unanimous approval by the British press except in
Natal, where there were serious reservations about unification.[24]

Kerr and his advisory committee responded to the publication
of the provisional constitution with the issuance of a "Special
Constitutional Number" of the *State* dated February 12. In addition to the complete text of the charter, it contained an "Analysis
and Explanation of the Constitution" by Patrick Duncan, an article on "Proportional Representation" by Brand, and an unsigned
explanation of "A Model Election (By the System of Proportional
Representation) ." Though all references to the provisional
constitution were favorable, no editorial stand on the matter
was announced, for according to an editorial in the preceding
issue, the *State* as organ of the Association of Closer Union Societies could only reflect the attitude of that parent body. In that
regard, the members of the closer union societies were reminded
that at the inaugural meeting of the Association in Durban the
preceding October it had been agreed that when the National
Convention ended there should be another meeting to plan a
united policy. For without unity it would be impossible for the
various societies to fulfil "their function not only to debate the
problems of Union among themselves but to endeavour to educate and lead public opinion on the subject."[25] Another meeting
of the Association would enable delegates to consider the national, rather than the provincial, effects of the proposed constitution. Following that,

> they will be able to go back to their own districts and do much to
> prevent the greatest danger which will beset the Constitution, that

23. Thompson, *Unification of South Africa*, pp. 240 f.
24. *Ibid.*, p. 311.
25. "The Month," *State*, I (Feb., 1909) , 118.

it may be criticized by every interest from its own point of view
alone instead of from the broad standpoint of South Africa as a
whole.[26]

This second convention of the Association of Closer Union
Societies met March 3 through 5 in Johannesburg, attended by
111 delegates from 53 local groups.[27] At this meeting, "for which
the Kindergarten is mainly responsible," wrote Robinson, "we
have had to play up at entertaining delegates and keeping their
noses straight."[28] The meeting was carefully stage-managed by the
kindergarten from beginning to end: every effort was made to
send the delegates home convinced that the provisional constitution should be accepted without amendment by the colonial legislatures. Bi-"racial" harmony was symbolized by welcoming
speeches by Farrar and Smuts in which both urged the delegates
to support the constitution as reported out by the Convention.[29] "I
hope," Smuts remarked, "that as a result of your discussions in
that broad South African spirit we shall see a great education of
public opinion. We will kill provincialism, and we will see pushed
to the front that spirit of union which alone will make union
possible."[30]

When all preliminaries had been gotten out of the way and the
proper atmosphere of Boer-British cordiality had been created,
Patrick Duncan moved that the Association record its approval of
the provisional constitution and recommend its adoption without
amendment by the colonial governments. There followed three
days of debate during which delegates offered objections to various provisions of the draft charter only to see them voted down
by the convention. Most of the delegates—British and Boer—
apparently agreed with Duncan's assessment of the situation:

> I do not say that it is the best Constitution from a theoretical
> point of view, but it is the best Constitution we are likely to get a
> general agreement upon, and, that being so, having regard for the
> paramount importance of union for South Africa, it will be run-
> ning a serious risk to endanger the document by sending it back
> again [for amendment].[31]

26. *Ibid.*, p. 132.
27. Closer Union Societies, *Proceedings*, p. iv.
28. Robinson to "Aunt Kitty," March 7, 1909, Dawson Papers.
29. Closer Union Societies, *Proceedings*, pp. 1–14.
30. *Ibid.*, p. 2.
31. *Ibid.*, p. 15.

On the final day of the convention Duncan's resolution was passed unanimously.[32]

Despite the best efforts of the kindergarten and the Association of Closer Union Societies, however, unqualified approval of the draft constitution by the colonial legislatures was not unanimous. Amendments proposed by the legislature of Natal were of relatively little importance, but those of the Cape Parliament touched the very heart of the compromise implicit in the draft constitution, and did in fact threaten the process of unification. In the special session of the Cape legislature called in late March to consider the report of the National Convention, Boer extremists were able to push through demands that, if acceded to by the other colonies, would have completely undermined the kindergarten rationale for unification. Changes demanded by the Cape Boers would have caused the abandonment of proportional representation and the establishment of rural legislative constituencies as much as 30 per cent smaller in voter population than those in the urban areas. If adopted, these amendments would have destroyed any possible restoration of British power through immigration. Perpetual Afrikaner domination of South Africa would thus have been assured.[33]

In the face of this crisis the Milnerites acted with energy to defeat these proposals at a meeting of the National Convention called to consider the Cape Colony and Natal amendments. Before the delegates gathered in Bloemfontein in early May, the kindergarten labored through the closer union societies to convince South Africans of the danger which would result from tampering with the electoral provisions of the draft constitutions. And the *State* in its May issue joined most other English-language publications in decrying any attempt to place the rural voters in a position of permanent power:

> The clauses as they stand in the Constitution represent, with the clause giving equality to the two languages, the fundamental basis of the settlement between the two races. They are a compromise which can only be tampered with at the risk of wrecking Union itself. Any alteration of the manifest intention of the clauses means that one or other of the two races is to give up the rights

32. *Ibid.*, p. 48.
33. Thompson, *Unification of South Africa*, pp. 327–62.

which the first Convention unanimously agreed ought fairly and justly to be theirs.[34]

It was through personal persuasion, however, that the members of the kindergarten made their most strenuous efforts to prevent disaster. In concert with Fitzpatrick, Farrar, and other Transvaal Progressive leaders, members of the group in the weeks just before the Bloemfontein session tried to convince leading Boers— particularly those from the Transvaal—of the threat to union posed by the Cape amendments.[35] Even Lord Selborne, who until this point had been able to maintain a pose of non-partisan aloofness, was moved to join with the other Milnerites in this campaign. Writing to Botha, he insisted that a constitution containing the Cape amendments "will produce disaster to South Africa, and that it will be much better for the Transvaal and the other Colonies to continue in disunion than to unite on such a false basis." This being so, he was prepared to ignore the political neutrality which tradition had imposed upon his office if the amendments were adopted by the Convention. "There is no sacrifice or effort which I would not . . . make to prevent the consummation of an Union, which I know would bring disaster and not happiness to South Africa."[36]

This Milnerite fear that the Transvaal Boers might follow the lead of their associates to the south was needless. In the meeting at Bloemfontein the Afrikaner delegates from the Transvaal remained true to their entente with their Progressive colleagues, and joining with British delegates from the four colonies, opposed the crucial amendments. The result was an impasse in the Convention which for a while seemed insurmountable. An acrimonious dissolution of the Convention was averted, however, by a compromise proposed by Sir John Henry de Villiers, president of the Convention and later the first chief justice of the Union of South Africa. De Villiers's proposal would permit the retention of the original clause creating constituencies of more or less equal voter

34. *State*, I (May, 1909), 484.
35. Robinson's diary, April, 1909, Dawson Papers. Thompson, in *Unification of South Africa*, p. 364, cites letters from Curtis to de Villiers, May 2, 1909, de Villiers Papers; and Brand to Botha, Smuts, and H. C. Hull, April 28, 1909, Transvaal Archives, Prime Minister, LX (ii).
36. Selborne to Botha, April 29, 1909, Transvaal Archives, Prime Minister, LX 44. Halpérin, *Lord Milner*, p. 200.

population, but remove from the draft constitution the planned proportional representation.

The reaction of the Convention to this suggestion has been thoroughly examined for the first time in Professor Thompson's recent study.[37] It remains only to be said, therefore, that members of the kindergarten on May 5 and 6 took part in the deliberations of what Merriman called "the rump of Milnerism."[38] They were, in fact, involved in the decision to accept de Villiers's compromise on one condition: and that was that the constitution also be amended to require that all bills designed to change the electoral section be submitted to the Crown for approval. The acceptance of this condition by the opposition on May 7 broke the deadlock and led quickly to the conclusion of the National Convention.[39]

What followed was anticlimax. In June the amended draft constitution was approved by the legislatures of the Cape Colony, the Transvaal, and the Orange Free State. And before the month ended the voters of Natal had indicated their agreement in a referendum. In August the Imperial Parliament approved the constitution in the form of the South Africa Act, and on May 31 of the following year (the eighth anniversary of the Treaty of Vereeniging), the Union of South Africa was formally established.

Less than four years after members of the kindergarten meeting at Moot House decided to work for immediate unification, the goal was thus achieved. In those four years Milner's young men worked tirelessly at their task. By political manipulation, public education, and outright propaganda they did everything in their power to unify South Africa. And South Africa was unified. But the question remains: To what extent is the kindergarten due the credit—or blame? Some members of the group were in later years willing to accept much of the responsibility. For instance, Richard Feetham, writing about Patrick Duncan in the *Dictionary of National Biography*, mentioned that "he shared with them [the kindergarten] in the discussions which produced the Selborne memorandum of 1907 and eventually led to the National Conven-

37. Thompson, *Unification of South Africa*, pp. 369 ff.
38. Merriman's diary, May 6, 1909. Quoted in *ibid.*, p. 371.
39. Thompson, *Unification of South Africa*, pp. 362–84.

tion of 1908–09 and the South Africa Act of 1909."[40] In an obituary of Kerr in the *Round Table,* the anonymous author—almost certainly a member of the kindergarten—described the *State* as "the most important factor in creating the public opinion that carried the Union through."[41]

If members of the kindergarten were generous in giving themselves credit for the achievement of unification, those who wrote about them were downright lavish. Paul Knaplund in 1924 wrote that "it appears certain that without the aid of the young Britons trained in the neoimperialistic school of Chamberlain and Lord Milner the union could not have come into existence at this early date."[42] According to Sir Evelyn Wrench, ". . . it is impossible to over-estimate the importance of the part played by the members of the Kindergarten, in paving the way for closer union of South Africa after Milner had left."[43] "It was principally through their efforts," wrote Vladimir Halpérin, "that the Union of South Africa came into being."[44] Their friend and associate Leo Amery recorded in his memoirs that "Union [was] achieved . . . largely by their exertions. . . ."[45] For it was they who initiated "that astonishing campaign of scientific propaganda and personal persuasion which led . . . to the fusion of all the South African Colonies into a single unitary state."[46]

These claims made by and for the kindergarten are clearly unjustified. It is obvious from the account just presented that Milner's young men did not unite South Africa. Their efforts were important in bringing closer union to the attention of the general population and keeping it there. And members of the group did exert some influence upon those, both British and Boer, who determined the final form of the constitution. But forces far more

40. *Dictionary of National Biography,* 1941–50, p. 223.
41. *Round Table,* No. 122 (March, 1941), p. 202. See a review of Butler's biography of Lothian by A. L. Burt in the *Journal of Modern History,* XXXIII (Sept. 1961), 342.
42. Paul Knaplund, "The Unification of South Africa: A Study in British Colonial Policy," *Transactions of the Wisconsin Academy of Sciences, Arts and Letters,* XXI (July, 1924), 20.
43. Wrench, *Geoffrey Dawson and Our Times,* p. 53.
44. Halpérin, *Lord Milner,* p. 200.
45. Leo Amery, *My Political Life,* I, 269.
46. *Ibid.,* p. 318.

powerful than anything the kindergarten could muster were responsible for South African unification.

Even so, it would not be fair to assume that in making such claims the young men were displaying a greedy desire for public praise. Nor should one charge the historians and biographers who made similar statements with conscious misstatement. Clearly, both groups were unaware of some of the developments which were taking place, particularly within the camp of the Boers. And so they logically assumed that it was the Selborne Memorandum, the closer union societies, the *State,* and other projects growing out of those long discussions in Moot House back in 1906 that brought about the unification of South Africa. Only recently have historians such as Thompson and Hancock been able to refute the claims of the kindergarten and its admirers. Information found in the personal papers of Smuts, Botha, Merriman, and others shows that South Africa was unified at that time because political leaders of both factions saw in unification advantages to their group, whose interests they identified with all South Africa.

This misinterpretation of recent South African history by members of the kindergarten is of more than incidental interest. Even before the South Africa Act had cleared the Imperial Parliament, they had begun to direct their attention to a much wider field of activity. And in so doing, the young men entered a new project, planning to use methods which they were sure had been largely responsible for the creation of united South Africa.

Chapter Eight. The kindergarten widens its horizons

With the achievement of South African unification Milner's young men turned their attention to a scheme which was to become the central theme of their group activities and which largely accounts for the historical significance of the kindergarten. That scheme of course was to unify the British Empire by the use of the same methods which they assumed had been responsible for recent events in South Africa.

The genesis of this plan is obscure. Surviving letters and diaries contain no record of how it originated. Nor are there any minutes of the many discussions on the subject which one may assume took place at Moot House and in fact wherever members of the kindergarten met. In a sense this appears strange, for one would suppose that such an important step should in some way have left its mark. According to Lord Brand, however, it was quite natural that no special note was taken of this decision. In describing the origins of the scheme half a century later, he pointed out that from the moment the kindergarten became interested in closer union in South Africa it was understood that unification there would be only a first step towards the creation of a more rational organization of the Empire. Local British interests in South Africa were important considerations in shaping the kindergarten decision to work for closer union, he said. But the matter of overriding importance to the members of the group was the future of the Empire.[1] As Brand wrote in 1909 while the South Africa Act was being enacted into law:

> Those, . . . perhaps few in number, who were capable of grasp-
> ing the necessities not only of South Africa but of the British
> Empire, recognising the rapid development of the imperial situa-
> tion, and that the Empire's fate may well depend on the creation
> of some form of imperial union within the next twenty or thirty
> years, foresaw how greatly the difficulties of any action would be
> increased if no single government were responsible for the affairs
> of South Africa. South African union is in itself a great step

1. Interview with Lord Brand, London, May 3, 1960.

forward in the direction of imperial consolidation. It simplifies at once all imperial problems and particularly that of defence, which for the safety of the empire and its component parts must be grappled with at once.[2]

Curtis substantiated Brand's assertion that from the first the group had in mind a plan to unite the Empire. "As you know," he wrote to Richard Jebb while the National Convention was meeting in Cape Town, "it has always been our idea to unite South Africa & then try to make some scheme for closer Imperial Union grow out of it." This being so, he cautioned Jebb not to "lose sight of the important impetus towards closer Imperial Union which the movement here may give. At any rate it is giving a certain number of people some practice in the art of uniting communities."[3]

This desire to duplicate on an Empire-wide level the achievement of the South African closer union movement seems to have been almost inevitable. Certainly the members of the kindergarten had received a splendid education in the administrative difficulties and governmental inefficiency caused by disunity. As young civil servants with "a general interest in public work,"[4] they had constantly faced problems caused by friction among the competing colonial governments. In municipal and imperial administration, in the operation of the railroads, and in the management of native labor matters they had seen their efforts frequently frustrated by conflicting regulations and provincial jealousies. As young men driven by "a keenness to serve the British Empire,"[5] they had thus become convinced that governmental centralization, whether among the colonies of South Africa or the dominions of the Empire, was an essential ingredient of efficient government.

Though important in explaining kindergarten involvement in the drive for imperial unity, the practical considerations of the bureaucratic mind cannot stand alone. This explanation ignores the force of an ideal which, far more than the practical concern for administrative efficiency, explains their desire to unite the

2. Robert H. Brand, *The Union of South Africa* (Oxford, 1909), p. 12.
3. Curtis to Jebb, Dec. 6, [1908], Jebb Papers.
4. Dove, "The Round Table: A Mystery Probed," p. 6b.
5. *Ibid.*, p. 7.

Empire. The ideal for which the young men of the kindergarten yearned was the creation of a commonwealth of British nations able to maintain the peace throughout the world and bring civilization and progress to millions who might otherwise live out their lives in poverty and darkness. Essential to this was a centralized government representing in its parliament British subjects in all the self-governing parts of the Empire. The kindergarten was by no means unique in its devotion to this ideal. In the three decades before the Great War millions shared their dream of a great community of British nations serving both its own citizens and all mankind. There were, in addition, dozens of groups whose members were convinced that only through some sort of closer imperial unity could this goal be achieved. But in the case of the kindergarten this ideal was given additional intellectual force by Lord Milner and F. S. Oliver, the former mainly through personal contact and the latter primarily through his writings.

Oliver, whose biography of Alexander Hamilton is credited with having inspired the Selborne Memorandum and the South African closer union movement, was unknown to most of his contemporaries in Edwardian England. He held neither elective nor appointive public office. He was a dry goods merchant whose firm (Debenham and Freebody) was sufficiently successful to permit him the leisure to involve himself in Conservative causes. Circumstances, however, forced Oliver to remain always behind the scenes. According to his widow, it was a bitter disappointment to him that poor health prevented him from assuming the active role in public affairs for which he felt otherwise well suited. Even so, Oliver had what John Buchan called "a real and enduring influence on political thought."[6] As unofficial adviser and con-

6. Buchan (Lord Tweedsmuir), *Pilgrim's Way*, p. 210. The true dimensions of Oliver's influence remain to be assessed. What has been written about him has almost all come from the pens of those who, like the members of the kindergarten, were his close friends and admirers. Gollin's recent *Proconsul in Politics* does contain information about Oliver's behind-the-scenes activities which was heretofore mostly unavailable except in scattered references found in memoirs and biographies of far better-known men. Even so, much remains to be known about his career and particularly about his part in bringing about the formation of Lloyd George's War Cabinet. This obscurity will probably remain, however, for Oliver during the last years of his life destroyed his personal papers. According to his widow, the papers suffered water damage at the time of a fire. Oliver, by then too weak to comb through them to save those of value, and fearing embarrassment to some of his friends if the papers were not judiciously edited, decided to destroy them all.

fidant to leading political figures his ideas were carried to the seats of power. But it was primarily through his writings that Oliver came to exercise some of the public influence denied to him through more direct channels by poor health. In the early years of the twentieth century he began to manifest his zeal for imperial reform in pamphlets and magazine articles of great force. "For a decade he was," according to Buchan, "the ablest pamphleteer in Britain."[7]

His writing and his interest in imperial affairs soon brought Oliver into association with Leo Amery. This intimate friend of many of the members of the kindergarten was at that time laboring at *The Times History of the War in South Africa* while attempting in association with Milner and others to generate enthusiasm for tariff reform. According to Amery, it was he who first suggested the career of Hamilton to Oliver as a topic around which to mold a magazine article promoting imperial preference. The initial suggestion seemed to have been received favorably, and Amery assumed that Oliver had set to work. "From time to time in the next three months," Amery wrote, "I asked when the article was going to appear and only got the reply that he was studying the material. Then one day he surprised me by saying that he had embarked on a full-scale life of Hamilton."[8] The resulting biography[9] was the most significant work of Oliver's literary career. According to his obituary in the *Times*—which was undoubtedly written by one of his admirers in the kindergarten:

> The book had probably more influence than any other political work of the decade. It became a text-book for all those up and down the Empire who were giving their mind to Imperial reconstruction, and it had a very special and direct influence on the group who conceived and carried through the Union of South Africa.[10]

7. Buchan, *Pilgrim's Way*, p. 208.
8. Leo Amery, *My Political Life*, I, 268–69. In contrast to Amery, Mrs. Oliver attributed the idea to a novel based on Hamilton's life entitled *The Conqueror*. According to Mrs. Oliver, her husband read the book on her recommendation, saw in Hamilton's actions an object lesson for modern Englishmen, and decided to pursue the subject. The American edition of the Hamilton biography is dedicated to the American author of *The Conqueror*, Gertrude Atherton.
9. Oliver, *Alexander Hamilton: An Essay on American Union.*
10. June 5, 1934.

It is the subtitle—*An Essay on American Union*—which betrays the real topic of the work, for what is on the surface a biography of Hamilton is more accurately described as a five-hundred-page plea for imperial unity. Oliver gave his reader warning of this in the introduction:

> To subjects of King Edward the history of the Union of the States should be of profound interest at the present time. Under many aspects the problems in America at the end of the eighteenth century and in the British Empire at the beginning of the twentieth bear a startling likeness to each other. In the memoirs of the chief actors we find a frequent echo of our own phrases. The attitudes of men, according to their various temperaments, are the same. There are the same enthusiasms and the same suspicions; the same vehement desires, indignant against all the race of sceptics; the same pleas of insuperable obstacles and the imprudence of a rash initiative.[11]

From beginning to end Oliver presented Hamilton's career in a way designed to make obvious these similarities. Though he reviewed all aspects of his subject's life, he dwelt upon the young Federalist's part in the creation of the United States Constitution. And as he did so, he described instance after instance in which Hamilton, sometimes with the support of like-minded patriots but often singlehanded, fought to win for the new country a central government powerful enough to make the nation prosperous and secure. Were it not for a statement to the contrary by Dougal Malcolm,[12] one might assume that the book had been written expressly to encourage the kindergarten in its unifying activities. Oliver seemed to be openly exhorting young men of his day to meet the problems of their generation with similar energy and determination. Not content with mere encouragement, he offered specific advice drawn from Hamilton's experience on ways by which young men of little influence might shape the affairs of nations. Hamilton had, for instance, accomplished much by simply explaining in the *Constitutionalist* and *Federalist Papers* the nature of the problems which faced the United States and the pressing need for centralized authority able to cope with them. With "boyish confidence undaunted in the grimmest difficul-

11. Oliver, *Alexander Hamilton*, p. 6.
12. "Frederick Scott Oliver," *Dictionary of National Biography*, 1931–40, p. 657.

ties,"[13] he had thus helped to shape history. "The *Federalist* is pure advocacy," Oliver wrote,

> but it is the greatest and rarest advocacy, for it appears to the reader to be a reasoned judgment. Confident in their cause, the authors never shrank from a fair statement of opposite opinions; so that, to the modern, its wisdom and justice are apt to obscure the amazing skill of the counsel who conducted the case.[14]

Oliver warned, however, that those who follow Hamilton's path should be prepared to receive the scorn of those in power. Despite the skill and force with which their arguments favoring unification were expressed, the young Federalists of the eighteenth century were assured "that the plan was fantastic and unworkable; that it was but the wild experiment of 'visionary young men.' Every pamphlet and every platform of the opposition echoed with this tremendous charge. . . ."[15] Even so, Hamilton in the end prevailed. His success prompted Oliver to comment with satisfaction that "young men who see visions may, if we consider the result, take comfort throughout the ages."[16] One can only speculate about the effect upon the kindergarten of Oliver's remark that

> there are few more conspicuous examples in history of the maxim that when people are struggling towards a decision the man who will take the pains to think out and elaborate his own plan in a clear consistency is apt to reap a reward entirely beyond his hopes, in the domination of his drilled ideas over the undisciplined aspirations of his enemies.[17]

Willing to leave nothing to chance, Oliver ended the book with a fifty page "conclusion" in which the obvious was made explicit. Here the method of instruction by parable gave way to a pedantic lecture on the need for modern Hamiltonians to act vigorously to reform the constitution of the Empire as Hamilton and his associates had done that of the United States.

> The work of Hamilton's life was the solution of problems which we have not yet found any means to solve. That, for us, is the chief

13. Oliver, *Alexander Hamilton*, p. 86.
14. *Ibid.*, p. 169.
15. *Ibid.*, p. 176.
16. *Ibid.*
17. *Ibid.*, p. 160.

interest of his career. Admitting frankly and fully that what he achieved is no precedent to govern our actions, his example is inspiring. We may draw morals from his fortitude and find encouragement in his success. And here and there, as we read his words upon the events and difficulties of a bygone age, the darkness and perplexity of the situation in which we find ourselves is lit up with sudden, luminous flashes which pierce to the four corners of the canopy.[18]

It is not surprising, therefore, that Oliver's book had a telling impact upon the kindergarten. "I shall never forget the effect which *Alexander Hamilton* had on me when I read it," Curtis wrote years later. "He came into our lives as a great inspiration at the moment when we most needed it in South Africa."[19] "Here we were trying to work out a new philosophy of the State and behold an unknown linen draper who had done it all for us."[20] And so, as Amery put it, *"Alexander Hamilton* became the Bible of the young men of Milner's Kindergarten."[21] For years thereafter Hamilton's example and Oliver's injunctions related thereto helped to mold the thinking of the group and, as will be seen, shaped the very tactics by which Curtis and his friends attempted to unify the Empire. Oliver himself soon became acquainted with the young men who, unknown to him, had found inspiration in his words. Following their return to England after unification of South Africa was assured, they drew him into their circle, where he remained as adviser, host, and generous supporter until his death in 1934.

While Oliver's intellectual influence upon the kindergarten attitude towards Empire was primarily derived from his writing and only secondarily from his personal contact, the impact of Milner's ideas in this regard came almost entirely from intimate association in South Africa and later in England. Day after day, by both precept and example, the disciples absorbed his passionate concern for the welfare of the Empire. They were awed by the extent to which the subject dominated Milner's life. But they understood that "he worshipped it [the Empire], not because he liked to see the map painted red, but because . . . he saw in . . .

18. *Ibid.,* p. 443.
19. Quoted in Gwynn, ed., *The Anvil of War,* p. 16.
20. Curtis, quoted in Wrench, *Geoffrey Dawson,* p. 94.
21. Leo Amery, *My Political Life,* I, 268.

its . . . ideals the principal hope for the progress of mankind."[22] It was this idealistic element so prominent in Milner's attitude towards Empire that members of the kindergarten found most congenial.

Articulate statements of this Milnerian philosophy of Empire are not difficult to find, for Milner wrote and spoke on this topic throughout his life. One statement, however, stands out from the rest. During World War I he wrote to his friend J. L. Garvin of the *Observer* that those who had an interest in his imperialist philosophy should study carefully his farewell speech to the citizens of Johannesburg made at the time of his retirement. "This long screed," he informed Garvin, "still expresses my views better than I could reproduce it. . . ."[23] In that unhappy hour, as he departed South Africa convinced that resurgent Afrikaner authority would presently sweep away his whole reconstruction program, Milner urged "those who may attach some weight to my words" to remain faithful to the one last hope for South Africa—"the great ideal of Imperial Unity." In considering this ideal, he told his audience,

> we think of a group of States, all independent in their own local concerns, but all united for the defence of their own common interests and the development of a common civilization; united, *not in an alliance*—for alliances can be made and unmade, . . . —*but in a permanent organic union.*[24]

Though he admitted the difficulty of achieving that ideal ("The goal may not be reached in my lifetime—perhaps not in that of any man in this room"), he nevertheless insisted it was neither visionary nor unattainable. His final words, charged with an emotion rarely displayed by the phlegmatic Milner, urged his listeners not to dwell on the problems and frustrations that lay ahead.

> But think, . . . of the greatness of the reward; the immense privilege of being allowed to contribute in any way to the fulfilment of one of the noblest conceptions which has ever dawned on the political imagination of mankind.[25]

22. Philip Kerr, "Lord Milner," *Nation and Athenaeum*, May 23, 1925.
23. Milner to Garvin, May 27, 1917 (copy), Milner Papers.
24. Italics added.
25. Headlam, II, 546–47. This speech is found in its entirety in Lord Milner, *The Nation and the Empire: Being a Collection of Speeches and Addresses with an Introduction* (London, 1913).

In this farewell speech to the Johannesburgers Milner did not spell out in so many words just how this "permanent organic union" could be achieved and what form it would take. Nor did he ever do so in later public statements. The failure of the Imperial Federation League of his youth had made him skeptical of popular appeals on behalf of the Empire. And what he considered to be the gross indifference to imperial interests on the part of Westminster politicians had convinced him that under the circumstances only failure could result from an effort to find a solution in the political arena. Thus little could be gained and considerable harm might be done by going into detail in print and on the platform concerning imperial unity.

The possibility of damage to the cause stemmed from the revolutionary nature of the changes which Milner considered necessary. Nothing less than a complete reorganization of the governmental structure of Great Britain and the nations of the Empire—which Milner referred to as "the system"—would make possible the "organic union" for which he yearned. These thoughts, though far too radical to be made public, were freely expressed by Milner to intimates.

> I am strongly impressed by two things [he wrote in 1901 to his old friend and Imperial Federation League associate George Parkin] 1) that the heart of the nation is sound, as I believe firmly is also *that* of the *British* Colonials everywhere & 2) that our constitution & methods are antiquated & bad, & the real sound feeling of the nation does not get a chance of making itself effective. I would rather not say what I think of the House of Commons as an Imperial Council or of the effect of our rigid party system on national affairs. The experience of life has been to confirm extraordinarily my belief in the doctrines wh. we both held & preached theoretically, as young men, only I am more radical & revolutionary than I then was & less induced to trust in the growth of Federal union from a small beginning.
>
> The existing Parliaments, whether British or Colonial, are *too small* & so are the statesmen they produce . . . for such big issues. Until we get a real Imperial council, . . . with control of all our *world business* we shall get nothing.[26]

26. Milner to Parkin, Sept. 13, 1901 ("Private"), Parkin Papers.

As time passed, the specific faults of "the system" became increasingly clear to Milner, so that in 1903 he was able to list five of the more serious defects:

1. A legislative process which gives "ultimate power on all matters . . . [to] an *ignorant* people."

2. Indifference on every level of government to "trained knowledge and complete information."

3. A political structure dominated by parties without issues and leaders without principle—"hence a pure struggle of ins and outs without any inner meaning . . . whatever."

4. A cabinet made overlarge to accommodate party placemen, and thus inefficient and downright dangerous in time of crisis. For "in a storm shifting ballast may sink a ship. The inert stupid mass wobbles over, . . . and you have disaster."

> *5.* Above and Before All. No grading of the 100,000 questions, no separating of the local and Imperial, the great and the small, but all ultimately centring in the same unwieldy Cabinet, which, muddling a pension or a 'row in the Guards,' may be shaken in its dealing with a national question of the first moment, and in any case cannot give *continuous thought and study* to the *vital,* being eternally distracted by the local and *temporary,* even when not by the absolutely *petty and parish pump,* order of questions.[27]

These criticisms of "the system" and the philosophy of Empire which engendered them were of course important in shaping the attitudes of the kindergarten. Milner was to the members of that group more than just an employer. Long before his retirement he had become both father-figure and Socrates to those who as members of his staff were with him day and night. And to the others—those who arrived in South Africa too late, or whose duties did not bring them into frequent contact with the High Commissioner—the effect of his ideas and his personality was no less noticeable. Like their more fortunate colleagues, they considered him to be the fountainhead of political wisdom and the greatest statesman of the Empire. They all took great pride in their membership in that small band called—at first sneeringly—

27. Milner to Lady Edward Cecil, May 16, 1903, Milner Papers. This letter and others of a similar vein addressed to the future Lady Milner are to be found in Headlam, II, 446–49, and Edward Crankshaw, *The Forsaken Idea: A Study of Viscount Milner* (London, 1952), pp. 133–36.

Milner's kindergarten. Though certainly not undeviating in their adherence to his philosophy, the members of the kindergarten coterie nevertheless demonstrated in their efforts to unite the Empire the extent to which they were in fact "Milner's young men."

Armed with the imperial outlook of Milner and Oliver, and emboldened by their apparent success in South Africa, the kindergarten in 1908 began to work out detailed plans for their new project. As the success of the South African closer union movement became assured, members of the group, led by Curtis, sought to develop a strategy with which to transform their dream of imperial unity into reality. The first indication of this groping for a new program reached Milner in a letter from Curtis written in late October. Unable at that time to speak for any but himself, he described his intentions:

> I feel that the right thing to do [following South African unification] will be to throw what strength and experience one has into the Imperial problem, but in any case I propose to do this as a South African colonist, because it is better that those who can should push the Imperial cause from the colonies. There are men enough like Jebb and Amery to push it from England. It becomes more and more apparent every day to my mind that the various countries included in the Empire must come to some definite business arrangement for the support and control of Imperial defence and foreign policy or the Empire must break up.[28]

These general intentions of Curtis were quickly worked into a detailed scheme and broadened to include all the kindergarten. By the end of March, 1909, Curtis and his friends had, in fact, evolved a step-by-step plan by which—subject to the amendment and approval of their associates in England—they intended to unify the Empire. Needless to say, the new plan was greatly influenced by the experience of the group in their South African closer union activities. In a sense it was simply an extension and expansion of the strategy used in South Africa, with modifications dictated by the geographical and political peculiarities of the Empire. In South Africa the kindergarten had created the Selborne Memorandum, the closer union societies, and the *State*; in the new plan can be seen a desire to duplicate on an imperial

28. Curtis to Milner, Oct. 31, 1908, Milner Papers.

scale all these devices. Clearly, the group believed that what appeared to have worked so well in South Africa should prove equally successful on an Empire-wide level.

Details of the scheme reached London in a long letter from Curtis to Leo Amery.[29] Written while the colonial legislatures in South Africa were debating the draft constitution, it was meant to apprise friends of imperial union in England of kindergarten plans now "that our hands will probably be free soon to join forces with you." What he and his friends had accomplished in South Africa was admittedly "rather showy," Curtis said, but they were only too conscious of how minor it was in light of all that remained to be done. In South Africa they had merely "acted as an advance party of sappers sent out to build a vital section of the road over which the main force will have to travel later on. . . ." Thus little credit was due them, for "the Kindergarten is like Mary Magdalen of whom it was said 'she hath done what she could.'" But now the sappers, having completed their path-finding, were ready—even eager—to put their knowledge and experience to work to lead the main force forward. In the belief that they might be invited to do so, Curtis wished to acquaint Amery—and through him others in England with similar interests—with the plans of the kindergarten.

The first task, according to Curtis, was to "state the Imperial Problem" in a carefully developed memorandum. In this way those who wished to initiate a movement of imperial consolidation would have a common vantage point from which to view the matter. Though they might not concur on the reforms required, they would agree on the nature of the flaws which threaten the Empire.

> *That* we have found is an excellent plan for arriving at a common policy and for getting a number of minds to move automatically in the same direction. In the case of Union here we had threshed out inch by inch what we wanted in this way, and so arrived at opinions which would hold water.

Here the kindergarten could be of great help. From the creation of the Selborne Memorandum the group had acquired the skills

29. Curtis to Amery, March 29, [1909], Leopold S. Amery Papers.

and experience "to prepare a written memorandum on the whole position as a basis for discussion." Curtis, who had visited all parts of South Africa gathering material and gleaning ideas for the Selborne Memorandum, was quite willing to resume his travels. "I have undertaken if so it seems desirable," he wrote, "to visit Canada, Australia and New Zealand successively as a sort of prospector." The other members of the kindergarten had agreed to function once again as an "editorial committee" and in conjunction with associates from England to hammer out a "statement of the Imperial Problem" which they could all accept.

Once an imperial counterpart of the Selborne Memorandum had been completed and adopted by those at the center of the movement it would be possible to approach others. Those throughout the Empire who were known to favor the preservation of the imperial connection and who were in positions of influence should then be asked to lend their support. "There is lots of fluid sympathy about," Curtis wrote, "but I have no thread on which to crystallise it." A logical, coherent exposition of the threats facing the Empire would provide that thread. Even as he traveled about gathering information for the new memorandum Curtis intended to discuss the matter informally and to locate in each nation of the Empire "the people who can be trusted to back us."

> The local editors are most important. Already I am getting hold of a series of local papers here whose editors will undertake to give common currency to the Imperial ideas . . . [promoted by the movement]. We must also get hold of some trustworthy members in each legislature who will undertake to master the information placed at their disposal and to raise a debate every year on the estimates.

Curtis thought this second circle of supporters might well be organized into local groups much like the closer union societies in South Africa. Speaking from experience, however, he urged Amery and those in London not to press for the early establishment of such groups.

> When you do I should lay much more stress on the quality than on the numbers of members it embraces. The active intelligent cooperation of a dozen men like Jameson, Duncan and Quinn in each dominion is worth long lists of sympathisers who put their names on paper and do nothing else.

Though he opposed the early creation of supporting groups, Curtis nevertheless insisted upon the need for a chain of publications throughout the Empire to disseminate the ideas of the movement. Patterned after the *State,* these monthly magazines would carry the gospel of imperial unity to the leaders of opinion in all the self-governing countries of the Empire. Centralized supervision was essential, however, if they were to remain free from the provincialism which threatened the goals of the movement. "I think," Curtis wrote, "there should be an office in London to feed them with pictures and stuff to make them readable and to look after the English 'Ads.' " Each local editor, whose primary responsibility would be the publication of his magazine, should also be charged with passing on to the London office all local material which might be of use to his colleagues in other parts of the Empire. "Philip Kerr, who thoroughly understands the whole business would be the man to run the central office, find the editors and keep the whole thing going." The plan was complicated, Curtis admitted. And the expense would be considerable. Even so, it would be well worth it, for such a chain of magazines offered unique opportunities for educating colonial opinion. Once established, "everyone concerned in the movement from Lord Milner downwards will have at their [*sic*] disposal a medium through which the same train of thought can be set in motion through all the self governing colonies of the empire at the same time."

These plans which Curtis and the kindergarten had developed were only tentative. Their implementation depended upon the extent to which they were supported by friends of imperial unity in Great Britain. Lest this be misunderstood, Curtis concluded his letter with an appeal for an early meeting at which the plans which he had described might be examined in the light of conditions as seen at the center of the Empire.

> These are a few ideas jotted down for your consideration against the time of our meeting. Naturally they are the fruit of a limited experience here, and I shall be quite prepared to find that some or all of them are by no means applicable to the wider problem. But of this I am convinced that before we build we should get plans carefully drawn out on paper and agreed upon amongst ourselves.

An opportunity to get plans drawn out and agreed upon occurred shortly thereafter. Within a few months after Curtis's letter to Amery and their London friends the unification of South Africa became a fact. As a result, those members of the kindergarten who did not intend to make South Africa their home began to drift back to England. There, under the constant prodding of Curtis, they and their associates hammered out the details of a scheme that came to be called the round table movement.

Chapter Nine. Lord Milner's part in founding the Round Table movement

Not all the kindergarten chose to leave South Africa when unification was achieved in 1909. Hugh Wyndham had for several years been devoting most of his time to his farm near Standerton and intended to remain. Both Duncan and Feetham planned to pursue legal careers in Johannesburg. Though they did not think of themselves as committed to South Africa indefinitely, Dove, Perry, and Robinson chose to stay for some time: Dove as director of certain immigration projects established by English Milnerites, Perry as chairman of the Rand Native Labour Association, and Robinson as editor of the *Star* until his return to England late the following year. Dougal Malcolm, Selborne's private secretary, was in 1909 the only member of the kindergarten still employed by the government.

On the other hand, three of the band—Curtis, Brand, and Kerr—were determined to return to England at the first opportunity to examine career possibilities there. Of course all three intended to do everything they could to locate and organize support for the kindergarten scheme to unify the Empire. And Curtis expected for some time to come to devote his full time to the project. But the former executives of the Intercolonial Council had other plans as well. Brand looked forward to a position with Lazard Brothers, the internationally powerful banking house,[1] while Kerr planned to run for Parliament. According to his biographer, the young Kerr thought that with the support of highly placed Conservative friends and relatives he should be able to win a Scottish constituency despite the political handicap of his Catholic faith.[2]

Before their departure, however, they had to dismantle or dispose of the machinery created by the kindergarten to promote South African unification. In the case of the Association of Closer Union Societies and the branch organizations which it comprised,

1. *Times*, Aug. 24, 1963.
2. Butler, *Lothian*, p. 35.

no action was necessary, for that complex of groups disintegrated the instant unification was assured. The *State*, however, was another matter. In the few months of its existence it had flourished, demonstrating the truth of Curtis's contention that there was great need for such magazines throughout the Empire.[3] There was, in fact, no logical reason why the *State* should not have been retained by South African Milnerites and used as one link in a chain of such publications. But for some reason this was not done. The July number carried an announcement that since unification was now assured, and since the closer union societies which fathered the magazine had ceased to exist, the *State* would inaugurate a new series. Beginning with the October issue it would become a general purpose magazine containing short stories, poetry, and articles on a wide variety of subjects. The editors would pursue a policy of strict political neutrality, striving only to provide South Africans with a magazine equal in quality to those published in Great Britain. It appears that at this time the financial support of Abe Bailey was withdrawn, for the price per issue doubled from six pence to a shilling.[4]

Though there was no reference to it in the columns of the *State*, Kerr relinquished his editorial chair with the publication of the July issue. His place was taken by B. K. Long, who had earlier edited the kindergarten-sponsored collection of federal constitutions entitled *The Framework of Union*.[5] At that time the kindergarten control of the *State* came to an end. For a year thereafter Kerr contributed a column called "Over-sea Notes." But even this tenuous connection ended in August, 1910, with an editorial notice that Mr. Kerr "has found himself unable to continue to contribute."[6]

With the matter of the *State* thus settled, Curtis, Kerr, and Brand were free to return to England. Curtis sailed in the first

3. Curtis to Amery, March 29, [1909], Amery Papers.
4. *State*, II (July, 1909), 24.
5. Butler, *Lothian*, p. 33.
6. *State*, IV (Aug., 1910), 307. Just four months after the kindergarten relinquished control of the *State* Robinson took a curious way of disassociating his paper from the magazine which he had helped to create. In an editorial on October 5, 1909, he made the acid comment that the *State* "has lamentably fallen away in its editorial columns from the 'broad South African' promise with which it started and is now little better than a reflection of Capetown gossip . . ." (Johannesburg *Star*, Oct. 5, 1909). In December, 1912, the *State* ceased publication.

week of June, arriving in London on the twenty-sixth.[7] Brand and
Kerr waited until the last of the month, however, so that they
could accompany the representatives of the four South African
colonies on their way to London to present the draft constitution
for parliamentary approval. This was done, according to Kerr, so
that they might "impregnate" Botha and Smuts "with proper
views about naval defence and so forth."[8] Upon their arrival the
three immediately established contact with Robinson, in England
from May to August to attend the Imperial Press Conference.
Together the four (the only members of the kindergarten who
were in England at that time),[9] set about trying to win support
for the new kindergarten project.

In this campaign much depended upon the attitude of Lord
Milner, whose opinions as patron of the kindergarten were crucial. His prestige among the members of the group was such that
only under the most unusual circumstances would they defy his
advice on imperial matters. Nor were they blind to the fact that
Milner's concurrence was essential if they were to recruit the
support, particularly financial, needed to turn a bold plan into a
great movement to unify the Empire. Members of the kindergarten were themselves not without influence. They knew men of
wealth and power who were inclined to support projects of this
sort. Some of them—Brand and Kerr—were in fact from influential families whose assistance might be called upon in the campaign. Even so, the kindergarten depended upon Lord Milner in
this matter. A word from him would bring to the project the sort
of support which the young Milnerites themselves could never
command.

Even in retirement—and in the eyes of some, in disgrace—
Milner was still a potent force among those in Great Britain who
placed the welfare of the Empire above all other public considerations. In that circle, whose numbers were much reduced by the
Edwardian reaction to the imperialism of the late Victorian era,

7. Robinson's diary, June 26, 1909, Dawson Papers.
8. Quoted in Butler, *Lothian*, p. 33.
9. Hichens, though he had returned from South Africa in 1907, was then in
Rhodesia as chairman of a government commission investigating public service
facilities.

no name stood higher. The financiers, merchants, and members of the nobility who provided the funds if not the brains of the imperial cause in those years considered him the obvious heir to Chamberlain's place of leadership. Yet the attitude of the Edwardian imperialists towards the brilliant, rather donnish bureaucrat was in a sense quite different from their attitude towards the great Colonial Secretary. Chamberlain was a far more important figure in British and imperial affairs than Milner, and far more powerful. But Chamberlain was a politician and thus a captive of the masses of the British people. His recognition of the facts of political life and his willingness to abide by those facts in some ways separated him from many of the leading imperial enthusiasts. He was their leader, and he remained so until his health broke in 1906, but he never established the sort of bond with his supporters which might create a deep personal attachment.

Milner, on the other hand, was a man with whom the imperialists of the Edwardian era could identify. Like Chamberlain he had devoted his adult life to serving the Empire and protecting British interests throughout the world. But in contrast to Chamberlain, Milner was not a politician. By temperament and conviction he opposed party politics, believing it to be the greatest enemy of the imperial cause. Many assumed that party politics—in a broader sense "the system"—had in fact wrecked Milner's own career. His supporters were certain that as a result of "the system" he had been removed from high office, slandered by press and public alike, and abused on the floor of the House of Commons by political opportunists not suited to dust his shoes. The man the public knew as an unyielding, ruthless administrative dictator, they recognized as a gentle, scholarly bachelor who had dedicated his life to the service of the Empire. While the public occasionally heard him on the platform lecturing his audience in a wooden manner and a reedy voice which betrayed his contempt for the mass of his compatriots, his closest supporters frequently observed the ease with which this man of character and earnest good sense could bring unity to a room full of divided partisans. In those years when "Empire, once the shrine of all aspiring Tories, had become the temple of coteries only—

powerful enough in the arcana of Conservative politics, but without public support,"[10] Milner became the personification of the imperialist movement. The result was what Sir Henry Campbell-Bannerman called the *religio Milneriana*.[11] Around this unlikely figure gathered men loyal to the ideas which he represented, but perhaps more important, loyal to the man himself. At a word from him these members of the Milnerian cult would gladly offer their influence, assistance, and wealth to an organization of the sort proposed by the kindergarten.

The loyalty of Milner's followers remained constant despite his reluctance—even refusal—in the years following his retirement to assume the leadership of a great public crusade to save the Empire. The reader will recall that to the disappointment of many of his followers, he would neither head a non-party organization like the old Imperial Federation League to which he had devoted the energies of his youth, nor lead them in the formation of a new political party dedicated to the welfare of the Empire. "The day might come . . . ," he wrote before his retirement,

> when I should have the opportunity of pointing out, *why* we make such a mess of things, and make the burden on the true-hearted servants of the country so unnecessarily heavy; *where* the system is wrong. But I should not attempt that for a long time, not until I could see my own experiences at a true perspective, till personal bitterness had died out of me, as it readily does, with rest and time, and I could speak of it all coolly, with balance, with calm and therefore carrying a conviction, which I could not carry while still heated from the fray and when people might think that anger, disappointment or some personal interest clouded my judgment. From a calm distance, as a man out of the fray for ever, with nothing to gain or lose, I think I might, if I lived and things so shaped themselves, make my experience of use to future labourers.[12]

This attitude, reinforced by fatigue and a natural distaste for politics, caused Milner to play a very limited part in public affairs for several years after his return from South Africa. It was, in fact, not until the constitutional crisis of 1909 that he began to partici-

---

10. A. P. Thornton, *The Imperial Idea and Its Enemies: A Study in British Power* (London, 1959) , p. 131.
11. J. A. Spender, *Life of Sir Henry Campbell-Bannerman* (London, 1923) , I, 264.
12. Milner to Lady Edward Cecil, April 24, 1903, Milner Papers.

pate in the party struggles which he found so repugnant. His refusal to provide public leadership for his supporters, however, was in contrast to his attitude towards unpublicized, even secret, activities on behalf of the Empire. In fact, from his return to England in 1905 Milner was deeply involved in a number of enterprises which, though known to a very few, were designed to pave the way for a great movement in support of imperial unity and reform. As he departed South Africa in 1905 he remarked to the people of Johannesburg that opportunities to serve the Empire awaited those willing "to work quietly in the background, in the formation of opinion rather than in the exercise of power."[13] Having been forced into the background and denied the exercise of power, Milner sought during his years in the wilderness to prepare for the day when he and other "true-hearted servants of the country" might explain to the public "*why* we make such a mess of things."

In these behind-the-scenes activities Milner's effectiveness was enhanced, one might almost say determined, by the wealth of Milnerites in England and throughout the Empire. Though he had no fortune of his own, he was almost always able to raise money for various imperial efforts. It came from a wide variety of admirers and fervent imperialists; but from 1905 until Milner's death in 1925 the bulk of this money was provided by the Rhodes Trust. Milner was an original trustee, having been chosen by Rhodes shortly before the latter's death.[14] His fellow trustees were Earl Grey and the Earl of Rosebery; L. S. Jameson; Alfred Beit, Rhodes's associate in the diamond industry; and Sir Lewis Michell and Bourchier F. Hawksley, Rhodes's banker and legal adviser respectively. Though prevented by his official duties from actively participating in the formation of the scholarship program, Milner soon after his retirement became deeply involved in the affairs of the Trust. From 1905 until well after the end of World War I he remained at the center of all Rhodes Trust affairs, the most active and influential of the trustees. "If the vision was Rhodes'," Amery wrote, "it was Milner who over some twenty years laid securely

13. Farewell speech to the people of Johannesburg, March 31, 1905, Milner Papers.
14. Earl Grey to Milner, Dec. 18, 1901, Milner Papers.

the foundations of a system whose power in shaping the outlook and spiritual kinship of an evergrowing body of men throughout the English-speaking world it would be difficult to exaggerate."[15]

Amery might also have written that it was Milner who took a particularly keen interest in those unpublicized projects into which the Trust poured funds acquired by the estate but not needed for scholarships. Time after time the Trust contributed this money to groups and individuals closely identified with the former proconsul. One such instance has been previously described in this study: that was the support of kindergarten efforts to unify South Africa. Unnoticed so far, but perhaps of greater historical importance, was the use of Rhodes Trust money to manipulate the newspaper press in South Africa. Letters in the Milner papers leave no doubt that on several occasions Milner acted on behalf of his South African supporters to secure funds with which to maintain both Afrikaans and English newspapers; in one instance the money almost certainly came from the Rhodes Trust.[16] Shortly thereafter he and his fellow trustee Lord Grey sought money from the Trust to encourage and support speakers able to carry to the dominions—particularly Australia and Canada—the message of imperial reform.[17] In 1908 the Trust at Milner's behest agreed to provide £1,000 over the next four years to a fund being organized privately to hire the geographer Halford Mackinder to conduct research on imperial matters. It was planned that Mackinder should analyze the problems which might face the next Imperial Conference and collect statistical ammunition for the supporters of imperial unity if it should be decided to push for constitutional reform at that time.[18]

15. In a foreword to Halpérin, Lord Milner, p. 16.
16. Milner to Selborne, May 10 and Sept. 23, 1905 (copies); Fitzpatrick to Milner, Feb. 5, 1906; Arthur G. Barlow to Sir John Fraser, n.d.; and an unaddressed, unsigned, and undated letter draft in Milner's hand which reads in part: "I have seen Beit, who is strongly in favour of keeping the 'Bloemfontein Post' going efficiently, and will communicate in that sense with Fitzpatrick. As regards 'Land en Volk,' we think that, if it could be shown that £6,000 would really put that paper on its legs, and not merely stave off collapse for a little while, we could find that amount here."
17. Copies of unsigned memoranda dated Feb. 16 and April 6, 1907, Milner Papers. Internal evidence indicates that Grey, at that time the Governor-General of Canada, was the author of both.
18. Amery to Milner, March 30 and April 4, 1908; Mackinder to Amery, May 22, 1908, Milner Papers. Very little is known about these surplus funds. The two

In most of these projects Milner was assisted by his young disciple Leo Amery. From the time of the Boer War when he went to South Africa as chief correspondent for *The Times*, Amery's association with Milner was exceptionally close—closer than that of any member of the kindergarten except perhaps Robinson. Though prevented from joining Milner's band of young men by his commitments to Printing House Square, Amery later took great pride in his association with the group, remarking near the end of his life that while in South Africa gathering material for his famous history of the Boer War he spent much time "lending a hand in the work of Milner's *Kindergarten.* . . ."[19] In London he was able during the years of South African reconstruction to prove his devotion to the cause of Empire in several ways. He was active in both the National Service and Tariff Reform Leagues and an original member of "a curious little talking and dining club"[20] called the Coefficients. This last named organization was founded in 1902 by Sidney Webb to find a common ground upon which all supporters of the Empire—whether socialist, free trade, or tariff reform—might stand. Among its members were Bertrand Russell, H. G. Wells, Richard Haldane, Sir Edward Grey, Bernard Shaw, and Milner. The prolixity of Wells and Shaw made discussion difficult; and the division within the group caused by Chamberlain's resignation from the government in 1903 and the resulting tariff-reform crusade made agreement impossible. As a consequence, nothing was accomplished.[21] Though they continued to dine together regularly for five or six years, "the Coefficients, as a brains trust with a definite political object, petered out almost as soon as they began."[22]

---

standard works on the Rhodes Trust—one by the longtime Scholarships Secretary of the Trust, Sir George Parkin, and the other edited by Lord Elton, the General Secretary of the Trust from 1939 to 1959—say almost nothing about the matter. Parkin virtually ignores all Rhodes Trust activities not directly related to the scholarships, while Elton makes only brief comments about the Trust's endowment of a number of academic chairs and colleges throughout the Empire and its support of "the Victoria League and other organizations" (George R. Parkin, *The Rhodes Scholarships* [Boston, 1912]; Lord Elton, ed., *The First Fifty Years of the Rhodes Trust and the Rhodes Scholarships 1903–1953* [Oxford, 1956]).

19. Leo Amery, *My Political Life*, I, 161.
20. H. G. Wells, *Experiment in Autobiography: Discoveries and Conclusions of a Very Ordinary Brain (since 1866)* (New York, 1934), p. 650.
21. *Ibid.*, p. 651.
22. Leo Amery, *My Political Life*, I, 224.

In an attempt to pick up the pieces, Amery in January, 1904, invited to his rooms in London those Coefficients who supported tariff reform along with several Chamberlainites not connected with Webb's group. Following a discussion of what might be done to promote Chamberlain's program, the twelve gathered there decided to form a club "to act as an energizing and propaganda body."[23] The name chosen for the new group—Compatriots' Club—perhaps contains a key to the goals towards which the organization intended to strive: it was derived from *Communis Patria,* the motto adopted by Milner upon his elevation to the peerage. His ideas clearly dominated the organization in succeeding years, and upon his return from South Africa in 1905 he himself became its president.[24]

When Milner retired, Amery was finally able to place himself directly under Milner's authority, becoming after 1905 a sort of administrative assistant to the former proconsul with particular duties in imperial affairs. From the time of Milner's retirement until Amery's election to Parliament in 1911, he divided his time between work for Milner and the completion of *The Times History of the War in South Africa.* For this service Amery received £1,200 annually from the Rhodes Trust.[25] The exact nature of his duties, like all such projects financed by the Trust, is obscure. Available material on the Rhodes Trust does not mention Amery's employment; nor is any reference to it found in his autobiography. Two letters in the Milner Papers, however, indicate at least part of his responsibilities.[26] It was Amery who, acting on behalf of Milner, recruited Mackinder to conduct research into imperial matters. He also wrote a number of pamphlets and articles on the need for fiscal reform aimed at promoting intra-Empire trade. But most of his time and effort seem to have been spent in attempting to develop the Compatriots' Club into a powerful device for the promotion of imperial preference.

The organization begun by Amery and his associates in January, 1904, quickly grew to include more than a hundred highly

23. *Ibid.,* p. 265.
24. *Ibid.*
25. Amery to Milner, March 30, 1908, Milner Papers. Amery was himself an active trustee from 1919 to 1955.
26. Amery to Milner, March 30 and April 4, 1908, Milner Papers.

placed tariff reformers. "We met for vigorous mutual discussion"; Amery wrote in his autobiography, "we arranged speakers for meetings; we gave courses of lectures . . . and published them in book form; we gave public dinners to eminent visitors from overseas."[27] Under Milner's direction, and with funds supplied by the Rhodes Trust, Amery in 1907 and 1908 sought to form branches of the London group in other parts of the Empire. In November, 1907, a South African Compatriots' Club was formed in Johannesburg at a dinner given by Fitzpatrick and attended by Amery.[28] Perhaps out of respect for their patron and friendship for Amery many of the kindergarten joined,[29] even though some who did doubted the wisdom of making tariff reform the central issue in a campaign whose ultimate goal was imperial unity.[30] Shortly thereafter, Amery reported to Milner that he was corresponding with Alfred Deakin, the Prime Minister of Australia and enthusiastic Milnerite, about the possibility of starting a branch there.[31] It is not known whether an Australian group was ever established; nor is there any indication that branches were created in other parts of the Empire. It is quite possible, however, that Milner himself made some effort in this direction in Canada while there on a speaking tour in late 1908.[32]

Milner's interest in indirect and unpublicized imperial projects and his involvement in small groups conspiring to revolutionize the Empire augured well for the four members of the kindergarten who returned to London in 1909 in search of support for their scheme to promote imperial unification. The approval and co-operation of their patron was apparently gained quickly, for in July and August Milner presided over a series of meetings at which the young men explained their project to small groups of the most

27. Leo Amery, *My Political Life*, I, 265. The only publication openly produced by the club seems to have been a book of eight lectures which appeared in 1905. The Committee of the Compatriots' Club, ed., *Compatriots' Club Lectures* (London, 1905).

28. Robinson to Milner, Nov. 10, 1907, Milner Papers.

29. An undated membership list found in the papers of Lord Lothian (Philip Kerr) at the Scottish Record Office, Edinburgh, contains the names of Brand, Dove, Kerr, Perry, and Wyndham.

30. Brand to Milner, Nov. 17, 1907, Milner Papers.

31. Amery to Milner, March 30, 1908, Milner Papers.

32. For a conflicting conclusion, see Carroll Quigley, "The Round Table Groups in Canada, 1908–38," *Can. Hist. Rev.*, XLIII, No. 3 (Sept., 1962), 204–24.

loyal Milnerites.[33] These meetings, attended by such fervent imperialists as Oliver, Lord Lovat, Amery, Jameson, and Lord Selborne (home on leave from South Africa), were in the best
tradition of the British ruling class events at which business was
mixed with pleasure. Except for several conferences at the London offices of the Rhodes Trust, they all took place over leisurely
meals at such London clubs as the Savile, Bachelors, and Brooks's,
or on long weekends at country homes such as Oliver's place at
Checkendon near Henley.[34]

As the end of the summer drew near, progress in the discussions
seems to have reached a crucial stage. All the leading figures in
Milner's circle had been informed of the plan; the time had thus
come to call together those willing to participate in the project to
work out organizational details and to contribute the needed
funds. A convocation of Milnerites was therefore planned for the
fourth and fifth of September at Plas Newydd, the Welsh seat of
Lord Anglesey. In final preparation for this important meeting
Milner gave a dinner at his club for Curtis, Kerr, and two fellow
Milnerites of their generation—William Marris of the Indian
civil service and Arthur Steel-Maitland, Milner's secretary. "We
had a very long discussion afterwards about Curtis's scheme,"
Milner wrote that night in his diary, "& I did not get home until
after midnight."[35]

With plans well laid, Curtis, Kerr, and Brand (Robinson had
returned to Johannesburg in August) were able, thanks to Milner's influence, to maintain control of developments at the Plas
Newydd meeting. The small group of imperial enthusiasts gathered at the Anglesey estate overlooking the Menai Straits adopted
a general program based upon the plans brought from South
Africa by Curtis and his friends. From this general program developed the round table movement. A detailed account of what took
place there would thus be of great value in understanding the
origins of this curious organization. Unfortunately, however, Milner's diary contains the only known description of this meeting,

33. Robinson's diary, Dawson Papers; Milner's diary, Milner Papers.
34. *Ibid.*
35. Milner's diary, Aug. 26, 1909, Milner Papers.

and his comments are frustratingly brief. On September 4 he wrote:

This is a purely male party, met to discuss Curtis's scheme. Those assembled at dinner, were, besides our host, Lovat, F. S. Oliver, Brand, Curtis, P. H. Kerr, Marris, Craik, Holland, Howick, & Wolmer. Jameson, who was expected, did not turn up. We had a long conference after dinner.[36]

And on the following day:

The conference of last night divided itself into several groups, to discuss different practical questions arising out of our talks, & these groups met successively this morning. Curtis, Kerr & I were present at all of them. We got a good deal settled.[37]

That evening the several groups combined to approve a series of statements which in effect made formal the general plans drawn up by the kindergarten in South Africa. Philip Kerr recorded these resolutions in a memorandum which was apparently distributed to those present.

It was agreed that the principle of co-operation was insufficient as a means of holding together the Empire. It was thought that in the long run some form of organic union was the only alternative to disruption. It was agreed that it was important to examine what form of organic unity was likely to be best suited to the facts of the situation. It was however also agreed that for the present, and until the situation was ripe for some constitutional measure, every effort should be made to extend the principle of co-operation. Organic unity would probably only be possible when people realised that the principle of co-operation had broken down.[38]

Inadequate though they are, the records concerning the general program adopted by the Plas Newydd group seem comprehensive when compared to those concerning the initial financial ar-

36. *Ibid.*, Sept. 4, 1909. George L. Craik was a New College friend of Milner's young men who had participated in some kindergarten activities in South Africa. Lord Howick, the heir to Earl Grey, was the son-in-law of Lord Selborne. Lord Wolmer was Selborne's son and heir. Holland is not readily identifiable. There were at that time at least half a dozen men in England by that name who might have been numbered among those invited to Plas Newydd. The most likely, however, was [Sir] Alfred Reginald Sothern Holland, a Cape Colony civil servant, secretary to Jameson when the latter was Cape Prime Minister, and Rhodes trustee from 1932 (*Burke's Peerage*, 1938).
37. Milner's diary, Sept. 5, 1909, Milner Papers.
38. Quoted in Butler, *Lothian*, p. 36.

rangements of the movement. According to Lovat's biographer, Sir Francis Lindley, the meeting in Wales was as much to raise funds as to hammer out policy.[39] And according to the former editor of the *Round Table,* Mr. Dermot Morrah, Sir Abe Bailey was from the first a generous contributor to the organization.[40] We may assume, therefore, that the necessary money came from both Bailey and those Milnerites at Plas Newydd. These contributions rather quickly proved to be inadequate, however, for in less than four years the kindergarten sought to get more money by widening the circle of contributors. Milner's diary on April 24, 1913, describes a dinner given by Oliver and Brand the previous evening at the Cavendish Hotel on Jermyn Street. To the twelve men of wealth and power gathered there the members of the kindergarten described the program of the round table movement and solicited their financial support. According to Milner, "we got promises of a good deal of pecuniary support for the 'moot.' "[41] The most generous of those attending seem to have been Lord Cowdray, Dr. Jameson, and Sir George Farrar, each of whom promised substantial annual contributions for a period of five years.[42] By the last year of World War I the five years had expired, and the goals of the movement were still unfulfilled. As a result, some thought was given to launching an appeal to the general public for financial support. Philip Kerr's private papers contain an undated typescript perhaps meant for publication in the *Round Table:*

> The Round Table movement in the past has depended on voluntary work and contributions and has been kept going because a number of generous supporters undertook 5 years ago to contribute so much a year for five years to ensure continuity for the work. This period is now at an end and the work must either cease or some means be found to continue it. The promoters of the Round Table movement, therefore, wish to appeal for further funds from those who are prepared to lend active support to the work. If they obtain the necessary financial support, they feel assured that the standard of Round Table productions can be maintained. The

39. Sir Francis Lindley, *Lord Lovat: A Biography* (London, n.d.), p. 114.
40. See "Sir Abe Bailey," *Round Table*, No. 120 (Sept., 1940), p. 745.
41. Milner's diary, April 24, 1913, Milner Papers.
42. Minutes of Moot, June 26, 1913, Round Table files, *Round Table* editorial office, London.

same people who made themselves responsible for the movement in the past are prepared to continue to conduct it in the future.[43]

No such public appeal for funds was ever made. The name of the benefactor or benefactors whose generosity made this step unnecessary, however, is not available. Certainly Abe Bailey was always ready to make his wealth available to the younger Milnerites; in fact, his will provided for a special endowment which would produce £1,000 a year for the movement.[44] But the extent to which Bailey was assisted by other wealthy imperialists is unknown.

In a recent article in the *Canadian Historical Review* Carroll Quigley pointed to the Rhodes Trust as the principal benefactor of the round table movement from its inception. According to his calculations, the Trust's contributions in the eleven and a half years from February, 1910, to July, 1921, amounted to almost £24,000.[45] This assertion deserves fuller documentation than the citation "Milner Papers, Rhodes Trust records" if it is to be accepted without question. Even so, the documented evidence of Rhodes Trust financial support of other imperial projects in which Milner was interested lends credence to these claims. Though this writer found no such specific references in the Milner Papers to Rhodes Trust contributions to the round table movement, there is no reason to believe that Milner and his fellow trustees should have been in this case any less generous to the kindergarten than in the past. It thus may be, as Quigley asserted, that the round table movement was financially dependent upon the wealth accumulated by Rhodes.

Regardless of how the money with which to operate the movement was raised, it is clear that some financial provision was made at Plas Newydd. For during the last day of the meeting it was agreed that Curtis and Kerr should be employed as full-time agents of the organization. In return for an annual salary and expense fund of £1,000 each, the two were expected to study just how organic unity of the Empire could best be achieved and to organize the machinery needed to promote such unity.[46]

43. Internal evidence suggests that the note was written in late 1918 or 1919.
44. Information provided by Mr. Dermot Morrah.
45. Quigley, *Can. Hist. Rev.*, XLIII, No. 3, 211.
46. Butler, *Lothian*, p. 37; Minutes of Moot, Feb. 12, 1914, Round Table files.

To gain a better understanding of Dominion opinion on matters relating to imperial unity, Curtis and Kerr requested and received permission from their Plas Newydd patrons to visit Canada. Milner agreed with the two young men that something of this sort was needed before the very general resolution adopted at Plas Newydd could be broadened into a comprehensive program upon which a great movement could be built.[47] Curtis of course had been yearning for such an opportunity ever since he and his kindergarten friends had conceived the South African closer union movement. For his part, Kerr even before the Plas Newydd meeting had made plans to visit North America. Since the date of the next general election was unknown, he had thought to prepare himself for a parliamentary career by examining conditions in Canada and the United States. His interests in that latter nation centered upon the place of the Negro in the South, a subject around which he proposed to develop a book.[48] Curtis and Kerr were accompanied on the tour by their friend and associate during their last years in South Africa, William Marris.

The three sailed for Canada on September 17, 1909, on what proved to be only the first of many such trips for the two full-time agents of the round table. From Quebec to Vancouver they met with leaders of opinion and gathered information about Canadian attitudes towards the proper relationship between "the oldest and most experienced of all the Dominions"[49] and the Empire as a whole. Though their mission was mainly to test the wind of Canadian opinion, the young imperialists could not refrain from impressing upon those with whom they came in contact the need for "a forward movement" lest the Empire break up on the shoals of Dominion nationalism.[50]

From Vancouver the three crossed the border to Seattle, where they separated, returning to England by different routes. Curtis and Marris chose to work their way slowly back to the eastern provinces, meeting with groups and individuals that the three had been unable to meet earlier. Kerr, on the other hand, returned

47. Milner's diary, Sept. 5, 1909, Milner Papers.
48. Butler, Lothian, p. 35.
49. Curtis, Letter to the People of India, p. 6.
50. Curtis to Kerr, July 21, 1910, Lothian Papers.

immediately to Ottawa for a visit with the Governor-General, Lord Grey, before re-entering the United States to spend almost a month studying the race problem. Neither the book on the American Negro nor the parliamentary contest which was to follow ever became a reality. During the trip Kerr learned that a general election would take place in January of the following year, yet he made no effort to qualify. "My ideas are clearing themselves about the wider Imperial issue," he wrote, "but I don't know yet whether my views are nearer those of the Liberals or of the Conservatives on that point. In any case the line I have been specialising on is not one which has yet become a matter for platform oratory or popular enthusiasm."[51]

Despite Kerr's refusal to be lured away from his commitments to the Plas Newydd group by the approaching election at home, Curtis returned to England convinced that his associate had failed to fulfil his responsibilities. The trip to the United States was, according to Curtis, a diversion which limited Kerr's effectiveness in Canada and drained his energies to such a degree that he might be unable to perform his duties.

> Our time is paid for by people who have subscribed liberally for a certain object [Curtis wrote to Brand]. Our duty is to fit ourselves for that object and to place it above all others. . . . So far as Philip is concerned Imperial Union is his business and the Negro question is a hobby. Philip would have trained himself far better for the work in hand if he had gone more slowly, taken more time to think, aimed at making fewer acquaintances and more friends. He flitted too fast in fact to gather honey, and like a bee a man has only one pair of wings and when those are worn out he is done for as a worker.[52]

This criticism should not be taken to indicate hostility on the part of the two young Milnerites. They were, in fact, the closest of friends and remained so throughout the rest of their lives. Curtis's remarks illustrate the frustration felt by a dedicated zealot for the talented amateur, the older brother for the younger. They occasionally differed on the fundamental matter of imperial philosophy, and they were frequently at odds over specific methods to be employed by the round table organization, but there was never a

51. Quoted without citation in Butler, *Lothian*, p. 41.
52. Curtis to Brand, Jan. 4, 1910. Quoted in Butler, *Lothian*, pp. 40–41.

diminution of the feeling of friendship which had developed during their South African days.

By January, 1910, Curtis, Marris, and Kerr had returned to London with reports on their findings. These memoranda were immediately turned over to Milner.[53] Though no copies of these documents have come to light, some indication of their contents may be gathered from remarks made later by Curtis. Speaking to the Toronto round table group in 1913 he said that on their 1909 tour he and his friends found that most Canadians failed to share their fear that the Empire must achieve some form of organic unity if it would compete in the world of the twentieth century. To the average Canadian "the difficulties which presented themselves to us were academic," for he was convinced that Dominion nationalism and imperial loyalty were in no way incompatible. The almost universal support of complete Dominion autonomy which they observed was thus balanced with the conviction that no matter what crises lay ahead tradition and emotional ties were sufficient to preserve the Empire.[54]

At the time Milner received these memoranda his life was more fully occupied with public affairs than at any time since his return from South Africa in 1905. The crisis precipitated by the Lloyd George budget of 1909 and the mounting tension over Home Rule had caused him to forget his usual distaste for party politics and to assume a leading place in Unionist affairs. It is understandable, therefore, that Milner's diary contains only the briefest of references to the return of his young friends and to the events relative to the round table which followed. On January 20, 1910, however, he did record that he had "perused carefully during the last day or two Curtis's, Marris's & Kerr's Reports on their Canadian experiences." And on that same day he mentioned having had a long talk with F. S. Oliver.

Though Milner and Oliver were both intimately involved in a number of schemes not directly related to imperial matters, it seems likely that the conversation centered upon what Milner had previously called "Curtis's scheme." For three days later in Mil-

53. Milner's diary, Jan. 20, 1910, Milner Papers.
54. Lionel Curtis, *The Round Table Movement, Its Past and Its Future: Address Delivered in the Senate House of the University to the "Round Table" Groups at Toronto,* Nov. 18, 1913 (Letchworth, n.d.), pp. 11, 12.

ner's quarters there took place a meeting of the greatest importance in the development of the round table movement. On January 23 Milner wrote in his diary that "at 3.0 there was a great
assembly in my rooms of Curtis, Kerr, Duncan, Feetham, Oliver,
Lovat, Craik, Hichens, Amery to discuss our Imperial Union
campaign. They stayed till past 7." Though the records are bare
concerning what transpired, it seems clear that at this meeting,
and at one held two days later at the Rhodes Trust offices with
substantially the same group in attendance,[55] the reports of the
three travelers were considered and the specific program of the
movement was worked out. Agreement upon this program marks
the birth of the round table movement.

Few of what Curtis called "the fundamental documents in
which the principles of R. T. work had been defined"[56] have
survived the years. Even so, comments subsequently made in letters, speeches, and memoranda, when analyzed in this context,
reveal with surprising clarity the policies and plans adopted at
these January, 1910, meetings. Basically these policies and plans
represent an amplification of the Plas Newydd resolutions along
lines established by Curtis and his friends while still in South
Africa. Only on matters of detail, in fact, does one find variation
between the conclusions reached at those meetings and the proposals outlined by Curtis in his letter to Amery written in March
of the previous year. This is an important point inasmuch as it
suggests that it was the opinions of Curtis and his kindergarten
friends that dominated these seminal meetings, and not those of
Milner and the older associates of the group in London.[57]

According to a memorandum written by Kerr sometime during
the following year, the goal of the movement "as defined last
January" was "an organic union to be brought about by the
establishment of an Imperial government constitutionally responsible to all the electors of the Empire, and with power to act
directly on the individual citizens."[58] This was a call for more
than mere imperial federation; it was a statement in support of a

55. Milner's diary, Jan. 25, 1910, Milner Papers.
56. Curtis to Kerr, April 27, 1916, Lothian Papers.
57. For a contrasting opinion, see Quigley, *Can. Hist. Rev.*, XLIII, No. 3, 204–24.
58. Quoted in Butler, *Lothian*, p. 40 n.

unitary government for the Empire the likes of which had rarely been proposed. Its achievement would thus require intense effort and careful planning, and to this end the organization would serve by "the preparation and eventual publication of a scheme of union—if possible a constitution," and by "the encouragement of intermediate steps by the promotion of public measures contributing towards the consolidation of the Empire, and the education of public opinion in the truth about Imperial affairs, and the necessity for Union."[59]

Responsibility for the execution of this program was vested in a committee of Milner's closest imperialist disciples. In addition to the members of the so-called "moot" that had aided in South African unification, it included Selborne, Amery, Oliver, and from time to time Edward Grigg (Lord Altrincham), Reginald Coupland, and Lord Robert Cecil (Viscount Cecil of Chelwood). Primary duties of the new moot were to keep a hand on the pulse of the new movement and particularly to supervise the activities of its two agents Curtis and Kerr. At the January, 1910, meetings these two were assigned specific duties in keeping with the experience which each had derived from the recently completed closer union campaign in South Africa. Kerr was made responsible for the London office, the headquarters of the movement and the editorial center for the publication of a journal with much the same form as the *State* but with the whole Empire as its province. Curtis's original plan for a chain of journals linked together by a common purpose and by material supplied by a central office was during this period dropped as impractical. The single quarterly, edited by Kerr and published in London, was meant to provide contact among the various elements of the movement and to promote "education of public opinion in the truth about Imperial affairs, and the necessity for Union."

Once again it would be Curtis's job to travel about gathering information and ideas from which to draft memoranda— memoranda from which he, with the assistance of the moot, would create a specific program for the establishment of organic union. When this program—perhaps a draft constitution—was com-

59. *Ibid.*

pleted and agreed upon by the members of the moot, small groups of influential men would be recruited in each Dominion to study the plan and decide whether they were able to fight for its adoption. Then, with a blueprint for organic union in hand and a body of supporters standing ready in all parts of the Empire, the movement would take on a new tone. The quiet conspiracy would give way to a great crusade. All those techniques of a mass movement which had been refined and improved in behalf of countless great causes over the preceding century would be employed to rout the Little Englanders and Dominion chauvinists who were thought to stand in the way of organic union.

This generally was the plan adopted in January, 1910. None of those involved expected its fulfilment to be either quick or simple. It was understood that the obstacles in the way of uniting the Empire were infinitely greater than those that had to be overcome in South Africa. Even so, Milnerites in charge of the new movement were hopeful. With the experience acquired in South Africa and the wealth provided by fervent imperialists, the members of the new moot were convinced that the Empire might at long last be transformed into the sort of race-nation for which their patron and leader had devoted his life.

Chapter Ten. Curtis's initial tour of the Empire

Adequate funds and a well-conceived program were essential to the fulfilment of the goal agreed upon by the moot in January, 1910. But of equal importance was the effectiveness of the two members of the moot hired to devote their full time to the establishment of the movement. This was particularly so in the case of Curtis, for the round table was, as Milner put it, "Curtis's scheme," and many of its characteristics bore the imprint of his experiences in South Africa. What is more, Curtis, as roving representative of the group, was by the nature of his job required frequently to make important decisions on his own. During his travels consultation with the moot in London was sometimes impossible and at best meant a delay of several weeks. The decisions which he made under these circumstances, therefore, often did more to shape some aspects of the movement than the most careful deliberations of the parent body.

Curtis's travels on behalf of the round table—which occupied so much of his time in the following decade—began almost immediately after the January, 1910, meetings in London. His first task, according to the program agreed upon by the moot, was to collect opinions and facts from which to draft a report defining in specific terms the problems which beset the Empire. To facilitate the collection of such information, Curtis decided to draft a tentative assessment of the situation based upon the observations of Kerr, Marris, and himself on their recent tour of Canada. Such a composite statement, he believed, would be of great value in acquainting those with whom he came into contact on his travels throughout the Empire with the general approach of the group which he represented.

Curtis's travels began, however, before work on the memorandum could be begun. His plan to seclude himself with copies of the reports on Canada until his composite draft was complete was altered by events in South Africa. In the early months of 1910 the final meeting of the Transvaal Legislative Council was to take

place just before the formal establishment of the Union government. Curtis, a member of that body, decided to return for the
session. He felt that the trip out would provide time in which to
begin the memorandum on Canada; and during the legislative
session and after, he could discuss plans which had been recently
formed in London with those of the moot who were still in South
Africa.[1] Arriving in the Transvaal in early March, Curtis met on
several occasions with Perry, Feetham, Duncan, and
Malcolm—all members of the kindergarten—as well as with Leo
Amery, who was in South Africa on a business trip.[2] Though no
record of these meetings exists, one may assume that on these
occasions Curtis, with the aid of Amery, explained to his associates the decisions which had been made in London several months
before and sought their advice concerning the composite statement on Canada which he was at that time creating.

By May the statement was completed and on its way to London
for printing. Entitled *Memoranda on Canada and the British
Commonwealth*,[3] but more commonly called "the original Green
Memorandum" by all those associated with the round table, it
became the prototype for a series of round table memoranda
produced by Curtis in the following decade. Copies for distribution to those interested in the movement were bound with a blank
sheet inserted between each leaf of text. The reason for this
peculiar arrangement was explained in a note on the back of the
title page.

> The memoranda contained in this volume are printed for private
> circulation among a few friends, who are asked to be good enough
> to read their contents and to record their criticisms on the blank
> pages opposite the passages to which the criticism refers. Any
> general criticism should be noted on the blank pages at the end of
> the memorandum.
> This copy is numbered . . . and issued to . . . who is requested

1. Curtis, *A Letter to the People of India*, p. 7.
2. Robinson's diary, March 9, April 3 and 17, 1910, Dawson Papers; Milner's diary, Feb. 11, 1910, Milner Papers.
3. The copy examined by this writer at the Royal Commonwealth Institute in London contains no indication of author, printer, or date. In her bibliography of Curtis, however, Ruth Pryor gives Richard Clay of London as the printer and 1910 as the year (Ruth Pryor, "Bibliography of the Works of Lionel George Curtis: A Provisional List to the Present Date Submitted in Part Fulfilment of the Requirements for the University of London Diploma in Librarianship," May, 1955).

to be good enough to return it, when it has been read and annotated, to L. Curtis, Uplands, Ledbury, Herefordshire.

Called by Curtis "a collection of notes on the government of the Empire,"[4] the Green Memorandum might be more accurately described as a survey of Canadian relations with Great Britain and an urgent plea for their improvement. It began with a historical account of the development of British influence in North America from the seventeenth to the twentieth centuries. In this part, which was after all only background material for the real point which the author wished to make, Curtis again displayed the talent for prostituting history for propagandistic purposes which was so apparent in his work on *The Government of South Africa*. Historical objectivity was brushed aside as he described a great saga full of heroes but no scoundrels, high-minded statesmen but no scheming politicians. Events which were unpleasant were simply forgotten, and care was taken to offend no important groups in either North America or in Britain. It was this Empire Day pageantry dressed out as history that prompted a prominent London editor to write several years later that

> their history is wicked—how *dare* they do this sort of thing. It is really poisoning the wells. I am pulled up short at every page—always doubting their conclusions &, where I have any little knowledge *knowing* them to be awry. . . . Damn it if England is guided by the R. T. she becomes permanently second-rate intellectually among the great nations.[5]

With the background of British North American interests firmly implanted in his reader's mind, Curtis turned his attention to contemporary relations between Canada and Great Britain. He conceded that, as everyone knew, Canada now had broad powers to govern herself. Like the other Dominions, the eldest sister of the Empire had for some time been mistress in her own house. But contrary to the opinions of almost all Canadians with whom he and his associates conferred on their recent tour of North America, this self-government was far from complete. Everywhere on their travels they met Canadians who insisted that except for

4. Curtis, *The Round Table Movement*, p. 5.
5. Fabian Ware to Richard Jebb, Dec. 24, 1912, Jebb Papers. Years earlier Steyn of the Orange Free State had asserted that the Selborne Memorandum was "full of . . . bad history" (Thompson, *Unification of South Africa*, p. 77) .

certain ties of sentimental loyalty to the Empire their land was, in fact if not in theory, as sovereign as any on earth. This, wrote Curtis, was an illusion. And from this illusion had developed the present "Problem of the Empire." Contrary to what most Canadians believed, Canada was not at that time autonomous, nor had she ever been. Her growth had taken place behind the shield provided by the British navy, and upon the continued strength of that force depended the freedoms customarily enjoyed by her citizens. Without the protection of Great Britain, Canada would long ago have been overrun by an aggressive European power or swallowed up by her neighbor to the south. Under these circumstances Canadian claims of autonomy were hollow; a nation that could not provide for its own defense was in no position to determine that most important of all issues, whether in a given situation to make war or remain at peace. In the event of war between Britain and another power it was highly unlikely that Canadian neutrality would be recognized even if Ottawa wished to remain aloof. Her dependence upon Great Britain in matters of defense, in fact, would make it almost essential that Canada line up behind her protector lest her failure to do so cause the shield to be removed. Thus in the vital area of foreign affairs Canada, far from being autonomous, was actually the captive of Whitehall.

According to the Green Memorandum, this was the heart of the Imperial Problem. The relationship between Canada—or for that matter, any of the Dominions—and Great Britain was unnatural, illogical, and liable to cause great damage to the Empire in some crucial moment when the interests of the two nations happened to diverge. And with the situation in Europe being what it was, that crisis might arise at almost any day. It was essential, therefore, that some way be found to make Canada and the other Dominions truly independent by extending their powers of self-government to include foreign affairs generally and the decision for war or peace in particular. According to Curtis, this could be done in either of two ways. On the one hand, the political leaders of the nations of the Empire could create a unified imperial government which would enable the Dominions to contribute to the common defense in return for a voice in the determination of foreign policy. On the other hand, the Dominions could achieve their

independence by severing the imperial connection. There was no middle road to relieve the necessity for decision, only these two paths "between which the States of the Empire would have to choose—independence, or organic union."[6] This "pistol policy," as Kerr called it,[7] was presented in the Green Memorandum not as a full and final solution to the Imperial Problem, but only as a logical conclusion which must now be examined in light of information to be gathered in the other Dominions.

With his memorandum finished and off to the printer and with the final session of the Legislative Council ended Curtis was ready to approach residents of the other Dominions. Therefore on May 31, 1910, "the appointed day when the Union of South Africa came into being," Curtis wrote several years later, "I sailed for New Zealand."[8] Curtis's mission on this initial tour was relatively uncomplicated.

> Under the original idea, as we figured it out last year [Curtis wrote], my first visits were to be devoted for the purpose of collecting the necessary information for our studies and of making a reconnaissance in order to find out the kind of men who might be asked eventually to go in with us. The formation of the groups was to be left to a future visit.[9]

The information so collected would then be used in "getting out a statement and reducing it to finality, so far as the South African and English groups were concerned," before taking "that statement round to discuss with the other three Dominions, leaving the groups to be formed in the course of these discussions."[10]

During Curtis's absence from London, however, the moot apparently decided upon a change of plans, for by the time of his departure from South Africa Curtis had received new instructions which greatly complicated his actions in New Zealand and Australia. "Now," he wrote with some asperity, "it is the desire of the Moot, that the work should be accelerated, and that I should not only collect information, but actually form the organization on

6. Curtis, *Memoranda on Canada and the British Commonwealth,* p. xv.
7. Butler, *Lothian,* p. 37.
8. Curtis, *Letter to the People of India,* p. 7.
9. Curtis to Oliver, Aug. 15, 1910, Lothian Papers, Scottish Record Office, H. M. General Register House, Edinburgh.
10. *Ibid.*

my first visit."[11] Why this change of plans was made by the moot is not clear, though it may have been prompted by the conviction that the original program involved needless delays which only postponed what was after all the real purpose of the movement—the creation of a truly unified Empire. But whatever the reason, the altered plans certainly made Curtis's mission both more complex and more difficult. Now in addition to his original task of gathering information and assessing opinion he was expected to locate in each Dominion those who might support the general goals of the movement and form them into branches of the London group. Nor was this all. He was further instructed to secure regular correspondents for the magazine which was then taking form in London and to promote the sale of subscriptions to all who were interested in the welfare of the Empire.

While never ceasing to complain in his letters to London that the revised plans were largely impractical inasmuch as they represented an attempt to do too much too soon, Curtis set out on his travels in the Pacific determined to do what he could to carry out the orders of those who sent him.[12] To do this Curtis—always the master salesman—found it helpful to develop a "sales pitch" by which he hoped to carry off the sometimes conflicting parts of his mission. As he wrote from New Zealand, "the spectre which I am always having to exorcise, is the notion so easily provoked in the Dominions, that people are to be lured into some propaganda, the final upshot of which they do not see."[13] This was the same sort of problem which he and the kindergarten had had to face several years before as they struggled to establish the closer union movement in South Africa. Both conservative Boers and back-veld Englishmen had suspected that these young disciples of Milner were attempting to use them in some scheme meant to promote the interest of Britain and the British Empire. In a sense of course they were right. To veil this truth and to allay this suspicion, Curtis had told South Africans in every colony that he and his friends had no specific solutions to the problems facing that divided region, but that they were convinced that the problems were

11. *Ibid.*
12. Curtis to Kerr, July 21, and Curtis to Oliver, Aug. 15, 1910, Lothian Papers.
13. Curtis to Kerr, July 21, 1910, Lothian Papers.

largely an outgrowth of the governmental situation which existed there. The closer union movement, he had insisted, was meant only to provide South Africans with an opportunity to meet together and discuss these problems; decisions about how to solve these problems could be made only by South Africans themselves. Curtis had not felt constrained to point out that he and his Milnerite friends intended to do everything in their power to see that South Africans came to interpret these problems as the kindergarten wanted them to and to choose solutions which the Milnerites had favored from the beginning.

This sort of logic had convinced South Africans by the thousands. There was no reason to think that it would not work with equal success in the other Dominions—especially inasmuch as the "pitch" could now be improved thanks to the recent achievement of a union government in South Africa.

> I come here as a man identified with South Africa [Curtis wrote from New Zealand], I tell them how the South African group grew up in the last ten years, how our own domestic government having at length been set in order, we now feel impelled to make our external affairs the subject of accurate study before we commit ourselves to a line of policy. How we are, therefore, compelled to examine the lines of policy upon which Canada, Australia and New Zealand respectively have started. I go on to point out how, before we can arrive at any constructive policy for our guidance in South Africa, we must, if we are really in earnest in that policy dicover [sic] first of all whether it is one that is suitable also to the other partners of the concern. We are, therefore, trying to suggest to our friends in Canada, New Zealand and Australia, that they should form little groups of students, similar to our South African group, and that we should pursue these studies to-gether, with a view to the development of a policy of mutual relations which would fit the circumstances of all. I represent the establishment of a similar group in England, rather as the outcome of suggestion from South Africa, subsequently endorsed by the approval of friends we have made in Canada, and I feel that I can do so with perfect sincerity.[14]

14. *Ibid.* This account of the nature of the origins of the round table movement, with its emphasis upon Dominion rather than London influence and its constant reference to unbiased study groups searching for the truth, quickly became the authorized version. In later years it was repeated in virtually everything which was written about the beginnings of the movement by members of the moot.

In this approach the Green Memorandum played an important part. Though printed copies did not reach Curtis until he was in Australia, he was nevertheless able to circulate the report among some of those with whom he came in contact thanks to the efforts of his secretary, who "made six for me at the cost of much labour."[15] This document, redolent with an air of scientific and historical objectivity, lent credibility to his claim that the object of the group which he represented was "to apply the methods of scientific study to politics." "When I put in front of them our Canadian Reports," Curtis wrote from New Zealand, "I do so with . . . a request that they may be read with the object of picking holes in them."[16] Ruthless objectivity is absolutely vital, he explained to his Dominion acquaintances, for

> the very essence of our work is, that we are all conscious of an Imperial problem, but there is, as yet, no statement of that problem which we all accept. We in South Africa may have arrived at some clear idea in our own minds, as to what that problem is, but it would avail us but little until we are working hand in hand with groups of men like ourselves, in the other Dominions who have accepted the same statement of the problem and are aiming at the same solution. My first task, therefore, is to bring home the fact that, while every thinking person in all these countries admits the existence of such a problem, they have none of them a definite idea of what it is, nor what is the solution with which it can be met. Having established this point, I go on to argue that the problem demands accurate study. My next step is to point out, that such study to be worth anything involves the collaboration of students who are viewing the problem and the facts involved in it from the distinct standpoint of all the countries concerned: on that I base an invitation to a few suitable people to join in these studies.[17]

Once he became committed to this sort of presentation, Curtis found that his duties to the magazine then being established in London presented a problem. In his travels he could without appearing to be inconsistent request that each study group provide the *Round Table* with a quarterly report on imperial developments in that country. Colonials immediately saw "that it

---

15. Curtis to Oliver, Aug. 15, 1910, Lothian Papers.
16. Curtis to Kerr, July 21, 1910, Lothian Papers.
17. Curtis to Oliver, Aug. 15, 1910, Lothian Papers.

would be impossible to secure continuity from groups in five different countries and any uniformity of action between them unless there were established something in the nature of a common journal. . . ."[18] But Curtis found it difficult in light of the objective study group image which he was attempting to create to speak too frequently of a need for subscriptions. He had to be on guard constantly, he wrote Kerr, lest he leave the impression "that my real object is to found a new organ to serve the political and even commercial interests of its founders, whom I am representing."[19] To allay such suspicions he felt obliged to play down the role of the *Round Table* as an organ for general instruction on imperial matters and to stress its function as an esoteric means of communication among widely scattered groups of students.

> I always say [wrote Curtis], 'never get a man to take it in just to get an additional subscription. The journal is not a commercial undertaking and it is not to go to anyone whom [*sic*] you do not think will read it. . . .' [For] the first and most important object of the magazine for the present would be fulfilled if it were taken in and read by the few dozen men who as an inner circle were to take part in the work of study, and if they only read it, it is still worth doing.[20]

These problems and the delicate nature of Curtis's work made for slow progress. When he began his travels in early 1910 Curtis, like the other members of the moot, had innocently assumed that he could return home by the end of the year with his task accomplished. The alteration of his instructions by the moot, however, had changed all this. With his added duties Curtis found that it took far longer to complete his work than he and his friends had originally anticipated. In making this point to the moot Curtis left a revealing account of the way in which he went about establishing a new group.

> When I arrive at a place like this [Wellington], I may have a dozen introductions, but I should come to grief at once, if I went straight off to see each of these dozen and unfolded myself to them: it is seldom that more than half of them are of any use for

18. Curtis to Kerr, July 21, 1910, Lothian Papers.
19. *Ibid.*
20. *Ibid.*

the purpose in view. Very often the people who are the least use are those to whom I am most highly recommended. . . . When we have established a group, its prominence and efficiency will largely depend on one strenuous leading spirit, who has got round him men who are congenial to himself. I have, therefore, to decide who is the best man for the cause, and enlist his support. I then discuss with him the others with whom he wishes to work, some of them may be included in the six just men I have already met, but nearly always there are other people outside, whom [sic] he thinks are as good or better, to whom he introduces me and about whom we consult. Then, when we have tapped all these people, I ask them all to dinner and thrash the thing out with them generally.[21]

Despite his complaints of delays caused by decisions made by the moot, Curtis in the midst of his travels in the Pacific proposed a further revision in plans which, if it had been adopted by his associates in London, would have delayed his progress for months. The scheme which he suggested concerned the forthcoming Imperial Conference planned for the early months of 1911. At this meeting of Dominion prime ministers and representatives of the British government it was assumed that all would express their support of the imperial connection and speak glowingly of the sentimental ties which united His Majesty's subjects throughout the world. It was not likely, however, that any fundamental changes in the direction of greater imperial unity would result, for Dominion opinion—as well as that in Great Britain—was not at that time prepared for such a step. There was mild surprise, therefore, when it was announced in 1910 that Sir Joseph Ward of New Zealand planned to propose to the Conference the creation of "a council for advising the imperial government."[22] Though the specific nature of the body envisioned by Ward was not disclosed, it was clear that he had in mind only the mildest sort of council whose function was simply to improve communications between the Dominions and Great Britain and not to legislate imperial policy.[23]

Upon learning of Ward's plan in late July, Curtis, who was still

21. Curtis to Oliver, Aug. 15, 1910, Lothian Papers.
22. Richard Jebb, *The Britannic Question: A Survey of Alternatives* (London, 1913), p. 112.
23. Keith Sinclair, *Imperial Federation: A Study of New Zealand Policy and Opinion 1880–1914* ("Commonwealth Papers," No. II; London, 1955), p. 42.

in New Zealand, suggested to Kerr that this might offer a priceless opportunity "to bring back the discussion to the real matters at issue."[24] Curtis hoped to encourage Ward to propose not the weak advisory council mentioned in the recent announcement, but a more powerful body with constitutional authority to direct the affairs of the Empire. Though the acceptance of such a proposal by the governments involved was at this time very unlikely, Curtis insisted that the discussion of imperial issues which its presentation would provoke could only work to the advantage of those who struggled for the organic unity of the Empire.

It is not clear whether Kerr's reply of August 31 represented the thinking of the other members of the moot. Nor is there any evidence that Curtis's proposal was even submitted to the moot. It is obvious, however, that Kerr looked upon the plan with disfavor. "I have been a little alarmed by your letter of 20th. July . . . ," he wrote to Curtis, for "my present view is that time and the men are against us in 1911."[25] Neither Laurier nor Botha was disposed to favor any scheme which would reduce the autonomy of the Dominions, Kerr insisted. Nor would the idea receive support from the Liberal government in Great Britain, for

> there are too many people like Morley within and without the Cabinet, men who regard the establishment of Colonial autonomy (of which South Africa is the last example) as the noblest of Liberal achievements, for the Government to be a party to initiating a discussion on steps towards the constitutional unity of the Empire. They would follow if we could get up popular enthusiasm beforehand, but the domestic situation . . . is too ticklish for them to break fresh ground about the Empire—on their own. . . .

Therefore, Kerr insisted, to push Ward into some sort of alteration of his announced plans might do great damage to the movement. "It would be a pity," he wrote, "to force a discussion of the real issues, only to get a resolution endorsed by Asquith, Botha and Laurier to the effect that present arrangements work very well, and that no urgent step is necessary. . . ."

Perhaps to deflect Curtis's enthusiasm into more suitable areas,

---

24. Kerr to Curtis (copy), Aug. 31, 1910, Lothian Papers. Kerr quotes from a letter written by Curtis on July 20. That letter, however, is not found in the Lothian Papers.
25. *Ibid.*

Kerr pointed out that the forthcoming Conference nevertheless presented a welcome opportunity to those interested in the achievement of imperial union. "The value of the opportunity will be educational," he wrote, "and I think the opportunity can be seized better outside than inside the conference." Members of the moot were rich in personal contacts with those in high places, and their influence on the press in all parts of the Empire was great. It would thus be possible for them to put arguments favoring organic unity before the public "in the most unsuspicious way, without a trace of Downing Street interference. . . ." Under the circumstances, Kerr insisted, this approach was likely to be far more productive than the scheme proposed by Curtis. "If we wanted to get something *done* [at this time] it would be another matter. We don't; we want to make people familiar with the idea of federation, so that they will be all the more ready to swallow our gospel when it is published."

Kerr's disapproval apparently had little effect upon Curtis. During the weeks required for his letter to reach London and a reply to return to New Zealand Curtis in fact seems to have become convinced that Ward's announcement offered an opportunity which could not be permitted to pass. He apparently found the imperial situation in 1910 analogous to conditions in South Africa four years earlier. In a crucial moment in the development of South Africa Curtis and his friends had been able to use a complaisant colonial prime minister to present an analysis of relations among British colonies there and a plea for their unification. The result, as he understood it, was a chain of events which ultimately led to the establishment of the Union of South Africa. Might not a new Selborne Memorandum have similar results? Material from which to weave such a study was at hand in the Green Memorandum, and Ward, if approached properly, should prove adequate in the role previously played by Dr. Jameson. Not even Curtis was sanguine enough to expect that Ward's presentation to the Imperial Conference of a proposal for organic unity conforming to the wishes of the moot would produce immediate constitutional changes. Opposition from Botha, Laurier, and powerful forces within the Liberal government could not be routed overnight. Even so, such a proposal would in Curtis's opinion produce more public interest in organic union than he and the moot could create in years. He was therefore determined to pursue the scheme until he was able to learn the wishes of the moot.

News of a moot policy on this matter was slow in reaching Curtis. Only in October was an "Imperial Conference 'mootlet,' " as Kerr called it, held to discuss Curtis's scheme and to decide upon a round table position concerning the forthcoming meeting. The results were communicated to Curtis informally in a letter from Kerr written on October 14 which was prefaced with the legend: "Oliver has seen this & approved."

> I daresay it is not much good my writing to you about your manoeuvres with Islington [Lord Islington, Governor of New Zealand from 1910 to 1912] and Ward, as you may have committed yourself long before this letter can reach you. Your idea that we should use the opportunity of the Conference to re-focus public attention on the real issues before the Empire by publishing a new sort of Selborne memorandum has many obvious attractions, but there is a good deal to be said on the other side.
>
> As you admit the value of the proceeding would depend on the memo itself, and not on anything that Ward could add to it, or say about it in the Conference. In fact Ward is so little up to the job that everybody would be sure to be asking who the devil had written it. The only real connection between the memo and the Conference is that the Conference will attract people's attention to Imperial affairs, and therefore to a memorandum dealing with its business, which will so get a good send off. The Conference itself would probably undo rather than add to the effect, for I have not the slightest doubt that Asquith, Laurier and Botha between them would manage to handle the subject in such a way as to damp down any enthusiasm the memo might have created. Moreover if you depend on the memorandum and not on a man you may be stalemated by finding that it is not made public until after the Conference. If my recollections serve me right it has been the rule that nothing should be published before the Conference in order that the Conference itself might decide how much of its proceedings and how many of the documents laid before it should be given to the public. If that were the case the bomb would not be exploded until the crisis in the fever of imperial enthusiasm had been passed and everybody was going off on holiday.
>
> Unless, therefore, you think that Ward and Fisher [Prime Minister of Australia] can put up a decent fight, and force the hands of Laurier, Asquith and Botha and Co. and expose in all their

nakedness by discussion and speechifying inside the Conference and out, the facts of the present imperial situation, the publication of a memorandum will really only precipitate at once the crisis we have always contemplated for a year or so ahead. You will publish a half-boiled egg to which nobody has pledged his consent, instead of a real chicken, in the hatching of which people all over the Empire have taken their share.[26]

There is no way of knowing Curtis's reaction to this letter. No evidence has yet appeared to indicate whether he continued with his scheme despite the opposition of the moot, or whether he simply dropped the matter. Nor is it clear just how far he had progressed with his plans before receiving the October 14 letter from Kerr, though it should be noted that Kerr's reference to "your manoeuvres with Islington and Ward" leaves little doubt that an attempt was made by Curtis to draw the New Zealand prime minister into his plan. In contrast, however, the activities of Ward just before and during the Conference are a matter of record. Before leaving New Zealand Ward is reported to have promised that he would propose nothing more limiting to Dominion sovereignty than an advisory council.[27] On his way to London, however, he addressed a group of New Zealanders living in Sydney. To these compatriots he expressed himself in terms which were somewhat different. Ward explained the necessity to create some sort of Empire-wide agency which would enable Dominion representatives actually to participate in the determination of policies affecting foreign affairs and defense. As things stood, Great Britain could very easily become embroiled in a controversy which would drag the whole Empire into a costly war, thereby violating "the first principle of our constitutional system—that there should be no taxation without representation."[28]

Upon his arrival in London the remarks Ward had made in Sydney took on added significance, for on the first day of the Conference he presented a proposal for a change in imperial organization which was far more radical than anything his political associates in New Zealand had cause to expect. What he actually proposed was an "Imperial Council of State" containing

26. Kerr to Curtis (copy), Oct. 14, 1910, Lothian Papers.
27. Sinclair, *Imperial Federation*, p. 43.
28. "New Zealand Affairs," *Round Table*, No. 4 (Aug., 1911), p. 535.

popularly chosen delegates from all the self-governing areas of the Empire. This body would be responsible for foreign affairs, defense, and "such other Imperial matters as may by agreement be transferred to such Parliament."[29] In presenting his plan, however, Ward weakened his position by his clumsy approach. His presentation was disjointed and rambling and his references to the proposed body were contradictory. What he described in one breath as an advisory council to guide the British government in the establishment of policy became in the next an "Imperial Parliament of Defence" and even an "Imperial House of Representatives." Under the circumstances it was a simple matter for Asquith and Laurier to discredit the plan and force Ward to withdraw it in embarrassment.

In attempting to account for this fiasco, observers and interpreters have offered various explanations. Many assumed at the time that Ward's confused presentation resulted from the unhappy combination of a mediocre mind and a notorious inability at public speaking. The British government, however, was unable to accept this interpretation. Leading political figures in London, knowing Ward to be no fool, were inclined to search for some less obvious explanation. According to remarks made by Sir Edward Grey to a group of Milnerites, the Colonial Office supposed that the New Zealander had made his proposals "without conviction but with an obvious desire to test them in discussion with people outside."[30] The most respected Edwardian authority on Imperial Conferences—Richard Jebb—offered another explanation:

> The confusion which seemed to characterise his introduction of it to the Imperial Conference was due simply to an accidental circumstance. He had previously given notice of a motion in favour of creating quite a different thing, a council for advising the imperial government. Instead of withdrawing that motion—a course which possibly may not have been open to him—he endeavoured to make it the "peg" for the federation scheme, which he had obtained in the meantime from a special source and had decided to substitute for his original proposal.[31]

29. Quoted from the minutes of the Conference in the *Cambridge History of the British Empire*, III (1959), 432.
30. Robinson's diary, July 12, 1911, Dawson Papers.
31. Jebb, *The Britannic Question*, p. 112. See also his "The Imperial Conference: A Retrospect and Warning," *National Review*, LXIX (April, 1917), 181–88; and *The Imperial Conference, a History and Study* (London, 1911).

This "special source" from which Ward obtained his plan is now conceded to have been Lionel Curtis.[32] But the exact circumstances by which Curtis's ideas came to be reflected in the proposal made to the Conference are by no means clear. The correspondence between Curtis and his associates in London shows, as we have seen, that he wished to use Ward to present such a plan to the imperial statesmen and to the world and that he went so far as to approach both Ward and Lord Islington about it. There is good reason to suppose, therefore, that in the London meeting Ward's proposal, if not his words of introduction, represents a latter-day Selborne Memorandum created by Curtis.

It is significant, however, that Curtis later denied that he had willingly participated in the formulation of Ward's proposal. In *The Problem of the Commonwealth* he described Ward's behavior at the Imperial Conference without making a single comment about any interest which he may have had in the matter. He implied, in fact, that Ward, though good-hearted and well-intentioned, had blundered badly not only in the way in which he had presented his plan but in presenting it at all, for according to Curtis, it should have been obvious to any perceptive observer that well-entrenched opposition made success highly unlikely.[33] In a letter to Sir Charles Lucas written in 1913, Curtis did admit involvement, but insisted that his part in the affair was indirect and unintentional. The Green Memorandum, he wrote, was made available to a New Zealand minister "owing to the indiscretion of one of the New Zealanders who had engaged to study the matter." This minister, thinking that the memorandum expressed the "unavowed policy of the Imperial Government," encouraged Ward to press for constitutional changes far more extreme than those he had originally planned to propose.[34] Why Curtis hid the truth about his part in the matter is not clear. Though he had the usual quota of flaws in his character, cowardice was not one of them.

It is obvious, however, that Curtis's infatuation with the scheme to produce a new Selborne Memorandum delayed his progress

32. Sinclair, *Imperial Federation*, p. 43; and J. D. B. Miller, "The Utopia of Imperial Federation," *Political Studies*, IV (June, 1956), 196.
33. Lionel Curtis, *The Problem of the Commonwealth* (Toronto, 1916), pp. 100 ff.
34. Curtis to Lucas, April 29, 1913. Quoted in Sinclair, *Imperial Federation*, p. 43.

through the Pacific Dominions. As the weeks passed he fell farther
and farther behind the schedule agreed upon before his departure
from London. Despite Curtis's claim that much of the fault lay
with the moot for increasing his responsibilities during this initial
tour, the London group remained insensitive to his requests for
more time. Insensitivity turned to vexation when a letter from
Curtis arrived asking that he not be required to return home by
Canada as planned, but rather that he be permitted to progress
through Australia at his own pace, return to New Zealand if
necessary, and finally make his way back to London the following
spring via India and Egypt. He justified this request by pointing
to the need for a great amount of additional research—
particularly in the two great dependencies of India and Egypt—
before he and his associates could work out a blueprint for unification acceptable to leaders throughout the Empire. "As I have
told Philip," Curtis wrote,

> when we have got a confession of faith so tested and accepted, I
> am prepared to spend the rest of my life in Canada if necessary
> propagating it, but until that time, I am tied hand and foot. Every
> day I see more clearly, that we cannot get to work until we have
> reached that point.

A second visit to Canada without such a confession of faith would
be, according to Curtis, "a positive mischief."[35]

Curtis's request was denied by the moot. To hasten the completion of his work in the South Pacific so that he might get to
Canada at the first opportunity, it was decided even before Curtis's plea reached London to send out John Dove to help. Dove
had recently returned to London to establish a private immigration society backed by wealthy Milnerites. Almost before he could
get settled, however, he was pressed into emergency duty as Curtis's assistant. After a long talk with Milner at the *Round Table*
offices,[36] Dove sailed for Australia in July where he participated in
the establishment of groups in Sydney and Melbourne.[37] With
part of his burden thus removed, Curtis was able belatedly to
arrive in Canada in early 1911. In the two months before he sailed

35. Curtis to Oliver, Aug. 15, 1910, Lothian Papers.
36. Milner's diary, July 15, 1910, Milner Papers.
37. Letter to this writer from R. L. Stock, secretary of the Melbourne round table
group, Aug. 29, 1961.

for home in March he accomplished a great deal in a short time there thanks to hard work and to the contacts established on earlier trips to Canada by Milner and Curtis, Kerr, and Marris. Groups were formed in Montreal and Toronto to study the Green Memorandum, provisions were made for a quarterly article to be published in the *Round Table*, and subscriptions to the journal were sold in numbers sufficient to satisfy the moot.[38] Initial members of these groups, some of whom later became important in imperial affairs, were drawn largely from educational and financial circles. Among them were Edward Kylie and G. M. Wrong, both of the faculty of history at the University of Toronto; Arthur Glazebrook, a Balliol friend of Milner's who had lived in Toronto since the eighties; (Sir) Edmund Walker, President of the Canadian Bank of Commerce; (Sir) Edward Peacock, an old associate of George Parkin's and a figure of growing importance in Canadian financial circles; and (Sir) John Willison, the journalist and Canadian correspondent for *The Times*.

The method of operation used by Curtis in Canada was essentially the same as that used in New Zealand except that in Canada he was spared the tedious sniffing about for reliable men. The previous experience of moot members provided him with a considerable amount of information about individuals who might be suitable for membership in the local groups. In Toronto he was able to hold the customary organizational dinner less than six weeks after his arrival in Canada. This event had an inspiring effect on at least one of those who attended. G. M. Wrong left this brief record of his feelings about the affair:

> A Committee in each of the Divisions of Greater Britain is working on the problem of finding out the common interests of the various parts of the British Empire and the possibility of organization to meet them. At present we think that Defence, and flowing from it, Foreign Affairs, exhaust the interest that we all have in common. Curtis asked me to act as the Chairman of the Toronto Committee to make the study of this part of the Canadian prob-

38. The aspect of the kindergarten-round table development which has been most adequately studied by members of the history profession is that relating to the origins of the movement in Canada. Two articles based upon original research in unpublished material have appeared recently in the *Can. Hist. Rev.* James Eayrs, "The Round Table Movement in Canada, 1909–1920," XXXVIII (March, 1957), 1–20; and Carroll Quigley, "The Round Table Groups in Canada, 1908–38," XLIII (Sept., 1962), 204–24.

lem. About twenty of us are engaged in the study. If we can
achieve anything our gathering to-night will be epoch-making in
the history of the world. On beginnings so slight do great issues
sometimes depend.[39]

With the groups in Toronto and Montreal started and Canadian matters relating to the journal taken care of, Curtis returned
to London without delay. Robinson's diary on March 27, 1911,
records that "Lionel just arrived from Canada within a day of
John Dove's arrival from Australia." Dove, it might be pointed
out, was near physical collapse when he reached London. He had
gone to South Africa years earlier to recover his health, but hard
work on behalf of first the city of Johannesburg and later the
Transvaal Land Settlement Board had only weakened his condition. No sooner had he arrived home from South Africa than he
was rushed off to Australia by the moot to shoulder part of
Curtis's burden. His last reserves of stamina were exhausted by
the time of his return to London in March, 1911, and shortly
thereafter he underwent a major operation which obliged him
"for some years to live quietly until his strength was restored."[40]

Nevertheless, Dove as well as Curtis was, according to Robinson, present on April 4 at "a full Moot w. the returning 'Der-
vishes' (L. C. & J. D.) begun at 5 in 175 Piccadilly [the first address
of the *Round Table* editorial offices] & continued at Oliver's
house in Hereford Garden where we all dined."[41] The reports
presented by Curtis and Dove prompted an extended debate
about the progress of the movement in general and "the best
method of ultimately producing the Egg" in particular.[42] The
term "egg" in this case of course referred to the projected proposal
for organic unity of the Empire. At the organizational meetings
the previous year it was agreed that such a proposal was necessary
before the activist phase of the movement could be begun. Back
then it had all seemed so simple; upon completion of his initial
tour of the Dominions, Curtis, with advice and assistance of the
moot, would set to work on a scheme of union which, after careful

39. Wrong's diary, Feb. 15, 1911, Wrong Papers. Quoted in Eayrs, *Can. Hist. Rev.*,
XXXVIII, 2.
40. "John Dove," *Round Table*, No. 95 (June, 1934), p. 464.
41. Robinson's diary, Dawson Papers.
42. *Ibid.*

study by interested individuals and groups throughout the Empire and amendment where amendment seemed necessary, would then become the charter for a great imperialist crusade.

The experience of the past year, however, had shown that the creation of such a scheme would not be easy. The moot had hoped that the Green Memorandum might serve as a first draft from which Curtis as draftsman might design the final plan, thereby using work which had been done earlier. But Curtis soon realized that that document—based as it was upon Canadian conditions and experiences—would be of little value in the creation of a plan applicable to the whole Empire. His friends in London suspected as much when the memorandum was first sent to them from South Africa, and Curtis himself was forced to admit it as he traveled through the Dominions. Everywhere he found among Dominion residents a diversity of opinion on imperial matters for which his previous experience had not prepared him. Later, therefore, he was not surprised to find on the blank leaves of those copies of the Memorandum which were returned an extent of criticism which convinced the moot that it was "necessary to re-write it from beginning to end."[43]

Curtis and the moot, now chastened by the discovery that a platform for constitutional reform agreeable both to themselves and to the residents of the Dominions was more difficult to create than they had originally assumed, adjusted their plans accordingly. Following a brief rest Curtis went into retirement to study the information he had acquired in his recent travels and as soon as possible to draft a new statement which hopefully would satisfy all concerned. Shortly thereafter he found a convenient place as Beit Lecturer in Colonial History at Oxford. This position, in addition to providing him with the leisure to work on the new egg, enabled him to bring the gospel of organic union to the young men who it was assumed would one day take their places as leaders of Great Britain and the Empire.[44]

Difficulties with the egg were not the only problems to plague the moot at this time, however. In its own way the journal pre-

43. Lionel Curtis, *Memoranda on Canada and the British Commonwealth* (London: Richard Clay [printer], 1912) , p. xx.

44. "Lionel Curtis," *Round Table*, No. 182 (March, 1956) , p. 106.

sented challenges which were equally pressing. For while Curtis was drifting from place to place in the Dominions Kerr, with the help of those members of the moot who were available, was hammering into shape the *Round Table*, a quarterly meant to be the house organ of the moot and later the herald of the great crusade.

Chapter Eleven. The *Round Table*

Upon his return to London from Canada and the United States in January, 1910, Kerr had found himself exhausted by his travels and badly needing a rest. Even so, he forced himself to complete his report to Milner and his associates and to attend the vitally important meetings in late January at which the tactics of the round table movement were defined. The holiday which followed was a short one, for about the time Curtis left Britain in mid-February on his tour of the Empire, Kerr established himself in London to begin the strenuous task of creating a new magazine.[1]

The matter of living quarters for the young editor presented no problems. His good friend and former superior on the Intercolonial Council, Robert Brand, having recently begun his long association with Lazard Brothers, offered to share with Kerr his bachelor quarters at 14 Wyndham Place. This domestic establishment proved to be very satisfactory. With the later addition of John Dove and Lionel Hichens, it continued until Brand's marriage in 1917 to Phyllis Langhorne, the sister of Mrs. Waldorf Astor.[2]

Editorial offices for the new publication were found at 175 Piccadilly. Here Kerr, with the constant advice and assistance of those of the moot who lived in London, began to repeat many of the steps which he had taken in Johannesburg when he established the *State*. Plans were made to publish quarterly and to entitle the magazine the *Round Table*. Macmillan and Company contracted for the printing, and the price per copy was set at half a crown. Of far greater importance, however, were decisions concerning the contents of the magazine and the nature of the reading public to whom it was addressed. In the meetings of the moot which followed the return of Curtis, Kerr, and Marris from North America these matters had been discussed at length. At that time it had been found impossible to do more than outline policies in the broadest terms, leaving the specific decisions to be made as

1. Butler, *Lothian,* pp. 40–42.
2. Interview with Lord Brand, May 3, 1960.

circumstances required.[3] As the development of the magazine progressed, however, some decision on these questions was found to be necessary. General editorial policy had to be translated into a practical program, one which in this case would harmonize with the activities of Curtis to promote the goals of the movement.

The nature of that practical program was defined in April, 1910. On the twenty-fifth of that month at a moot attended by several Canadian Milnerites Kerr presented a memorandum which specified the sort of magazine which was needed and the steps by which such a publication might be created.[4] Despite an absence of evidence, it seems likely that the provisions of this memorandum were agreed upon five days before at a smaller moot. At this meeting on April 20, Kerr, Oliver, Brand, Craik, and Marris met with Milner, who had recently returned from a six weeks' holiday in Egypt.[5] In light of the contents of Kerr's memorandum there is good reason to suspect that the document which was presented to the moot and its Canadian guests on the twenty-fifth was actually a committee report, threshed out in Milner's presence on the twentieth and worked up into draft form by Kerr. It further seems obvious that Kerr, as he worked on the phrasing of the memorandum, had in mind an audience larger than the moot. The hortatory style and simplified explanation of events and concepts well-known to his associates suggest a desire to convert. He probably thought to create an *aide-memoire* for the moot while at the same time preparing for publication a pamphlet to promote the *Round Table*.[6]

The memorandum began with an argument for "a well-informed and well-balanced periodical review of imperial politics" able to counterbalance the narrow, provincial outlook of the press in both Britain and the Dominions. "Ordinary newspapers and magazines run for profit," Kerr remarked, "are bound to allow the greater part of their space to matters of special interest to the

3. Kerr to Curtis, Oct. 14, 1910, Lothian Papers.
4. Kerr to A. J. Glazebrook, April 25, 1910, Papers of Sir Edmund Walker at the Library of the University of Toronto.
5. Milner's diary, April 20, 1910, Milner Papers.
6. There is no evidence that it was ever published in the form in which it circulated to the moot. Nevertheless, Curtis, in a letter to Kerr, July 21, 1910, mentioned receiving "your . . . printed circulars" concerning the subjects and comments contained in this memorandum.

district in which they circulate, and to treat of imperial and foreign affairs from a local point of view." This condition was made inevitable by the scrappy and politically biased nature of the cable news circulated within the Empire and by the unenlightened attitudes of editors and leader writers who "are not in a position to acquire a real understanding of the world forces playing upon the Empire, while they are only too conscious of teacup storms near by."

There was thus a real need, Kerr insisted, for an informative, balanced publication with a wide circulation among those who determine the editorial policies of the Empire's press.

> What is wanted is a quarterly review, severely detached from the domestic party issues of the day, and written anonymously with the sole aim of exchanging information and ideas about the imperial problem among people interested in all parts of the British dominions.
>
> To achieve its purpose such a review must be produced where the best news from all the world is most easily accessible. This is clearly London, which is also the nerve centre of the Empire. Preliminary arrangements have therefore been made for the publication in London in the near future, of a quarterly review—to be called "The Round Table" or "The Moot." This review will not compete with ordinary magazines. No attempt will be made to obtain a large circulation among the general public by popular methods or flag-wagging. It is intended only for people who are genuinely interested in the problem of imperial organization, and it will therefore deal solely with imperial affairs. So far as can be stated at the present time each number will contain a survey of the internal and external relations of the empire during the preceding three months, and three or four special articles on different aspects of the imperial problem.

But "if the scheme is to be fruitful," Kerr continued, those in London who declared their willingness to absorb the inevitable financial loss must be assured of two conditions:

> In the first place an adequate number of subscribers (minimum 300) must be found in each of the self-governing dominions. Unless it can be ensued [*sic*: ensured] that practically all men of real influence in politics, journalism, business, etc., who are in any way sympathetic, subscribe with the intention of reading the review, it is not worth while making a start.

Secondly, it was necessary that in each Dominion local supporters should establish and maintain at local expense an agency with a paid secretary in charge. These offices, Kerr wrote, "will supply information and articles to the editor, obtain subscribers, and distribute the review in their own countries." It was hoped that in time they might become

> valuable centres through which people interested in imperial poli-
> tics in each dominion could be brought into touch with one
> another and with visitors from outside; and at times when impe-
> rial questions were to the fore they might prove invaluable agen-
> cies for the interchange of ideas between the different parts.

The London office would serve as a sort of clearing house for the whole.

Much depended upon the "initiative, keenness and energy" of the local secretary. "If he fails," Kerr remarked, "nobody else is likely to supply the drive when the first impetus has spent itself." Great care must be exercised, therefore, to find the right sort of person. Along with other qualities he "must know what is really going on in every important sphere of political and economic activity, and exactly where to obtain information when he does not possess it himself." Access to information not ordinarily available seems to have loomed large on Kerr's list of attributes essential to a local secretary:

> The value of the dominion offices, both as they concern the review
> and their local work will depend entirely on their efficiency as
> intelligence bureaus. It is essential that the information they
> transmit to London should be trustworthy, complete, and 'inside.'

Using Canada as an example, Kerr roughly estimated the annual cost of maintaining a Dominion office at between £375 and £660, including the salary of the local secretary.

Kerr's memorandum discussed at the moot of April 25, 1910, is important as much for what it does not say as for what it does. In it there is no reference to two aspects of the movement which were always emphasized by Curtis: the conviction on the part of those promoting the project that some form of imperial consolidation was essential if disintegration was to be prevented and the need for careful, unbiased study of the Imperial Problem by small groups in all parts of the Empire. Kerr's silence on these points may have resulted from a conviction that the two were practically, if not logically, exclusive. Perhaps he and those who took part in framing the memorandum considered it impossible for the moot to act as both advocate and jury in the matter of imperial reorganization. Regardless of his reasons, the fact that in his personal letters and printed material designed to introduce the new magazine Kerr failed to mention these points and that he approached the development of the *Round Table* in the terms found in the paper discussed by the moot on April 25 caused Curtis great uneasiness. In the earliest of a number of surviving letters to Kerr written from the South Pacific Curtis remonstrated with his sedentary associate over these matters, insisting that both Kerr's general approach to the development of the movement and his specific plans for the journal were in conflict with agreements made earlier that year in London. "The moment I got your letters and printed circulars," Curtis wrote, "I realised that since we parted our minds, under the pressure of totally different conditions under which we work, had been diverging until in some respects we were going in diametrically opposite directions."[7] Determined to face these conflicts lest they multiply and thereby destroy the movement, Curtis in this letter sought to define the points upon which he and Kerr differed and to explain what he felt to be the proper role of the magazine.

The heart of the matter concerned a disagreement about methods by which the goal of organic unity could best be achieved. Curtis had always been convinced, he reminded Kerr, that success depended upon unbiased and objective study of the Imperial Problem by carefully chosen groups in each of the Dominions. This, he said, was "the primary conception as to the method of our work which has figured most largely in my own brain from the very outset, and upon which I have worked constantly throughout." In this scheme the proposed magazine served an important though ancillary purpose. From the first it had been agreed that some means of maintaining contact among the groups was needed.

> The magazine was in fact to be, what the name you have chosen 'The Round Table' expresses. Once a quarter students in the five

7. Curtis to Kerr, July 21, 1910, Lothian Papers.

self-governing States and, if possible, in the two principal Dependencies were to communicate information to each other in their own words.

This was all; whatever the magazine might become after the popular crusade was begun, the fact was, according to Curtis, that it was initially conceived of as an esoteric publication of very limited circulation.

Yet it seemed to Curtis that the letters and descriptive material which he recently received from London referred to something altogether different. Nowhere was there reference to an Empire-wide association of study groups intent upon solving the Imperial Problem. Nor could he find a description of a forthcoming periodical devoted solely to the circulation of information and ideas relating to the activities of that association. In fact, he remarked,

> anyone who knew nothing of the movement, but what he learnt from these circulars could scarcely do otherwise than assume that the whole thing was engineered from England and was just a repetition of the pattern so often attempted before, and which have so often failed before.

There hovered over these introductory statements the implication that once again an attempt was being made to use imperial loyalty within the Dominions "to serve the political and even commercial interests of . . . [a group in London] whom I am representing."

The practical difficulties resulting from this situation were, according to Curtis, manifold. For instance,

> in proposing a project of preliminary study, I have always said that the students in each country must be few and their number must be kept down to a few dozens at most. I have gone on to say, that the first and primary purpose of the magazine will be served if it is taken and read by these few dozens.

Kerr, on the other hand, was cutting the ground out from under him by appealing for the greatest number of subscriptions possible. In evidence Curtis quoted from one of Kerr's pamphlets that

> the purpose of the review will not be achieved unless *a great majority of men of real influence* in politics, journalism, business, etc., take it in with the intention of reading it. Efforts are therefore being made to obtain at once a circulation among the people

who count in order that *from the outset it may reach a large number of readers.*[8]

Another instance of conflict cited by Curtis concerned the extent to which the contents of the magazine would originate in the Dominions. It had been his understanding from the very first, Curtis insisted, that the bulk of each issue would consist of articles on local conditions in various parts of the Empire or reports of research conducted by the study groups on some aspect of the Imperial Problem. The London editor and his associates might provide in each number a lead article summarizing the Dominion contributions and commenting upon events of the previous three months as seen from the center of the Empire. The editor's main function, however, was to see to the publication of material sent to him from the local groups and to serve as co-ordinator of the whole project.

But according to Curtis, Kerr seemed to have drifted away from that plan. He referred the editor to a recent letter from London in which Kerr spoke of a need to edit material from the Dominions to make it conform to the editorial policy of the moot. This, said Curtis, would destroy the movement, for it would alienate those on whom success depended—the loyal but intellectually independent colonials who would refuse to see their words trimmed to fit a pattern the exact nature of which they did not understand. Since the writing of that letter, however, Kerr's plans had apparently diverged even farther from the understanding reached the previous January. In the most recent pamphlet sent to him from London "the articles originated in the Dominions had," according to Curtis, "dropped out altogether," leaving the promoters of the magazine open to the charges of devious self-serving which he had sought to pre-empt with his study-group approach.

These and other disagreements about the development of the magazine required prompt attention, Curtis insisted, for the implementation of Kerr's ideas and the circulation of his introductory pamphlets throughout the Dominions would undermine the whole movement. Canadians, South Africans, and New Zealanders to whom he had talked would surely become suspicious of a

8. Emphasis provided by Curtis.

project which bore all the markings of a scheme to manipulate Dominion opinion for some devious purpose.

Curtis's letter of July 21 apparently had an effect upon Kerr and his associates in London. Basic differences remained to trouble the development of the movement throughout its formative period, but steps were quickly taken to paper over the most obvious fissures. In describing these modifications to Curtis, Kerr admitted the extent to which the two had drifted apart in their thinking.

> The truth of the matter of course is that nobody had thought out sufficiently clearly what the Magazine was to be like before you left England. If we had reduced the practical proposal to your present idea we should never have started the Magazine until you had perambulated the Empire far further than you could have done last June. Last February we all of us contemplated its circulation in Canada, the minutes of the moot contemplate its distribution to all editors and statesmen! That being so, as I have explained before, we had practically no option but to do what we have done. But in order that the Magazine should compromise you as little as possible in the future selection of your group we have confined our activities . . . solely to the Magazine. . . . Apart from the fact that the decision of the moot to start a magazine at once tied our hands, I think that the Magazine may do much good apart from its service as a link between selected enthusiasts all over the world. If last February we had agreed that the Magazine was only to fulfil the part which you propose for it in New Zealand I think there would have been no question that we should have agreed to postpone the first publication, at any rate till the end of this year and possibly until after you had made another expedition to Canada, distributing memoranda and so forth to serve as links between the groups meanwhile.[9]

In practical terms the adjustment produced a compromise. The moot decided that the new magazine was to receive the widest possible distribution, and, as we have seen, Curtis was instructed to secure as many subscriptions as possible in the Dominions. In the format of the *Round Table,* on the other hand, one can detect an effort by the London group to meet the needs expressed by Curtis in his letter to Kerr on July 21. As Curtis wished, each issue was to contain an article from each of the nations within the

9. Kerr to Curtis (copy), Oct. 14, 1910, Lothian Papers.

Empire along with one or more articles concerning imperial conditions as a whole. As a matter of policy the material from London, like that from the Dominion groups, would be published anonymously, for it was assumed that all articles would be committee projects. In the tradition of the kindergarten in South Africa, one hand might produce the final draft, but the dialectical process by which the work was created would be collaborative. "Under such a system," John Dove remarked years later, "the writer's name hardly matters."[10]

The first number of the *Round Table* appeared in November, 1910. Subtitled "A Quarterly Review of the Politics of the British Empire," it contained a lead article concerning the potential threat to the Empire posed by an increasingly militant Germany followed by reports from correspondents on local conditions in Canada, South Africa, and Great Britain. Prefacing the number was an article entitled "The Round Table," which purported to explain the origins of the magazine and the policies guiding its development.[11] Valuable insights into the thinking of the editor and his associates may be derived from this statement, for it illustrates the limited extent to which they intended to take the reader into their confidence.

According to the editor, the creation of another magazine in an admittedly overcrowded field was justified because of inadequate news coverage of imperial affairs. Existing magazines and newspapers, either by design or unavoidable circumstance, were not serving to dispel an all-pervading ignorance about affairs in other parts of the Empire or about imperial fortunes as a whole. "This ignorance naturally leads to misgivings, and people are frequently involved in disputes and controversies about the Empire which in most cases would immediately be solved if the facts were known." Overcoming this condition was no simple matter, however.

> That would be a task to be entrusted to a council of the wisest men to be found. But we are practical people who dislike creating governments to rule over us unless we are quite certain that we shall be the better for them, and we have got on very well hitherto with an arrangement by which the Imperial Government has no

10. Dove, "The Round Table: A Mystery Probed," p. 4.
11. Pp. 1–6. Butler, *Lothian*, p. 323, assigns authorship to Kerr.

authority over the larger part of the Empire which it may be called upon to defend.[12]

Having thus obliquely disassociated the movement from those groups which would promote radical constitutional change within the Empire, Kerr proceeded to explain how his publication intended to mitigate the disputes and controversies resulting from widespread ignorance of imperial affairs:

> Failing, therefore, a body which can speak for every part, we must contrive a makeshift, and the makeshift is *The Round Table*. The aim of *The Round Table* is to present a regular account of what is going on throughout the King's dominions, written with first-hand knowledge and entirely free from the bias of local political issues, and to provide a means by which the common problems which confront the Empire as a whole, can be discussed also with knowledge and without bias. For that, in the opinion of the promoters, who reside in all parts of the Empire, is what is most needed at the present day.[13]

To emphasize the impartial nature of the magazine the editor asserted that

> *The Round Table* does not aim at propounding new theories or giving voice to ingenious speculations. It will serve its purpose if it contributes to the better understanding of the problems of the Empire and to their solution, and if no one ever raises the charge against it that it has distorted the truth for its own ends.[14]

Nevertheless, Kerr wrote,

> The founders of *The Round Table* have an uneasy sense that times are changing, and that the methods of yesterday will not serve in the competition of to-morrow. They feel that if the various communities of the Empire have common interests they are singularly badly equipped to pursue them. If there is a conflict between the political systems of the British Empire and of Germany, as the writer on foreign affairs thinks, . . . it is an anomaly that there should be no means of marshalling the whole strength and resources of the Empire effectively behind its will, when its mind is made up. . . . If there is a common problem, . . . there should be some other means than the circulation of formal official despatches, or a meeting of Premiers only once in four years,

12. *Ibid.*, p. 2.
13. *Ibid.*
14. *Ibid.*, p. 6.

whereby it can be publicly discussed, and a decision quickly reached.[15]

Only to this extent did Kerr and his associates admit to the reader that the promoters of the *Round Table* were interested in changing the constitutional structure of the Empire. They were even less candid in admitting their plan to submit the Imperial Problem to the scrutiny of study groups scattered throughout the Empire. Despite the central part this scheme played in the thinking of the moot and particularly Curtis, no reference to study groups, moots, eggs, and ultimate crusades to reform the Empire can be found in Kerr's preface unless one could so interpret the remark that those who were founding the magazine hoped gradually to "accumulate the material on which a sound judgement of the Imperial problem can be based."[16]

With this rather disingenuous introductory statement the *Round Table* began publication. Though circulation figures have never been made public, it is clear that as the years passed the magazine gained a respectable following both in Britain and throughout the Empire. The Great War formed a watershed in the development of the *Round Table,* however. Though its format remained the same, in succeeding years its purpose changed. With the decline in chiliastic enthusiasm for organic unity during and after the war, the magazine became increasingly involved in describing the events leading to the establishment of independent nations from former British colonies and in analyzing international developments which only indirectly related to the Empire. Gradually it became one of the most widely respected English-language publications devoted to the general topic of international politics.

It is the few years of *Round Table* publication which came

15. *Ibid.,* pp. 3 f.
16. *Ibid.,* p. 5. For several years thereafter each number carried the following "note" inside the title page: "*The Round Table* is a co-operative enterprise conducted by people who dwell in all parts of the British Empire. Their aim is to publish once a quarter a comprehensive review of Imperial politics, entirely free from the bias of local party issues. The affairs of *The Round Table* in each portion of the Empire are in the sole charge of local residents, who are also responsible for all articles on the politics of their own country. It is hoped that in this way *The Round Table* will reflect the current opinions of all parts about Imperial problems, and at the same time present a survey of them as a whole. Opinions and articles of a party character will be rigidly excluded."

before World War I, however, which are germane to this study. A composite of moot attitudes for that time may be derived from the lead articles which appeared in the early numbers. According to Kerr's biographer, the editor wrote two articles for each of the first three issues and a total of ten for the first eight numbers.[17] But other members of the moot made contributions as well. In fact, from hints found in the minutes of prewar moots one might conclude that virtually everyone who was active in the affairs of the London group submitted material.[18] None of these articles, however, could be considered the work of an unaided individual. Even those of the editor were stamped with the impress of the collegial system by which the kindergarten had created its works of inquiry and propaganda in South Africa. Early moot minutes show that much time was devoted to the discussion of articles drafted by one of the members and previously circulated among the others. As a result, the pages of the *Round Table* display a remarkable consistency. Though articles submitted by Dominion groups varied greatly and even conflicted with those originating in London, the editorial position of the magazine remained throughout the years before World War I much as had been agreed upon at early moots. The reader was constantly reminded of deficiencies in imperial administration which imperiled the future of the Empire. The irrational organization of the British parliament, the ineffectual nature of Imperial Conferences, and the injustice of a system which gave to Britain war-or-peace authority over supposedly self-governing nations were frequently examined. In fact, the whole body of Milnerian criticism was rehearsed time after time by Milner's disciples, and usually the Milnerian solution was offered. It was time, they insisted, for all elements of responsible opinion in all parts of the Empire to face up to the "growing necessity for constitutional reform." Some means had to be found by which illogicalities, inconsistencies, and

17. Butler, *Lothian*, p. 323.
18. Curiously enough, Curtis seems to have been an exception. In 1917 he claimed that "personally I have never written a word in it," *A Letter to the People of India*, p. 50. And in her bibliography of Curtis, Ruth Pryor lists nothing of his in the *Round Table* prior to 1948. "Bibliography of the Works of Lionel George Curtis: A Provisional List to the Present Date Submitted in Part Fulfilment of the Requirements for the University of London Diploma in Librarianship," May, 1955.

injustices of the present system might be overcome if the British connection was to be preserved.

In justifying this need for constitutional reform, however, the *Round Table* refused to become committed on one of the central issues of Edwardian politics which many considered to be an integral part of the movement for imperial unity. At no time did the magazine take a position on the matter of tariff reform. This cause, for which Joseph Chamberlain had resigned from the government in 1903 and to which Milner had devoted a part of his time and attention after his return from South Africa, was to most imperial enthusiasts the essential first step leading to effective reform. The *Round Table* disagreed. "The problem of Empire is a political problem, to be determined not by the standard of wealth, but by that of national well-being." This being so, "neither the past history nor the future destiny of the Empire can be tested in the economic crucible. A great nation cannot be governed 'on the maxims of the counter.' "[19]

This refusal of the *Round Table* to adopt the economic determinist attitude of the tariff reformers is difficult to explain in light of the strong support which Chamberlain's campaign received from some of the moot, particularly Amery, Oliver, and Milner. The matter undoubtedly provoked many heated discussions at moots in both South Africa and England. No records exist, however, to explain how and why it was decided to insist on the pages of the *Round Table* that tariff reform and organic unity were not necessarily two sides of the same coin. In the absence of documents one is thus restricted to speculation. The most likely explanation rests not in any opposition—or even indifference—to preference among members of the moot but in the belief that commitment one way or the other would be inexpedient. A cornerstone of the round table movement upon which all hopes for success depended was the conviction that it should always remain aloof from the political controversies which beset Great Britain. Time and time again members of the moot had explained to each other that organic unity of the Empire would suffer the fate of a hundred good causes which remained unfulfilled unless it could

19. "Ethics of Empire," *Round Table*, No. 11 (June, 1913), p. 485.

be lifted above the sordid squabbles of political factions. Only by being presented as a cause too vital for party controversy could organic unity win the support of the mass of the British people. But equally important was the need to convince leaders of Dominion opinion that they were not being used as pawns in a political contest at Westminster. Members of the moot assured each other that the merest hint that there was a connection between the round table movement and the political ambitions of any faction in Great Britain would wreck the movement in the Dominions. These practical reasons for shunning any sort of connection with a tariff reform movement which was deeply involved in the complex party struggles of Edwardian Britain were reinforced by the record of Chamberlain's campaign. By the time Milner's supporters had begun the creation of the round table movement it had become clear to perceptive observers that the great mass of the British people opposed any program which threatened to increase the cost of living. Opponents of tariff reform skilfully characterized it as a protectionist device of the manufacturers which would result in the much dreaded "dear loaf." For better or worse, therefore, tariff reform had proved to be a dangerous argument for those whose primary goal was the achievement of greater imperial unity.

Whether or not this explanation accurately reflects the reasons why the moot refrained from either supporting or condemning tariff reform, the fact remains that in the pages of the *Round Table* the ardent disciples of the late Colonial Secretary could find little comfort. This undoubtedly cost the round table movement a great amount of support, particularly in Great Britain. Among those who otherwise might have been expected to play a part in the movement there were many who considered the position of the *Round Table* on preference to be inexcusable. Austen Chamberlain, who must be numbered among those in this group, left a record of his feelings. In a letter to his stepmother he described a dinner in 1913 attended by a group of leading Milnerites at which he spoke on the relationship between tariff reform and imperial union:

> I went there determined to let them know as politely as I could that while they had done a lot of good work, they had also, in my

opinion, done a lot of mischief and to beg them in future not to "crab" *any* movement which led in the direction of Imperial Union. I expect some of them did not like it and it was not exactly a proper guest speech, but I am sick of being told that this or that Round Table man or the Round Table as a whole does not want Preference. It is really all traceable to Curtis, of whom they have a tremendously high opinion, who is certainly very much in earnest and wholly unselfish, but seems to me to think that he discovered in 1909 what Father preached from 1895 onwards, and because he had a share in framing the South African Constitution thinks that he can settle a policy for us on every conceivable subject. If the cobbler would stick to his last, I should have no complaint, but he at once annoys and amuses me when he tells me that what Birmingham needs is a parliament for the midland counties, and he does not amuse me at all, but simply irritates me—nay rather, angers me—when, because he thinks he can get organic union without our policy [preference], I have him flung at my head at every turn as saying that Preference is unnecessary, undesirable, bad. His business is, on his own showing, to encourage *every* movement towards Union and to discourage none.[20]

The editorial consistency of the early *Round Table* is especially remarkable in light of the personal difficulties experienced by Kerr in the years just before World War I. Less than a year after the appearance of the first number he began to suffer from a series of maladies—mostly mental—which denied to the new magazine the editorial continuity so important to the development of a young publication. In the fall of 1911 Kerr set off on a round-the-world tour on behalf of the *Round Table*. His purpose was to arrange for correspondents, promote circulation, and establish in some of the African and Asian colonies the sorts of contacts made by Curtis in the white Dominions. The trip had only just begun, however, when Kerr realized that he was suffering from "I suppose . . . what they call brain-fag."[21] Attributing this condition simply to overwork in South Africa and since, he continued his travels through the Mediterranean, the Near East, India, Southeast Asia, the China coast and Japan, and finally Canada and the United States. He even managed to draft two articles for the

20. Quoted in Sir Austen Chamberlain, *Politics from Inside: An Epistolary Chronicle 1906–1914* (London, 1936), p. 553. Leo Amery's estrangement from the round table movement over the tariff reform issue is examined in chap. xii below.
21. Kerr to Brand, Dec. 28, 1911. Quoted in Butler, *Lothian*, p. 49.

Round Table under these strained circumstances.[22] A visit to a nerve specialist in New York, however, convinced Kerr that treatment was necessary. His arrival in London in August, 1912,[23] was followed in a matter of days by his departure for a sanitorium in Germany. "It is the penalty for 5 years overwork," he wrote, "and a week for each is not much of a price, if it means a permanent cure."[24]

But the cure was not permanent. Continuing mental fatigue combined with an unhappy romance and religious doubts about his Roman Catholic faith rendered him still unfit upon his return to London to resume his editorial duties. In January, 1913, he went to St. Moritz on what turned out to be the beginning of another year and a half of inactivity. The moot gained partial compensation for the loss of Kerr's services, however, for during this period of enforced inactivity Kerr developed an intimate friendship with Mr. and Mrs. Waldorf Astor. Lord and Lady Astor (he succeeded to his father's title in 1919) were quickly drawn into the moot circle where they played an active part in round table affairs. As time passed their relationship to the group became closer. Brand's marriage to Phyllis Langhorne (Lady Astor's sister) and Kerr's conversion to Christian Science (Lady Astor's faith) were partly responsible. Soon Cliveden, the Astor estate near London, became the center of moot activities and the scene of frequent weekends at which the round table group was joined by a varied assortment of guests drawn by the splendor of the house and the wit of the hostess. It should be pointed out here, however, that the connection between the Astors and the moot really has no place in this study, for their association with the group was a wartime and postwar development.[25]

It was not until two months before the beginning of the war that Kerr felt well enough to return to 175 Piccadilly and the editorial desk of the *Round Table*.[26] During his intermittent

22. Butler, *Lothian*, p. 323.
23. Milner's diary, Aug. 27, 1912, Milner Papers.
24. Quoted in Butler, *Lothian*, p. 50.
25. Useful antidotes to the myth of the "Cliveden Set" and its pernicious influence upon British affairs may be found in Butler and also in Maurice Collis, *Nancy Astor: An Informal Biography* (New York, 1960).
26. Minutes for the moot of May 30–June 2, 1914. (These minutes from January, 1913, are in the files of the *Round Table* editorial office.)

absence over a period of almost three years the affairs of the magazine were directed by other members of the moot. Kerr retained his title as editor until January, 1917, when he resigned to become private secretary to Lloyd George, but during the early part of his absence Brand and Oliver ran the *Round Table*. And in June, 1913, the moot appointed as joint editor Edward Grigg (later Lord Altrincham), a New College friend of many of the group and at that time the imperial affairs editor of *The Times*.[27]

The impact of the *Round Table* in the years before World War I is difficult to gauge. Circulation figures, even if they were available, would be of little value in assessing the influence of a publication which denied having any interest in large numbers of subscriptions. Scattered comments have survived, however, which suggest that the magazine quickly gained the respect of that group at which it was aimed—the shapers of policy and opinion in both Great Britain and the Dominions. Less than two years after the *Round Table* began publication, the *Spectator,* in commenting upon its integrity and freedom from party domination, remarked that it had already passed "from an adventure into an institution."[28] By the middle of 1915 the American ambassador was prompted to write that *"The Round Table,* is the best review, I dare say, in the world."[29] Perhaps the highest accolade—certainly the sincerest form of flattery—came from a fellow imperialist and onetime associate of the kindergarten, Richard Jebb. Unable to accept what Kerr called the pistol policy of organic union or disintegration of the Empire, Jebb refused to participate in round table activities. He worked instead for a form of imperial unity based on what he sometimes called association and sometimes co-operation. This he defined as a family of free nations bound together by ties of loyalty and tradition and by an effective system of imperial preference. The effectiveness of the *Round Table* so impressed Jebb, however, that in 1912 he began to discuss with Fabian Ware, a former subordinate of Milner in South Africa and from 1905 to 1911 the editor of the *Morning Post,* the possibility

27. Minutes for the moot of May 28, 1913.
28. "The Round Table," *Spectator,* Sept. 14, 1912, p. 364.
29. Walter Hines Page to Arthur W. Page, July 25, 1915. Quoted in Burton J. Hendrick, *The Life and Letters of Walter H. Page* (Garden City and New York, 1924), II, 84.

of creating a similar publication to promote association.[30] By the following year the plan had begun to take form. "What seems to me to be required," Jebb wrote in September of 1913,

> is . . . that our view should have some definite organ of publicity to which our adherents or critics could look regularly for comments on current affairs of Britannic interest. The centralists possess such an organ in the *Round Table,* which was founded for the purpose of combating the ideas and influence of the other school.[31]

In May of 1914 Jebb's organ of publicity was born. Called the *Britannic Review,* his answer to the *Round Table* served for a short time as a soundingboard for associationist views. The *Britannic Review,* however, did not survive World War I.[32]

30. Jebb to Ware (copy) , June 2, 1912; Ware to Jebb, Dec. 24, 1912, Jebb Papers.
31. Jebb to the editor of the *Nineteenth Century and After* (copy) , Sept. 25, 1913, Jebb Papers.
32. Miller, *Richard Jebb,* p. 26.

Chapter Twelve. The failure of the movement

Before examining the climax of the round table movement—Curtis's labors to complete the egg and the ironic circumstances which made impossible its implementation—it is necessary to consider the careers of those members of the kindergarten who remained behind when Curtis, Kerr, and Brand departed South Africa in 1909. Even before South African unification was achieved, three of the *kinder* had decided to make their home there. Hugh Wyndham was farming in the southwest Transvaal, and both Richard Feetham and Patrick Duncan were members of the Johannesburg bar. All three remained active in South African politics during succeeding years. Though they attended moots when in England and retained their early intimacy with other members of the kindergarten, they nevertheless played a negligible part in round table affairs.

The rest of those who stayed behind in 1909, however, were back in England by early 1911. The first to return was John Dove. The physical collapse which followed his trip to Australia to assist Curtis restricted his activities for years, making it impossible for him to attend moots or assist in the establishment of the round table movement.[1] By the last year of the war, however, his health had recovered sufficiently for him to serve in France in the Intelligence Department. In 1920 he became editor of the *Round Table*, and from then until his death in 1934 he remained at the heart of all round table activities.[2]

Dougal Malcolm, Lord Selborne's private secretary throughout his tenure as High Commissioner, returned to England in 1910. Following his marriage in June of that year he and his bride left for Ottawa, where he served for a little more than a year as secretary to Lord Grey, the Governor-General of Canada.[3] By 1912 he was back in London working at the Treasury, but the

1. According to moot minutes preserved at the *Round Table* editorial offices, he attended only three moots from January, 1913, to December, 1919.
2. "John Dove," *Round Table*, No. 95 (June, 1934), pp. 464–65.
3. Robinson's diary, June 20, 1910, Dawson Papers.

following year he received an offer to become a director of the British South Africa Company, Rhodes's great enterprise created to marry capitalism to idealistic imperialism in central Africa. In later years these responsibilities took Malcolm away from London for long periods of time. Even so, he attended almost every moot from 1913 to 1920, and he remained an active participant in round table affairs until his death in 1955.[4]

Perry and Robinson, on the other hand, remained in South Africa almost a year after Malcolm's return to England. As secretary of the Rand Native Labour Association and editor of the Johannesburg *Star* respectively, they were active in South African political affairs until their departure. Both, in fact, were keenly interested in the outcome of the initial election of the Union legislature, which occurred in September, 1910. As loyal Milnerites they were of course eager to see a victory for the Unionist party over a coalition of parties supporting the Botha government. This interest was especially acute inasmuch as three of their kindergarten colleagues—Duncan, Wyndham, and Feetham—were standing for election. In his diary Robinson left ample evidence of the intense effort which he and others made on behalf of the Unionist cause in general and the candidacy of his friends in particular. There were almost daily references to political meetings and conversations and to editorials written for the *Star* in support of the Unionist Party.[5]

In these months before the election Robinson frequently recorded in his diary comments about a plan on which he and Perry were working to establish a new magazine. Apparently unable to assume direction of the publication themselves, they recruited as their partners two men identified by Robinson only as Macleod and Lloyd.[6] These four met several times a week from June to September, 1910, to discuss the development of what was at first called the "bulletin"[7] and later the "Observer."[8] Progress was

4. "Dougal Orme Malcolm," *Round Table*, No. 181 (Dec., 1955), pp. 3–5.
5. See also Robinson to Milner, Sept. 18, 1910, Milner Papers.
6. According to the Director of Archives, Pretoria, they were almost certainly Lewis Rose Macleod, an Australian journalist who came to South Africa in 1905, and A. W. Lloyd, a cartoonist and journalist. In 1911 Macleod and Lloyd founded the *Sunday Post* (Director of Archives, Pretoria, to G. A. le Roux, May 2, 1963).
7. Robinson's diary, June 3, 1910, Dawson Papers.
8. *Ibid.*, July 28, 1910, and thereafter.

slow, however, for it was not until the week of the election that the first number of the weekly *Observer* appeared.[9] This initial issue contained—in addition to news of the world of society, sports, fashion, and entertainment—a considerable amount of political comment favorable to the Unionist cause and to the development of stronger imperial ties. The life of the *Observer* was short. It lasted for only thirty-four issues, the last appearing on April 27, 1911.[10]

In considering this unsuccessful venture one wonders if it had anything at all to do with the round table movement and the campaign for organic union. The answer is not clear. On the negative side, there is no evidence of any direct connection. Nowhere in the letters, memoranda, minutes, and diaries seen by this writer is there any mention of the *Observer* except in the diary of Robinson. On the other hand, there is circumstantial evidence to suggest that the *Observer,* like the emigration schemes and the plan to influence Ward's presentation at the 1911 Imperial Conference, may have been one of a number of peripheral projects which from time to time interested the members of the moot. Curtis was in South Africa during the weeks just before the first entry in Robinson's diary about the "Bulletin." He had come down to attend the last session of the Transvaal Legislative Council and to organize support in South Africa for the round table scheme before sailing for New Zealand and Australia. It may be that he originated the plan, promoting the necessary money from wealthy South African Milnerites and winning the assistance of Robinson and Perry.

Though the matter of the *Observer* and its relation to the round table is obscure and will probably remain so, it is clear that Perry left South Africa shortly after the appearance of the first issue of the publication. Following the election of September 15, in which Feetham's defeat only partly dampened the happiness of the Milnerites over the victory of Duncan and Wyndham, Perry resigned as secretary of the Rand Native Labour Association to return to England. With his departure from South Africa his

9. Vol. I, No. 1 is on file in the Library of Parliament, Cape Town. According to the librarian there, inquiry in other archives failed to uncover other issues. (T. Roos, Librarian, Library of Parliament, Cape Town, to this writer, Oct. 5, 1963.)

10. Director of Archives, Pretoria, to G. A. le Roux, May 2, 1963.

career becomes obscure and his connection with his old friends of the kindergarten tenuous. Apparently Brand was able to find a place for him with Lazard Brothers, for in early 1912 he left England for Montreal to represent the firm there.[11] There are references to his having visited England from time to time during subsequent years, and on those occasions he was included in moot activities.[12] But there is no indication that he took more than a passive interest in the development of the movement in Canada. James Eayrs does not even mention Perry in his account of the origins of the round table movement in Canada.[13] Vincent Massey, who was active in the movement in those years, remembers him but adds that "I cannot recall his having taken any part in the formation of groups."[14] Clearly, Perry drifted to the very edges of the movement after his departure from South Africa and even seems to have gradually lost contact with all of the kindergarten save Brand. His death in February, 1935, went unnoticed in the pages of the *Round Table*.[15]

Robinson, like Perry, left South Africa shortly after the Union election of September, 1910. Relinquishing his editorial duties at the *Star*, he sailed for home, arriving in London in the early days of 1911. His diary contains no explanation for this move, nor does it indicate his plans for the future. According to *The History of "The Times,"*[16] however, the latter issue was settled almost immediately upon his return with his employment at Printing House Square. George Earle Buckle, editor of *The Times* since 1884, was then failing in health. But more importantly, he was finding it increasingly difficult to get along with Lord Northcliffe, who in 1908 had come to the financial rescue of the foundering paper by buying an enormous amount of stock. In January, 1911, therefore, Northcliffe instructed C. F. Moberly Bell, the managing director, to begin a search for Buckle's replacement. Attention quickly centered upon Robinson.

11. Robinson's diary, Feb. 17, 1912, Dawson Papers.
12. Moot minutes show that he attended eight meetings from 1913 to 1921.
13. James Eayrs, "The Round Table Movement in Canada, 1909–1920," *Can. Hist. Rev.*, XXXVIII (March, 1957), 1–20.
14. The Right Honorable Vincent Massey to author, Aug. 2, 1961.
15. The month and year of Perry's death were supplied by Mrs. Henry Parker, former secretary to the editor of the *Round Table*.
16. Vol. III: *The Twentieth Century Test 1884–1912* (New York, 1947), pp. 741–42.

The former Johannesburg Correspondent, Geoffrey Dawson (then Robinson), a young man who had been serving *The Times* since 1906, had permanently returned to London at Christmas 1910. He possessed the advantage of Northcliffe's acquaintance. He had naturally looked into the office, seen Bell and told him that as he was still interested in Imperial problems he was prepared to continue working for the paper in any new capacity that might be open and agreeable. Having reported these facts to Northcliffe, Bell was instructed to try him in a position in the Imperial and Foreign Department. Dawson was invited to Sutton Place [Northcliffe's country house] and there talked to at every available moment of an entire week-end about a place on *The Times* that might be his. On February 14, 1911, Dawson came into the office on trial for, it was explained, a possibly high editorial position in the not distant future.[17]

The high editorial position mentioned by Northcliffe was not long in coming. In an effort to infuse new blood into the anemic newspaper, Northcliffe and John Walter IV, proprietor of *The Times* Publishing Company, decided in 1912 to delay no longer in forcing retirement upon Buckle, the last of the "old gang" which held sway during a generation of decline. On July 28, 1912, Robinson was notified by the proprietor that he would become editor in September.[18]

Robinson was of course not the first Milnerite to serve at Printing House Square. Years before his arrival, Leo Amery had come to report the negotiations in South Africa between the Transvaal Republic and the British government. He had stayed to head the contingent of *The Times* correspondents covering the Boer War and then to work in the Foreign and Imperial Department while writing most of the seven volume history of that conflict published by the *Times*.[19] Amery had resigned from the staff to enter politics, however, by the time of Robinson's return to London. Thus the two were never staff associates at Printing House Square. Their careers with *The Times* were nevertheless interrelated to a remarkable degree. It was, in fact, on the advice of Amery that Moberly Bell appointed Amery's good friend and All Souls col-

17. *Ibid.*
18. *Ibid.*, p. 768.
19. Leo Amery, ed., *The Times History of the War in South Africa,* 7 vols.

league, Robinson, a South African correspondent in 1906.[20] And according to Amery, it was he who urged Robinson's name on Northcliffe when the latter was searching for a successor to Buckle. Northcliffe first offered the job to him, Amery recorded in his memoirs. "I declined, but suggested Geoffrey Robinson (Dawson) whose journalistic capacity as editor of the Johannesburg *Star* had greatly impressed me while I was out there."[21]

Another loyal Milnerite at Printing House Square was Edward William Grigg. A New College friend of almost all the kindergarten and from June, 1913, until the war a joint editor of the *Round Table*, Grigg first became associated with *The Times* in 1899. He became Buckle's secretary in 1903, left *The Times* in 1905 to travel throughout the Empire, and served for a year as assistant to J. L. Garvin, at that time the editor of the *Outlook*. In 1908, however, Grigg returned to *The Times* to take charge of imperial affairs so that Amery might devote his full time to the completion of the history of the Boer War. From then until the outbreak of war in 1914 "Grigg was responsible for Imperial affairs, and most of the leading articles on the Empire which appeared between 1909 and 1913 were from his pen."[22]

In the early years of the twentieth century the editorial attitude of *The Times* concerning matters relating to the Empire underwent a noticeable change. The rather reluctant approval of colonial expansion only when it was thought to be economically essential gave way to expressions favoring imperialism as a positive good. In the words of *The History of "The Times,"* "while in Victorian times the paper took little pleasure in 'painting the map red,' it later foresaw that British civilization, prosperity and power, firmly established in the four corners of the earth, would justify itself in its capacity as a guarantor of peace."[23] This gradual conversion to the idealistic imperialism of Chamberlain and Milner of course affected the editorial position concerning specific issues confronting the British people. In the years before World

20. *The History of "The Times,"* Vol. IV: *The 150th Anniversary and Beyond 1912–1948* (London, 1952), p. 11.
21. Leo Amery, *My Political Life*, I, 324.
22. *History of "The Times,"* IV, 17. For a guarded account of his relationship to the round table movement, see "Edward, Lord Altrincham," *Round Table*, No. 182 (March, 1956), pp. 110–12.
23. *History of "The Times,"* IV, 1–2.

War I *The Times* was thus found on the side of improved communication between the nations of the Empire, a greatly strengthened navy, Dominion co-operation in matters of imperial defense, a sympathetic examination of Chamberlain's demand for imperial preference, and fundamental reform of the imperial constitution in the interest of imperial unity. The paper opposed self-government for the former Boer Republics so soon after the South African War, home rule for the Irish, closer relations between Canada and the United States, and naïve faith in the power of sentiment to hold the Empire together.[24] *The Times*, in other words, came to have opinions on imperial matters which were almost the same, point for point, as those of the Milnerites of the round table movement.

Was this similarity of outlook simply a natural occurrence which resulted from the historical circumstances of the time? Or, was it rather a result of a conscious effort by Robinson, Amery, and Grigg—and other Milnerites on the staff such as A. W. Jose in Australia and (Sir) John Willison in Canada—to use the prestige and considerable influence of *The Times* to promote the goals of the moot? Of course no definitive answers to these questions are possible. Several fragments of information do exist, however, which suggest that members of the moot viewed *The Times* with the same sort of proprietary interest which they had previously shown for the Johannesburg *Star* and certain other South African papers over which they had influence. These bits of evidence indicate that on a number of occasions decisions were made within the moot which, probably unknown to Northcliffe, molded the editorial attitudes of *The Times*.

One such example is found in a letter of congratulations written by Oliver to Robinson upon the announcement of his appointment as editor.

> I think you had better found a sort of little 'India Council' for yourself consisting of wise Philip, Socratic Bob, & the indomitable policeman [G. L. Craik, the chief constable of the metropolitan police?]. You can invite me when the discussions are not too serious & Curtis when they are not too [word indecipherable].[25]

24. *Ibid.*, pp. 1–34.
25. Oliver to Robinson, Aug. 8, 1912, Dawson Papers.

In these remarks Oliver may have been attempting only to be humorous. It should be noted, however, that Oliver was an elitist who despised democracy and looked with optimism on the ability of a small group of men with vision and character to carry the day.[26] It thus would have been in keeping with his character if he had been serious. The "India Council," however, never materialized.

Moot influence at Printing House Square was further demonstrated by a note recorded in the minutes of a moot held in early January, 1917. At that meeting discussion centered around a recent round table study of German economic policy. For various reasons it was thought best not to publish it in the *Round Table*. It was decided instead that it should appear in the pages of *The Times*.[27]

The most direct connection in these years between the moot and *The Times*, however, developed from the dual career of Edward Grigg. Until May, 1913, Grigg was employed full-time in the foreign and imperial department of *The Times*. At a moot on May 28, however, he was chosen joint editor of the *Round Table*. It is the conditions of his new employment which are important here: in return for an annual salary of £1,000 Grigg was expected to take charge of the moot publication while retaining his editorial position at Printing House Square. In fact, his work on the staff of *The Times* was to be an important part of his service to the moot. According to the minutes, he was to

> write two articles a week, or their equivalent, on colonial subjects [for *The Times*], and to advise the Editor of the Times on colonial correspondence; but . . . any remuneration received by him from The Times to be deducted from the above-mentioned salary.[28]

From mid 1913 to 1914 when he went to France on military service, Edward Grigg was thus employed by the moot to influence the editorial policies of the Empire's most influential newspaper as he prepared for press the quarterly numbers of the *Round Table*, of which he remained nominal editor until 1916.

In the years just before and during World War I the members

26. See Oliver to Milner, Dec. 26, 1914, Milner Papers.
27. Minutes of the moot of Jan. 4, 1917.
28. Minutes of the moot of May 28, 1913.

of the moot were of course frequently together on social occasions. The friendships of Oxford and South Africa had if anything grown stronger with the passage of time.[29] It is probable, therefore, that much of business of the movement was handled informally at such meetings. Official meetings of the moot nevertheless played an important part in the development of the movement, for it was at these moots that the full membership of the group was brought together once a month to review developments and give direction to the editor and general secretary. These moots were frequently held late in the afternoon at the *Round Table* offices, 175 Piccadilly. But when the number expected was large, or when it was thought that the meeting might extend into the evening, the moot convened for dinner at Brooks's Club, the Cavendish Hotel, or the London house of one of the better established members. Moot weekends in the country were frequent, with visits to Hatfield House as guests of Lord and Lady Salisbury, to Checkendon, the Berkshire home of Oliver, and after 1913 to Cliveden.[30]

Membership in the moot was flexible. Like the kindergarten before it, the moot had no rigid organizational structure or membership requirements. As a result, there was a certain amount of fluidity, especially in the early days. Some, in fact, entered the movement only to drift away shortly thereafter. At the core of the organization, however, there was a basic membership which was remarkably stable. This "inner moot," as it was sometimes called, consisted of Lords Milner and Selborne, those members of the kindergarten who had returned from South Africa, and several close associates like Amery, Grigg, Oliver, and Craik. They attended meetings regularly, did most of the work, and provided the continuity which kept the organization alive. Before the beginning of the war two new names were added to the list of the inner moot: they were the scholars and publicists, Reginald Coupland and (Sir) Alfred Zimmern. In later years they both became indispensable to the organization, providing energy and drive which

29. Robinson's diary, as in South African days, recorded almost daily meetings with old kindergarten friends and fellow members of the moot.

30. This paragraph, and the one which follows, are based upon information derived from the diaries of Milner and Robinson, and the minutes of moots on file at the editorial offices of the *Round Table*.

partly compensated for the waning enthusiasm of several of the original members. The remaining membership was very irregular in attendance. It consisted in the main of returning *kinder* and visiting members of Dominion round table groups. Though always welcome at moots, they had little to contribute and in no way affected the progress of the organization.

There was in those early years only one defection of real importance to the round table movement. The loss of Leo Amery's energy and incisive thinking was keenly felt by the moot. Though he was active in the establishment of the movement and continued to attend moots from time to time until the end of the war, Amery gradually fell out of sympathy with the ideas which dominated the movement. Curtis's insistence that the Empire must unify organically or face dissolution was to Amery unrealistic and likely to provoke just the sort of disaster which it was intended to prevent.[31] But more serious than this to Amery was the attitude of the majority of the moot towards imperial preference. As a loyal supporter of Chamberlain's crusade, he was convinced that tariff reform was "the master key to the whole problem." He was certain, therefore, that ignoring "the question of Empire economic co-operation" was like "staging *Hamlet* without the Prince of Denmark," for it "gave to the whole movement an academic and unreal air."[32]

It is clear from the evidence found in the minutes that at these monthly moots the members were occupied with a variety of matters. Much time was devoted to discussions of material prepared for publication in the *Round Table*. The reader will recall that this was particularly important during Kerr's travels and subsequent illness. In addition, the moot had to attend to the administration of several projects to promote the emigration to South Africa and the other Dominions of young Englishmen possessing the happy combination of adequate capital and a fervent loyalty to the concept of imperial unity.[33] Attention was also given at these early moots to the need for educating the general pub-

---

31. Leo Amery, *My Political Life*, I, 348–49.
32. In the foreword to Vladimir Halpérin, *Lord Milner*, p. 14.
33. Perhaps because he was personally involved in this phase of round table work, John Dove gave these emigration projects special attention in his typescript "The Round Table: A Mystery Probed."

lic—as contrasted to the "molders of opinion" who were the usual
target of round table propaganda—to the need for closer ties
among the nations of the Empire. Efforts which were made in this
direction were usually in conjunction with other imperialist
groups such as the Victoria League, the Imperial Cooperation
League, and the Workers' Educational Association.[34] The matter
of publishing the 1913 Canadian debates on the naval question
was discussed but abandoned because the cost was thought to be
excessive.[35] Steps were taken to find a new Beit Lecturer in Colonial History in 1913 when Curtis decided to devote himself completely to travel and work on the egg. It was decided that the
name of Reginald Coupland should be proposed, and if selected,
"200£ should be found" from the General Fund to enable him to
travel in South Africa.[36] The moot also showed an interest in the
social problems which confronted Britain and the Empire. Matters of this sort were not thought to be within the province of the
moot itself, but since some of the younger members felt keenly
about them, it was decided to maintain a " 'Social Moot' . . . as a
parallel but independent organization." This group might use the
facilities of the *Round Table* editorial offices and was invited to
submit to the editor an occasional article on "social subjects."[37]

Certainly the greatest portion of the moot's attention in these
years, however, was given to the labors of Curtis as he struggled to
create a statement upon which the moot could base the great
crusade for organic unity. It will be recalled that following his
tour of the Dominions Curtis returned to England in 1911 and
the next year accepted an appointment as Beit Lecturer in Colonial History at Oxford. During the following academic year he
divided his time between work on the egg and his duties at the
University. In the latter capacity he was charged with conducting
a seminar in which he asked members of the group to suppose that
organic unification had just been accomplished and that each of
them was a Dominion minister confronted with the task of reor-
ganizing his department to conform to the new situation.[38] This

34. Minutes of the moots of Jan. 23, 1913, and Feb. 12, 1914.
35. Minutes of the moot of Sept. 25, 1913.
36. Minutes of the moot of May 29, 1913.
37. Minutes of the moot of Oct. 30, 1913. It appears that this "Social Moot" had a
short and uneventful life; no further reference to it is to be found.
38. Curtis to Richard Jebb, April 14, 1913, Jebb Papers.

assignment was undoubtedly meant to serve a double purpose of arousing the students' interest in imperial problems and in the best academic tradition of providing the instructor with raw material for a study in which he was involved.

Not content to pass up any opportunity to win converts to the imperialist cause, Curtis became involved in projects meant to bring the gospel of organic union to the young scholars of Oxford. His usual fervor and enthusiasm were so out of place in the restrained environment of Oxford, however, that he became something of a curiosity among the undergraduates. It was during Curtis's year as a don that Philip Kerr's younger brother David—killed in France in 1915—applied to him the nickname the Prophet. It apparently gained wide popularity among the Oxonians of the day and remained in use among an ever-widening circle of Curtis's acquaintances thereafter.[39] The most notable of these projects to interest undergraduates in the future of the Empire was a club organized by Curtis and H. E. Egerton, the Beit Professor of Colonial History. According to Curtis, it was meant to provide an agency through which the young men of Oxford might hear imperial issues discussed by "people from the Dominions and men of both parties in this country."[40] At the first of the club's fortnightly meetings in March, 1913, a group of about fifty gathered to hear remarks from Milner and Sir James Allen, the New Zealand statesman.[41]

Despite the time and effort which Curtis invested in such enterprises, he never lost sight of his first responsibility—the completion of the egg. Throughout this year at Oxford—in fact, from the time of his return from his first Empire tour—Curtis appears to have worked steadily towards that end. Though details of this labor are obscure, it is possible to piece together the outlines of the story from minutes of moots of the period, from a printed version of a speech made by Curtis in Toronto in 1913, and from occasional comments found in relevant diaries and correspondence.

39. A marginal note made by Curtis on a typed copy of a Harvard honors thesis by J. W. Shepardson entitled "Lionel Curtis." This document is in the archives of the Royal Institute of International Affairs at Chatham House.
40. Curtis to Jebb, April 12, 1913, Jebb Papers.
41. Milner's diary, March 4, 1913, Milner Papers.

It is clear, for example, that Curtis's conviction by the time of his return to London in early 1911 that the creation of the egg would be far more difficult than expected was strengthened by comments found in copies of the Green Memorandum returned to him from the Dominions. The complex and sometimes conflicting Dominion interests illustrated by these remarks forced the moot in early 1911 to revise its plans. The previous hope that an acceptable egg might be produced by simply revising the Green Memorandum to conform to Dominion opinion was recognized as illusory, and the need for a laborious reconstruction of the statement was accepted. Curtis was sent off to re-examine the matter in the light of his recent experience and to return with a scheme for constitutional reform agreeable both to the moot and to the Dominions which would be ready for publication "early in 1914."[42]

Until the new statement was ready it was decided that something should be done to maintain the interest of the recently created Dominion round table groups and to show them the complexity of the problem confronting those supporting imperial reform. Late in 1911, therefore, the moot had the Green Memorandum reprinted, but this time the leaves inserted between the pages of text were covered with marginal comments and criticisms taken from those copies of the original Memorandum which had by that time been returned to Curtis.[43] The resulting volume of over 800 pages contained an extensive index of both commentators—though not by name—and the subjects upon which they commented.[44] More than one thousand copies of this so-called Annotated Green Memorandum were printed for distribution to the groups and individuals that had received the original.[45] Probably for the same reasons the moot subsequently had printed two memoranda—on Australia and New Zealand respectively—containing Curtis's reflections on the problems peculiar to each of these Dominions.[46]

42. Selborne to Kerr, Aug. 12, 1912, Lothian Papers.
43. Curtis, *A Letter to the People of India*, p. 9.
44. This second printing of *Memoranda on Canada and the British Commonwealth* was further identified on the title page as "Round Table Studies, first series, No. I."
45. Curtis, *A Letter to the People of India*, p. 9.
46. No copy of the memorandum relating to Australia is known to exist. However, Curtis's bibliographer described a document entitled New Zealand Notes, printed in 1913 by W. H. Smith, the Alden Press, Letchworth. (Ruth Pryor, "Bibliography of

Curtis's work on the egg itself appears to have gone slowly. By the end of his tenure at Oxford, however, it is clear that he had completed a rough outline of the full study—including the all-important conclusion with its proposals for constitutional revision—and several portions meant to provide the reader with background information about how the Problem of Empire had developed. Like other moot documents, these completed portions of the egg were printed privately for circulation among those involved in the movement,[47] while the outline of the remainder of the study and the nature of the conclusions were apparently communicated to the Dominion groups in private correspondence.

The printed introductory portions of the egg contained a series of oversimplified historical accounts of early colonial developments similar to those which appeared in the earlier Green Memorandum. This material was apparently meant to salve the feelings of Dominion nationalists while describing the steps by which the present imperial situation had developed.[48] There was nothing controversial here; one may thus assume that it was received with little adverse comment from either the moot or the Dominion groups. The outline of the remaining portions of the egg, however, was another matter. Though no direct evidence exists to substantiate this assumption, it seems obvious from subsequent developments that Curtis's projected conclusion advocated constitutional changes which were far more revolutionary than anything many members of the moot would then dare to propose. One can only speculate about the specific nature of these proposed changes, but it is probable that among them was one for the

---

the Works of Lionel George Curtis: A Provisional List to the Present Date Submitted in Part Fulfilment of the Requirements for the University of London Diploma in Librarianship," May, 1955.) It was probably to one of these memoranda that the minutes of the moot of February 20, 1913, referred when it was mentioned that the next installment of "the Round Table Studies" would be ready in March. In 1914 the two were reprinted in one volume with notes and comments made by those who had previously read them when circulated separately. Called "Round Table Studies, first series, No. II," it was printed in London by Macmillan.

47. First printed separately in 1912 and 1913 as "Round Table Studies, second series, installments A through E," they were later reprinted—again for private circulation—in one volume entitled *The Project of a Commonwealth, an Inquiry into the Nature of Citizenship in the British Empire, and into the Mutual Relations of the Several Communities Thereof*, Part I (London, 1915).

48. Curtis later credited Egerton, H. A. L. Fisher, R. W. Seton-Watson, and Robert S. Rait with assistance in the historical portions of this work (Curtis, *A Letter to the People of India*, p. 6).

creation of a parliament for imperial affairs containing both British and Dominion representatives elected by, and answerable to, the voters and not the constituent governments.

The basis for these assumptions is to be found in the effect which Curtis's proposals had upon members of the round table in both London and the Dominions. Quite simply, many who had participated in the movement to this point were not prepared to accept anything so radical. This is obvious from the minutes of a moot in the fall of 1913 at which Curtis, aware of the hostility with which his conclusions had been received in the Dominions and sensitive to the lukewarm attitude of many of his London colleagues, offered a solution. Since neither London nor the Dominions was prepared to accept and support the statement which he had outlined, he proposed that a basic change in the program of the movement be adopted. The original program was based on the assumption that Curtis could create an egg to which the members of the moot could give their wholehearted endorsement, and which could then be sent around to the Dominion groups for discussion and criticism. Then, after everyone involved had had his say, it would be published, with all those in the round table movement who could support its conclusions banding together to form the cadre of a popular army demanding organic union. Until recently it had seemed to be a workable plan, but the opposition from the Dominions and the coolness of the moot now convinced him that it was out of the question. Curtis suggested, therefore, that as soon as completed the egg should be published, not as the agreed statement of the London group, but merely as a report "by certain individuals at the instance of the Round Table groups." Concerning the Dominion groups, the reader should be told, Curtis continued, that though the egg was the result of "research upon which the Groups had agreed and to which they had all in some way contributed, it was not in itself an agreed document."[49]

Curtis's proposal to the moot was a radical departure from the scheme which he had presented to the original supporters of the round table four years before. It therefore must have been with a feeling of defeat that he offered changes which could only weaken

49. Minutes of the moot of Sept. 25, 1913.

the chances of ultimate success. Other members of the moot, however, apparently felt the original plan was not hopeless and that some way might yet be found to bring the egg into conformity with the feelings of the moot. For it was decided that a decision on Curtis's suggestion should be postponed and that the general secretary be sent on another tour of the Dominions in search of a modified solution to the egg which would be acceptable to all factions.[50]

By the middle of November Curtis had arrived in Canada. His private conversations with leading Canadian members of the movement appear to have passed unrecorded. There does exist, however, a printed version of a speech made by Curtis to the Toronto group on November 18, 1913.[51] In it he explained to his listeners the nature and purpose of the egg and the problems which were at that point hindering its completion. "Originally," he said, "our idea was to work like a royal commission. Some one person was appointed to prepare a draft report; the groups were then to consider that report and, having agreed upon it, were to take what steps might to them seem fit for giving effect to it."[52] This of course had not worked as expected. It had been impossible to communicate concurrently with groups scattered throughout the world. To circulate the first draft, receive comments, work these comments into a new draft acceptable to the London group, and then to repeat the process until the greater portion of those associated with the movement were satisfied would have taken many years. "I should require some magic which I do not possess," Curtis remarked, "in order to charm into verbal unanimity several hundred men, all accustomed to think freely for themselves."[53]

It had therefore become necessary, Curtis said, for him to abandon all hope of producing a statement satisfactory to nearly everyone associated with the movement. He had decided instead to

50. *Ibid.* He later claimed that this trip was made to establish some administrative organization among Dominion groups, for especially in Canada, "the enquiry had excited such interest in university circles that the groups each threatened to expand beyond a manageable size" (Curtis, *A Letter to the People of India*, p. 11).
51. Curtis, *The Round Table Movement, Its Past and Its Future.* The title page was marked "For Private Circulation Only."
52. *Ibid.,* p. 22.
53. *Ibid.,* p. 23.

concentrate his attention upon something far less significant—an examination of the Imperial Problem and an analysis of various possible ways of solving it. As projected, the study would be published in three volumes. The first—a historical account of how the Empire had developed—would consist of those portions of the egg which had already been printed and circulated among the groups; Volume II would contain an analysis of present conditions within the Empire; and the last would deal with ways by which the much discussed Imperial Problem might be solved.

It was of course the contents of the third volume which was the heart of the study and upon which attention would center. Here, Curtis said, he planned to lay before the reader what seemed to him to be the four possible courses of action open to the Empire. First, there was the option to follow the same path along which the Empire was then traveling. Let the relationship between Great Britain and the Dominions, and between the Dominions and the dependent Empire, continue undefined in the belief that time and circumstances will solve the problem. The second was to alter the existing situation by proclaiming the Dominions independent of Britain in matters relating to both defense and foreign affairs and then watch the imperial connection disintegrate and finally disappear. Third, to apply the policy of association or co-operation advocated by Richard Jebb. And last, to move directly towards the organic unity which could come only from sweeping constitutional reform.[54]

Each of these courses of action, Curtis said, had been proposed by members of the round table in their correspondence with the general secretary, and as a result he felt obliged to include them for consideration. He assured his listeners in Toronto, however, that he was far from neutral in the matter of which path the Empire should follow, and in the last volume of the egg he intended to make this point clear to his readers. He was convinced that continuing things as they were at that time or simply ending British influence in Dominion foreign affairs and defense without at the same time creating new constitutional ties were both out of the question. In either case the result would be the same: the destruction of the Empire. Though he could never accept this

54. *Ibid.*, pp. 16–18.

negative approach to the settlement of the Problem of Empire, he thought it essential that all points of view be presented to the members of the movement. He hoped, therefore, that someone who supported each of these courses of action would marshal the arguments for his position and present them in a statement similar to the one on which he, Curtis, was currently at work. He was convinced that only organic union and Jebb's co-operation offered any possibility of a positive solution to the Imperial Problem— that is, one which would strengthen and preserve the imperial connection—and that of the two, organic union was far more likely to meet the challenges of the twentieth century. As in the case of the first two suggested solutions, he hoped that someone strongly in favor of co-operation would present the case for that proposal in a well thought out study. As for himself, he said, "it is obviously impossible that I should endeavour to prepare a report which will harmonize these two, when experience and reason both seem to me to point to the fact that they are irreconcilable, and that our duty is to choose between them and to choose in time."[55]

Curtis emphasized, however, that he had no intention of presenting these conclusions as the agreed position of the round table organization. It was not his place to commit the groups to a specific plan of action by pretending to speak with an authority which he clearly did not possess. "I submit," he said, "that the 'Round Table' organization will have done an invaluable work if it succeeds in elucidating the possible alternatives, and places before its members, and afterwards before our fellow-citizens in each of these countries the best that can be said for each of them."[56]

Curtis's proposed tour of the Dominions was cut short by his return to London in January, 1914. Instead of visiting Australia, New Zealand, and South Africa before returning to England, he decided to go home directly from Canada.[57] The reason for this change of plans is perhaps to be found in a letter written to him by Brand. The tone of the letter and the fact that it was found appended to the minutes of a moot suggest that Brand wrote on

55. *Ibid.*, p. 22.
56. *Ibid.*, p. 23.
57. Robinson's diary, Jan. 15, 1914, Dawson Papers.

the instructions of his London colleagues.[58] In it he discussed the feelings of the moot concerning Curtis's suggestion made just before his departure for Canada that all hope of unanimous agreement on the conclusion be forgotten and that it be presented simply as a product of round table research which in no way committed the movement to a course of action. He pointed out that the moot understood why Curtis had despaired of gaining general support throughout the movement for a statement favoring organic unity. In fact, those in London were now as convinced as Curtis that the egg, scheduled for publication in 1914, should be presented without regard for the opinions of the Dominion groups. However, it was the opinion of the moot that Curtis should make every effort to win the approval and concurrence of the moot itself. This was essential, Brand wrote, "unless the egg is to appear under your name as your personal work. If it is to appear under the aegis of the Round Table those in England at any rate, who are known to be identified with the Round Table, must be able to advocate & defend it wholeheartedly." Such concurrence should not be difficult to achieve, he continued, if Curtis would work more closely with members of the group, conferring with them frequently and submitting his drafts to them for comment and criticism. "I would suggest therefore that you should do with Part III [of the egg] as you did with your documents in South Africa, i.e. send instalments of it frequently as they are written round to all members of the inner moot for their criticism."

The sentiments expressed in Brand's letter—which perhaps brought Curtis home before his intended tour of the Dominions—were reinforced by the discussion which took place on January 15, 1914, at a moot held shortly after Curtis's return. There it was emphasized to Curtis that, like it or not, all members of the moot were tied together in the minds of British and Dominion political and opinion leaders. For Curtis to assume at this point that he could rush into print with a grand scheme for repairing the Empire without involving the whole moot was unrealistic. No disclaimer printed in the preface would convince the reader that Curtis was not in fact speaking for the round table

58. Brand to Curtis, n.d. (copy attached to the minutes of the moot of Jan. 15, 1914).

organization. So far as the minutes indicate, the moot ended without any firm decision on what steps would be taken next.

By early March, however, Curtis had developed a plan which, if adopted by the moot, would end disagreement within the moot over proposals contained in the egg and would make possible within the current year the commencement of the great crusade. On March 9 there was a moot which was crucial in the development of the movement. The unusual nature of the meeting can be sensed from the minutes. Ordinarily the number attending was between six and ten, and the account of business transacted was brief. In this case, however, there were seventeen present including almost everyone in the inner moot, and the record of what was said was unusually full, as though the secretary was aware of its special significance. Curtis seems to have dominated the meeting from beginning to end. According to the minutes, he first described the meeting in Toronto and the speech there in which he announced his conviction that organic union was the only positive solution to the Problem of Empire. Since this belief was the basic tenet upon which the moot had been formed, and since disagreement between himself and certain members of the moot was only over details by which this goal might be achieved, Curtis announced that he planned to make organic union the conclusion of the egg despite the opposition which such a proposal generated in the Dominions. To win wholehearted support within the moot he intended to follow Brand's suggestion and circulate his material as soon as he finished it, thereby making it possible to adjust differences before they became insurmountable.

As far as the Dominion groups were concerned, Curtis suggested that the moot notify them of what was afoot and urge those who found organic union unacceptable to draft statements supporting an alternative. In all fairness then the moot should see to the circulation of dissenting statements so that participants in the movement might be apprised of the best thinking on both sides. Having done this, Curtis said, the moot's duty to scholarly objectivity would be ended. The egg should be prepared for publication before the end of the year (1914) as had been planned, and on the day of its publication the round table movement as constituted in 1909 should come to an end. All existing groups would be dissolved simultaneously and the administrative apparatus would be dismantled "to be reconstituted as a propagandist organization from all members willing to subscribe to the broad principles of the English Report."[59]

Whether Curtis's proposal was adopted immediately is not recorded. Nor is there any record of another moot for almost two months. At first glance this inactivity seems odd in light of the climactic nature of the March 9 meeting. It becomes quite easy to understand, however, if one considers the times. In the spring of 1914 the long series of constitutional crises and difficulties over home rule had brought Great Britain to the verge of civil war. In such circumstances the less immediate threat of imperial dissolution was thrust into the background. Members of the moot—especially Milner and Amery—were in the secret councils of those willing to take arms against the government rather than submit to a settlement which would put Ulster under the authority of an autonomous Dublin government.[60] Even Curtis, whose concentrated involvement in an effort to solve the Problem of Empire had up until this point left little time or energy for concern for events at home, was drawn into the crisis. As the spring of 1914 advanced, Curtis seems to have thought less and less about unifying the Empire as he threw himself into a search for some means of ending the crisis peacefully. At least one member of the moot seems to have found the general secretary's zeal and enthusiasm in this matter amusing. "Lionel [is] rushing around to interview leaders," Robinson wrote in his diary. And on the following day he noted that "Lionel C. & Grigg v. busy saving the State."[61] Under these circumstances, therefore, it is understandable that little immediate action resulted from Curtis's proposals made at the March 9 moot.

By the last of May, however, Curtis's plan had become the established policy of the moot. Though the circumstances by which this took place are unknown, it is clear that at a moot at Cliveden on the weekend of May 30 to June 2, 1914, the matter of proposals to be made in the third volume of the egg was no

59. Minutes of the moot of March 9, 1914.
60. This matter was recently examined in detail in Gollin, *Proconsul in Politics,* pp. 195–222.
61. Robinson's diary, April 30 and May 1, 1914, Dawson Papers.

longer of interest to the group. According to the minutes, the attention of the moot was directed towards a new project—to prepare a condensed and popularized version of the egg to be published at the same time the full study was made public. The feeling within the moot was that the three-volume egg, with its extensive statistical information and historical digressions, would influence the thinkers without whose support a crusade for imperial unity would fail. But something was needed to bring the message to the thousands of politicians, educators, journalists, and other molders of opinion who would never read through the egg. The need for such an abridgement had been discussed at moots for some time, but it was not until the weekend moot at Cliveden that a decision was made to press forward with the preparation of what the members of the moot dubbed "the omelette."

It is the irony of the round table movement that just as the moot was ready to bring the preliminary program to an end and launch the great crusade, events occurred which in the short run caused a postponement of the popular campaign for organic unity and in the long run rendered it futile. Curtis, the aspiring manipulator, was outmanipulated by history. In his Toronto speech he had expressed a fear that something of this sort might happen. "What we must pray for," he told his Canadian friends, "is that tremendous and swiftly moving events, which we have as yet no power to control, may not rush upon us like a thief in the night and precipitate a crisis which public opinion has not yet been prepared to face."[62] World War I more than justified his fears.

When the war began the moot tried to continue its operation uninterrupted. There were meetings almost every month, and the *Round Table* continued to appear quarterly. Soon, however, the effects of the war became apparent. First Amery, and then other members of the moot, became involved in war work, and the planned publication of the egg and omelette in 1914 was delayed. Volume I of the egg, entitled *The Commonwealth of Nations*, and the omelette (*The Problem of the Commonwealth*) were finally published in 1916,[63] but the all-important conclusion of the egg never appeared. And the great crusade, scheduled to begin in late

62. Curtis, *The Round Table Movement, Its Past and Its Future*, p. 30.
63. Both were published by Macmillan.

1914 or early 1915, was postponed and finally forgotten. The round table scheme which seemed logical and feasible in 1909 gradually came to have a quaint, legalistic—even utopian—ring to it as the events of the war years unfolded. The more realistic minds in the movement quickly saw that the sacrifices made by Dominion troops and the concurrent growth in Dominion nationalism were harbingers of a new imperial relationship unlike anything they had proposed. And nothing the round table movement could do could change these facts. By the time the war was drawing to an end even Curtis seems to have become reconciled to the hopelessness of the original plan. Though he never ceased to write and talk about the need for organic unity within the Empire, his words soon became those of a prophet crying in the wilderness, ignored by a people indifferent to the truth. Even before the war had ended he had begun to turn towards other matters the same single-minded enthusiasm which he had for the previous decade devoted to the drive for imperial consolidation. First came India, then Ireland, the League of Nations, and finally a religiously oriented brotherhood of man.

The end of the round table movement as it was conceived in 1909 gradually led to the dissolution of the moot. The friendships of an earlier day remained, binding together this expanded kindergarten until its ranks were depleted by death. But as a coterie with a clearly defined political program, the moot disappeared shortly after the war. The same men who had previously met each month as the inner moot continued to meet regularly thereafter, but both the name and purpose of their meetings were different. They now constituted the *Round Table* editorial committee, and their business as time passed became increasingly restricted to the affairs of the journal.

Thus the round table movement ended in failure, with only the quarterly magazine to mark the fact that it had ever existed. Probably it would have failed regardless of the momentous events of 1914–18. Even so, one can say that among the many lights that went out in that first week of August, 1914, one was that which had illumined the round table.

Bibliography

Primary sources

Private papers

Instead of simply listing the collections of private papers consulted, it might be useful in this case to comment on the location, condition, and accessibility of the papers of all the leading figures of the kindergarten–round table coterie. I shall mention first those persons whose papers did not survive or for some other reason were not available to me as I gathered material for this book.

Dove, Hichens, Malcolm, Wyndham

These four apparently did not save letters and similar papers from that period of their lives.

Perry

I was able to learn nothing of the papers—if any—of J. F. (Peter) Perry.

Oliver, Selborne, Curtis

Oliver's papers were destroyed at his order under circumstances previously described in a footnote. The early papers of both Selborne and Curtis were destroyed by fire. Curtis's papers which accumulated after the 1933 fire, along with a small amount of earlier material which survived the flames, were several years ago moved to the *Round Table* offices in London. At least three historians—Sir James Butler, Professor Carroll Quigley, and Professor A. M. Gollin —have been permitted to examine them. In no case does the use to which they were put suggest the existence of an important body of material concerning the kindergarten and the origins of the round table.

Duncan

Patrick Duncan's personal papers are the property of his sons, Messrs. Patrick and John Duncan, and are presumably still in South Africa. They were used extensively by Professor Thompson in his history of the unification of South Africa.

Brand

In response to my request for permission to examine whatever relevant material he might have, Lord Brand explained that he did not recall having saved any great amount of papers in the years before World War I. Before his death in 1963, however, he did turn over some material from this period to Sir James Butler for use in the preparation of his biography of Lord Lothian and to Professor L. M. Thompson for his study of South African unification. I assume that access to Lord Brand's papers is now controlled by his son-in-law and daughter, Major and Mrs. Edward William Ford.

Amery

Mr. Julian Amery has the personal papers of his father. Professor Gollin used them extensively in his study of Milner's career after his retirement from South Africa. I am grateful to Mr. Amery for providing me with a copy of a significant letter sent to his father by Curtis in March, 1909.

Feetham

Mr. Justice Feetham's papers have never been exploited by students of the period. I assume they are still in South Africa; I have no idea of their extent.

Milner

Milner's papers at New College, Oxford, are voluminous but difficult to use, because they have not been properly catalogued. Some items are mounted in scrapbooks, some are in old-fashioned letter boxes, but most are simply tied into bundles. A valuable part of the collection is the series of diaries which Milner kept throughout his adult life. His daily entries were frustratingly brief, however, usually consisting only of his appointments for the day and his companions in the evening. He almost never gave away his feelings on either personal or public matters. Even so, these volumes provide an invaluable chronology of the kindergarten and its activities.

In reading through these papers I got the feeling that considerable caution was exercised in preparing them for the archives—but whether by Milner or someone else is impossible to say. There are indications, for instance, that at one time Milner and Curtis corresponded frequently; yet the papers at New College contain remarkably few examples. There is evidence, furthermore, that some entries in Milner's diary were mutilated so as to make them illegible. Nevertheless, this collection forms the most comprehensive and useful source of information which I was able to use.

Kerr

The Lothian papers are at the Scottish Record Office, H. M. General Register House, Edinburgh. Kerr, like several of his kindergarten associates, kept few of the letters and other documents from this period. Except for a very important handful of letters which passed between Curtis and the London group in 1910 upon which much of Chapter Ten is based, there is little of interest in the collection for the student of the kindergarten. I subsequently learned of a substantial collection of letters written by Kerr to his family in the possession of Lady Margaret Kerr and Lady Minna Butler-Thwing. This correspondence may contain much of value.

Robinson

Geoffrey Robinson's personal papers are the possession of his widow, Mrs. Geoffrey Dawson. This collection is rich in personal information about members of the kindergarten, for Robinson—who corresponded frequently with his kindergarten associates—usually kept letters which he received and sometimes copies of those he sent. His diary, like Milner's, is bare of intimate secrets, containing only brief references to appointments and social engagements.

Jebb

Though not a member of the kindergarten–round table group, Richard Jebb was in close touch with Curtis and other imperial enthusiasts of the Edwardian era. His private papers thus contain some interesting comments about the kindergarten and its activities. They are filed at the Institute of Commonwealth Studies of the University of London.

Round Table

The files at the editorial offices of the *Round Table* contain little of real value to the student of the kindergarten except the minutes of the moots. Important though they are, these minutes frequently raise more questions than they answer. A typical minute contains only a list of those present and a brief description of the matters brought before the group. Seldom was there an indication of the decisions reached or the positions taken by the various members. It is particularly unfortunate that the first book of minutes—covering the time from the organization of the London group to January, 1913—has been lost.

Contemporary books

Brand, Robert H. *The Union of South Africa*. Oxford, 1909.
————, ed. *The Letters of John Dove*. London, 1938.
Committee of the Compatriots' Club, ed. *Compatriots' Club Lectures*. 1st Series. London, 1905.
Curtis, Lionel. *The Commonwealth of Nations*. London, 1916.
————. *The Government of South Africa*. 2 vols. South Africa, 1908.

Curtis's studies drafted for the moot and frequently circulated throughout the Empire present a number of problems to the bibliographer. In the first place, they were printed but usually not published in that they were never offered for sale. Secondly, several of them were simply annotated reprints of studies which had been previously circulated. Below are listed in chronological rather than alphabetical order those round table studies which seem to have been important in the development of the movement. A fuller though probably incomplete listing of these studies and a very valuable explanation of their relationship to each other may be found in Ruth Pryor's bibliography of Curtis listed below.

————. *Memoranda on Canada and the British Commonwealth.* London, 1910.

————. *The Project of a Commonwealth: An Inquiry into the Nature of Citizenship in the British Empire and into the Mutual Relations of the Several Communities thereof.* Part I. London, 1915. (Published the following year under Curtis's name as *The Commonwealth of Nations.*)

————. *The Problem of the Commonwealth.* London, 1915. (Published in 1916 in Toronto with Curtis named as author.)

————. *A Canadian Criticism on "The Problem of the Commonwealth" and the author's reply thereto.* London, 1916.

Gwynn, Stephen, ed. *The Anvil of War: Letters between F. S. Oliver and His Brother 1914–1918.* London, 1936.

Headlam, Cecil, ed. *The Milner Papers: South Africa.* 2 vols. London, 1931–1933.

Jebb, Richard. *The Britannic Question: A Survey of Alternatives.* London, 1913.

————. *The Imperial Conference: A History and Study.* London and New York, 1911.

[Long, B. K.] *The Framework of Union: A Comparison of Some Union Constitutions. With a Sketch of the Development of Union in Canada, Australia and Germany; and the Text of the Constitutions of the United States, Canada, Germany, Switzerland and Australia.* Prepared for and issued by the Closer Union Society. Cape Town, 1908.

Milner, Lord. *Constructive Imperialism. Five Speeches (Oct.–Dec., 1907).* London, 1908.

————. *England in Egypt.* London, 1892.

————. *Imperial Unity. Two Speeches (Dec. 1906).* London, 1907.

————. *The Nation and the Empire. Being a Collection of Speeches and Addresses with an Introduction.* London, 1913.

————. *Speeches delivered in Canada in the Autumn of 1908.* Toronto, 1909.

Oliver, Frederick Scott. *Alexander Hamilton: An Essay on American Union.* "New Edition." New York, 1921.

————. *What Federalism is Not.* London, 1914.

Williams, Basil. *The Selborne Memorandum: A Review of the Mutual Relations of the British South African Colonies in 1907. With an*

Introduction by Basil Williams. Oxford, 1925. (This contains the full text of the memorandum officially presented as "Papers Relating to a Federation of the South African Colonies." *Sessional Papers, 1907.* Vol. LVII [*Accounts and Papers,* Vol. XI]. Cd. 3564. July, 1907.)

Contemporary articles and pamphlets

Brand, Robert H. "Proportional Representation and Closer Union. A Lecture Delivered Under the Auspices of the Closer Union Society at Johannesburg," *Cape Times,* September 26, 1908.

Chaplin, F. Drummond. "The Labor Question in the Transvaal," *National Review,* No. 275 (January, 1906) , pp. 835–49.

Closer Union Societies. *Proceedings at the Annual Meeting of the Association of Closer Union Societies at Johannesburg. March 3, 4, and 5th, 1909.* Johannesburg, 1909.

Curtis, Lionel. *A Letter to the People of India.* Bombay, Calcutta, and Madras, 1917.

———. *A Letter to Philip Kerr, Secretary of the Round Table, 175 Piccadilly, London, W. November 13, 1916.* (Apparently printed in India and circulated to those interested in the movement.)

———. *The Round Table Movement, Its Past and Its Future: Address Delivered in the Senate House of the University to the "Round Table" Groups at Toronto, November 18, 1913.* Letchworth, n.d. (Marked "For Private Circulation Only.")

Duncan, Patrick. *Closer Union: Stirring Speech on Unification by Mr. Patrick Duncan.* No place, date, or publisher given. (Marked "Presented to the Natal Closer Union Society, Durban, by the Colonial Secretary of the late TV Government.")

[———.] *Suggestions for a Native Policy.* Johannesburg, October, 1912.

Feetham, Richard. "Some Problems of South African Federation and Reasons for Facing Them." (A typescript of a speech "read to the Fortnightly Club at its first meeting, in Johannesburg, on 4 October 1906.")

Jebb, Richard. "The Imperial Conference: A Retrospect and Warning," *National Review,* LXIX (April, 1917) , 181–88.

Kerr, Philip. "The Commonwealth and Empire," in *The Empire and the Future: A Series of Imperial Studies Lectures Delivered in the University of London, Kings College.* London, 1916. Pp. 69–89.

———. *What the British Empire Really Stands for: An Address Delivered by Mr. Philip Kerr at the Toronto Club to the Members of the Round Table on Tuesday, July 30, 1912.* Toronto, n.d.

Marcus, Herman W. "A Sketch of the Imperial Unity Movement," in *The British Empire Series.* Vol. V: *The British Empire, General.* New York, 1902. Pp. 584–613.

Milner, Lord. *The British Commonwealth*. London, 1919. (An address delivered at Oxford, August 1, 1919.)

Oliver, Frederick Scott. *The Alternatives to Civil War*. London, 1913.

――――. *Ireland and the Imperial Conference: Is There a Way to Settlement?* London, 1917.

"Transvaaler" [Robinson, Geoffrey]. "Political Parties in the Transvaal," *National Review*, XLV (May, 1905), 461–88.

The Round Table in Canada: How the Movement Began. What it Hopes to Accomplish. Toronto, February, 1917.

Secondary sources

Biographies, autobiographies, and memoirs

Amery, Julian. *The Life of Joseph Chamberlain*. Vol. IV: *At His Height of Power*. London, 1951.

Amery, The Right Honorable L. S. *My Political Life*. Vol. I: *England before the Storm 1896–1914*. London, 1953.

Barker, Sir Ernest. *Age and Youth: Memories of Three Universities and Father of the Man*. Oxford, 1953.

Buchan, John. *Pilgrim's Way: An Essay in Recollection*. Cambridge, Mass., 1940.

Butler, J. R. M. *Lord Lothian (Philip Kerr) 1882–1940*. London, 1960.

Cecil, Lord Robert (Viscount Cecil of Chelwood). *A Great Experiment: An Autobiography*. New York, 1941.

Chamberlain, Sir Austen. *Politics from Inside: An Epistolary Chronicle 1906–1914*. London, 1936.

Collis, Maurice. *Nancy Astor: An Informal Biography*. New York, 1960.

Crankshaw, Edward. *The Forsaken Idea: A Study of Viscount Milner*. London, 1952.

Curtis, Lionel. *With Milner in South Africa*. Oxford, 1951.

Gollin, Alfred M. *Proconsul in Politics: A Study of Lord Milner in Opposition and in Power*. London, 1964.

――――. *The Observer and J. L. Garvin 1908–1914: A Study in A Great Editorship*. London, 1960.

Halpérin, Vladimir. *Lord Milner and the Empire: The Evolution of British Imperialism*. (With a foreword by The Rt. Hon. L. S. Amery, P. C., C. H.) London, 1952.

Hancock, W. K. *Smuts: The Sanguine Years 1870–1919*. Cambridge, 1962.

Hendrick, Burton J. *The Life and Letters of Walter H. Page*. 2 vols. Garden City, New York, 1924.

Lindley, Rt. Hon. Sir Francis. *Lord Lovat: A Biography*. London, n.d.
Long, Basil Kellett. *In Smuts's Camp*. (With a foreword by Sir Dougal
O. Malcolm.) Oxford, 1945.
Riddell, Lord. *Lord Riddell's Intimate Diary of the Peace Conference
and After 1918–1923*. New York, 1934.
Spender, J. A. *Life of Sir Henry Campbell-Bannerman*. London, 1923.
Steed, Henry Wickham. *Through Thirty Years 1892–1922: A Personal
Narrative*. 2 vols. Garden City, New York, 1924.
Wells, H. G. *Experiment in Autobiography: Discoveries and Conclu-
sions of a Very Ordinary Brain (since 1866)*. New York, 1934.
Willison, Sir John. *Sir George Parkin: A Biography*. London, 1929.
Wrench, John Evelyn. *Alfred Lord Milner: The Man of No Illusions
1854–1925*. London, 1958.
———. *Geoffrey Dawson and Our Times*. London, 1955.

Other books

Amery, L. S. *The Empire in the New Era: Speeches Delivered during
an Empire Tour 1927–28, with a Foreword by Lord Balfour*. London, 1928.
———, ed. *The Times History of the War in South Africa 1899–1902*.
7 vols. London, 1900–1909.
Burt, Alfred Leroy. *Imperial Architects: Being an Account of Proposals in the Direction of a Closer Imperial Union, Made Previous to
the Opening of the First Colonial Conference of 1887*. Oxford, 1913.
———. *The Evolution of the British Empire and Commonwealth from
the American Revolution*. Boston, 1956.
The Cambridge History of the British Empire. 8 vols. Cambridge,
1929–1940.
Cheng, Seymour Ching-yuan. *Schemes for the Federation of the British
Empire*. New York, 1931.
Courtney, W. L. and J. E. *Pillars of Empire: Studies and Impressions*.
London, 1918.
Dawson, Robert MacGregor. *The Development of Dominion Status
1900–1936*. London, 1937.
Elton, Godfrey Elton, Baron, ed. *The First Fifty Years of the Rhodes
Trust and the Rhodes Scholarships 1903–1953*. Oxford, 1956.
Ensor, R. C. K. *England 1870–1941*. Oxford, 1936.
Halévy, Elie. *A History of the English People in the Nineteenth
Century*. Vol. VI: *The Rule of Democracy 1905–1914*. Translated by
E. I. Watkins. New York, 1961.
Hancock, W. K. *Problems of Nationality 1918–1936*. Vol. I of *Survey of
British Commonwealth Affairs*. London, 1937.
The History of "The Times." Vol. III: *The Twentieth Century Test*

1884–1912 and Vol. IV: *The 150th Anniversary and Beyond 1912–1948*. London, 1947 and 1952.

"Janitor" [Lockhart, J. G., and Lady Craik]. *The Feet of the Young Men: Some Candid Comments on the Rising Generation, with an Epilogue 1929.* 2d ed. London, 1929.

Jebb, Richard. *Empire in Eclipse*. London, 1926.

Keith, A. Berriedale. *Imperial Unity and the Dominions*. Oxford, 1916.

Kerr, Philip, and Lionel Curtis. *The Prevention of War*. New Haven, Conn., 1923.

Marais, J. S. *The Fall of Kruger's Republic*. Oxford, 1961.

Marquard, Leo. *The Story of South Africa*. New York, n.d. [1954].

Mendelssohn, Sidney. *Mendelssohn's South African Bibliography*. 2 vols. London, 1957.

Parkin, George R. *The Rhodes Scholarships*. Boston, 1912.

Pyrah, G. B. *Imperial Policy and South Africa 1902–10*. Oxford, 1955.

Robinson, Ronald, and John Gallagher (with Alice Denny). *Africa and the Victorians: The Climax of Imperialism in the Dark Continent*. New York, 1961.

Rowse, A. L. *Appeasement: A Study in Political Decline 1933–1939*. New York, 1961.

———. *The English Past: Evocations of Persons and Places*. New York, 1952.

Semmel, Bernard. *Imperialism and Social Reform: English Social-Imperial Thought 1895–1914*. London, 1960.

Thompson, L. M. *The Unification of South Africa 1902–1910*. Oxford, 1960.

Thornton, A. P. *The Imperial Idea and Its Enemies: A Study in British Power*. London, 1959.

Tyler, J. E. *The Struggle for Imperial Unity (1868–1895)*. (Imperial Studies, No. 16. A. P. Newton, ed.) London, New York, and Toronto, 1938.

Walton, The Hon. Sir Edgar H. *The Inner History of the National Convention of South Africa*. London, 1912.

Worsfold, W. Basil. *Lord Milner's Work in South Africa from its Commencement in 1897 to the Peace of Vereeniging in 1902: Containing Hitherto Unpublished Information*. New York, 1906.

———. *The Reconstruction of the New Colonies under Lord Milner*. 2 vols. London, 1913.

Pamphlets, articles, and speeches

Amery, The Rt. Hon. L. S. "Lionel Curtis 1872–1952." (A speech broadcast by Amery on March 7, 1952. Typescript at Chatham House library is marked "Record & only copy.")

Baylen, Joseph O. "W. T. Stead and the Boer War: The Irony of Idealism," *Canadian Historical Review,* XL (December, 1959), 304–14.

Beer, George Louis. "Lord Milner and British Imperialism," *Political Science Quarterly,* XXX (June, 1915), 301–08.

Brodribb, C. W. *Government by Mallardry: A Study in Political Ornithology.* London, 1932.

[Coupland, Reginald.] *Lionel Hichens.* Oxford, n.d.

Curtis, Lionel. "One of Milner's Young Men," *Ashridge Quarterly,* I (July, 1947), 34–39.

Dartford, Gerald P. "Failure of Federalism in the British Community," *Current History,* XXXIX (August, 1960), 108–13.

Donelly, M. S. "J. W. Dafoe and Lionel Curtis: Two Concepts of the Commonwealth," *Political Studies,* VIII (June, 1960), 170–82.

Gathorne-Hardy, G. M. *Lionel Curtis, C. H. 1872–1955.* (Publisher, place, and date are all unknown.)

Knaplund, Paul. "The Unification of South Africa: A Study in British Colonial Policy," *Transactions of the Wisconsin Academy of Sciences, Arts and Letters,* XXI (1924), 1–21.

Lower, A. R. M. "The Evolution of the Sentimental Idea of Empire: A Canadian View," *History,* XI (January, 1927), 289–303.

McInnis, Edgar. "The Imperial Problem in the Minds of Chamberlain and His Successors," *Canadian Historical Review,* XVI (March, 1935), 65–70.

Miller, J. D. B. *Richard Jebb and the Problem of Empire.* (Commonwealth Papers, No. III.) London, 1956.

———. "The Utopia of Imperial Federation," *Political Studies,* IV (June, 1956), 195–97.

Quigley, Carroll. "The Round Table Groups in Canada, 1908–38," *Canadian Historical Review,* XLIII (September, 1962), 204–24.

Schiller, Kathleen A. "Lionel Curtis—the Man," *Freedom and Union: Journal of the World Republic,* October, 1949.

Semmel, Bernard. "Sir Halford Mackinder: Theorist of Imperialism," *Canadian Journal of Economics and Political Science,* XXIV (November, 1958), 554–61.

Sinclair, Keith. *Imperial Federation: A Study of New Zealand Policy and Opinion 1880–1914.* (Commonwealth Papers, No. II.) London, 1955.

Walker, E. A. "Lord Milner in South Africa," a reprint from *Proceedings of the British Academy.* London, 1942.

Periodicals

Round Table, 1910–
Spectator, 1910–1915.

State, 1909–1912.
United Empire: The Royal Colonial Institute Journal, 1910–1919.

Unpublished theses and research essays

Conway, John. "The Round Table: A Study in Liberal Imperialism." Unpublished Ph.D. dissertation, Harvard University, 1951.

Dove, John. "The Round Table: A Mystery Probed. Notes for a History of the Round Table." (A typescript dated December 18, 1924, in the files of the *Round Table* editorial offices.)

Ellinwood, DeWitt Clinton. "Lord Milner's 'Kindergarten,' the British Round Table Group, and the Movement for Imperial Reform, 1910–1918." Unpublished Ph.D. dissertation, Washington University, 1962.

van Heerden, J. "Closer Union Movement 1902–1910." Mimeographed bibliography submitted to School of Librarianship, University of Cape Town, 1953.

Pryor, Ruth. "Bibliography of the Works of Lionel George Curtis: A Provisional List to the Present Date Submitted in Part Fulfilment of the Requirements for the University of London Diploma in Librarianship." Unpublished, 1955.

Shepardson, J. W. "Lionel Curtis." Unpublished honors thesis, Harvard University, 1949.

Index